Combating Mountaintop Removal

New Directions in the Fight against Big Coal

Bryan T. McNeil

University of Illinois Press

Urbana, Chicago, and Springfield

Library of Congress Cataloging-in-Publication Data
McNeil, Bryan T.
Combating mountaintop removal : new directions
in the fight against big coal / Bryan T. McNeil.
p. cm.
Includes bibliographical references and index.
ISBN 978-0-252-03643-9 (cloth)
1. Mountaintop removal mining—Appalachian
Region. 2. Coal mines and mining—Environmental
aspects—Appalachian Region. 3. Landscape protection—
Appalachian Region—Citizen participation. 4. Community
activists—Appalachian Region. 5. Environmentalists—
Appalachian Region. I. Title.
TD195.C58M38   2011
622'.292—dc22   2011006828

To my families,
at home and in Coal River,
and in memory of
Archie Green and Judy Bonds.

Contents

Acknowledgments

A great many people made this research and book possible. I am eternally grateful to the people of Coal River, West Virginia, for the hospitality and grace they offered me during my stay there, especially Judy Bonds, Patty and Butch Sebok, Freda Williams, and too many others to name. Thanks also to Coal River Mountain Watch, the Ohio Valley Environmental Coalition, and the Friends of the Mountains and its many member organizations. At the University of North Carolina, I thank the many people who influenced this project in ways direct and indirect, including Dorothy Holland, James Peacock, Carole Crumley, Glenn Hinson, Robert Cantwell, David Camp, Harry Watson, and the Curriculum in Folklore. Mary Hufford offered invaluable insight and collaboration. Special thanks to Archie Green, the Fund for Labor Culture and History, the University of North Carolina Graduate School, and the UNC Center for the Study of the American South, all of whom provided funding for the project. Thanks also to Harvard Ayers, Jeff Boyer, Kim Allen, Ann and Catherine Pancake, Mary Beth Fitts, and Alison McNeil.

I especially thank my family for their support, patience, and understanding throughout this effort.

Introduction

From Chestnut Strip you can see forever. The mountaintops of south-ern West Virginia rise toward the horizon like waves on the ocean. Butch, my guide for the day, is a member of the United Mine Workers who has worked underground for more than twenty-five years. Butch worked the morning shift before our Saturday afternoon meeting, when he took me to the place where he used to hunt grouse. Standing on the flat, grassy plateau left after the mountain was strip mined, we watched the slow but ceaseless movement of a dragline nearly ten miles away. Moving 100 tons of rubble with each scoop, the dragline performs mountaintop removal coal mining. Staring at the gray scar on the horizon, Butch told a story. "One Sunday afternoon in Da Nang, South Vietnam, all at once it sounded like freight trains coming over top of our head, and everything around us started blowing up, and huddled in a bunker in the dark I said, 'God let me get back to West Virginia.' And then when I got back here and I found out what they was doing, strip mining and stuff . . . ever since the first time I first realized this is what they get away with, this is what they do . . . this [makes] me want to puke."

* * *

Living in Appalachia's coalfields is an experience you feel. Natural forces like the cold of winter and the stifling humidity of summer, the beating rain and the rising river go hand in hand with the human activities that shape and reshape the mountains. Wind rushing off a speeding coal truck slams against an old coal camp house. The ground trembles under the force of distant explosive blasts. My spleen vibrates with the engine of a loaded coal train straining in the predawn.

The visceral experience of living in the coalfields extends far beyond the actual body. Natives of the region often describe an attachment to the land in romantic but vague terms. When someone delves deeper into the special relationship between the people and the land, they often make the connection in terms of bodies. Author Ann Pancake described the Appalachian Mountains as having a "closer likeness to a human body than any landscape I've ever seen." Over the generations, people have come to know parts of the land and the tools they use to work it like they know parts of their own body. The body of landscape, memory, and experience comes alive in the stories people tell about life in the mountains.

The offense taken by many residents to mountaintop removal coal mining also has a visceral referent, even beyond Butch's urge to puke. Coal executives frequently call it hyperbole stirred up by a few extremists and outside agitators. But locally, people often equate the profound violation of the social and physical landscape with rape. Towns that once flourished on Coal's bounty now languish before its insatiable appetite.[1] Whereas they once housed and sustained the legions of workers that made coal mining possible, these same communities now stand in the way of a largely automated earthmoving process. As companies buy people's property and make life unbearable for those who will not move, communities experience a gradual, creeping death. Dazed and emaciated, the remains of towns struggle to understand how the once life-giving fuel metastasized into a creeping killer.

*   *   *

As a case study, this book is about mountaintop removal coal mining and the ways people like Butch have reacted to it, including reimagining profound social and personal ideas like identity, history, and landscape. From a different perspective, this book is about the social processes that help create and continue to justify a monster like mountaintop removal, and about the social resources communities assemble to combat those processes. Often conflicts of this sort are associated with globalization. In this case, the term globalization may be counterintuitive. Globalization typically conjures images of closed factories and jobs flowing out of the United States to so-called export processing zones in Latin America or Asia. Unlike manufactured goods, coal cannot be moved to another country for mining and processing. Still, the same economic, political, and social forces have reshaped the Appalachian coal industry to create conditions similar to those sought by manufacturers over seas.[2] The process and its driving forces are the same, even if no national boundaries are crossed. I prefer to analyze mountaintop removal as the logical product of neoliberalism—one of the main ideas that has guided the development of globalization. Neoliberalism refers to the package of social, economic, cultural, and political ideas that have remade society in the image of a very specific business ideology in the past quarter century.[3]

This book shines light on the ways people experience in their daily lives the local effects of those global processes. In their opposition to mountaintop removal and other coal industry practices, local activists specifically articulate what is different between the coal industry they grew up with and their current terrifying reality. Citizen activists narrate as part of their cause a revised version of local and regional history to situate themselves and their position in relation to the black rock and its industry that fed them for generations. The retelling of history and social relations is a wonderfully clear revelation of a social process that is typically assumed and latent, rarely emerging in open discussion. By examining this case, we can see directly how ideas about economy and environment are woven into the underlying fabric of community and society. Because all culture is taken for granted, only when conflict arises are these ideas questioned.

To say the very least, mountaintop removal has given rise to conflict and laid bare conflicting understandings of community, economy, and environment. I present the resulting conflict not as a two-party fight with industry and miners facing off against activists. Rather, the conflict over mountaintop removal involves far-reaching social processes in which opposing understandings of self, history, community, and culture itself are being renegotiated. In the case of mountaintop removal, these processes have tentacles that reach from the hills and valleys of Appalachia to the federal government, global economics, transnational treaties, and back to living rooms and kitchen tables. Overlapping contours of political power, economic conditions, and cultural values, all having multiple forms and expressions, shape the debate.

My approach to conflict focuses less on confrontation than on everyday life in which people struggle with the process of reassigning meaning to their encounters with the coal industry. I follow fellow anthropologists Dorothy Holland and Jean Lave who argue that, through their daily practices and activities, people create political, economic, social, and cultural features of society; they both participate in and produce the cultural forms that make up and mediate the dense web of social relations—what we might call "community."[4] Within the field of anthropology such approaches are broadly referred to as practice theory. Bringing an analytical framework to everyday experience is particularly well suited to analyzing local conflicts in which people create and recreate the meanings of social issues through their practices and actions.

Many intertwined themes woven together make up the whole of any "community." Specific themes like economy, morality, or environment can never be distilled as discrete realms of activity separate from each other. With that in mind, separating these categories can provide analytical clarity not available when approaching a whole, complex, conflicted community. I have selected themes of community, economy, environment, and morality because those are common terms used by participants as they struggle to create new meanings and understandings of their own experience. Everyone has some sense of what these things mean, but meanings are never fixed within any one particular set of circumstances. In times of conflict, discrepancies lurking in assumed understandings of the most basic components of social life are laid bare. Cultural politics is the common term used to describe this continual, contested process of making meaning using these and other categories. For the sake of clarity, I will briefly explain how I use these concepts throughout this text.

"Community" may seem to be the most self-evident of all these terms, but the meaning of community shifts according to the context in which it is used. A community might refer to a geographic place (a neighborhood, for example) or it might refer to a group of people spread over vast areas (Citizens' Coal Council is a community of activists from around the United States who work on coal issues). In any case, some kind of common bond links people together in something they call a community. Rather than community as a place-based concept that is frozen in time, I borrow anthropologist Stephen Gregory's definition of community as a "power-laden field of social relations whose meanings, structures, and frontiers are continually produced, contested, and reworked in relation to a complex range of sociopolitical attachments and antagonisms."[5] I follow participants in the mountaintop removal conflict who emphasize particular features like environment, economy, and morality as issues within the "power-laden fields" of their lives.

Running throughout the conflict over mountaintop removal coal mining is a sense that conditions in Appalachia's coalfields violate basic expectations of how citizens should be treated in the United States. Of course, not everyone shares this view. Coal executives and their lawyers argue that abolishing mountaintop removal would fundamentally violate property rights. Many mine workers resent activist efforts because they feel it threatens their livelihood. I characterize this kind of dilemma as a moral process. This is distinct from morality as a metaphysical or religious concept, although many people see mountaintop removal in that way. What I call a moral process is the *social* process of deciding right and wrong within the framework of our (or any) society. Where social concepts like community, economy, and environment intersect, deciding right from wrong is fundamentally a social process that reflects a set of collective and, in some cases, contested values. In the case of mountaintop removal, this process has become a sometimes-bitter personal and public debate that is confounded by factors like industry's political and economic dominance; state, local, and national politics; and legal traditions like property rights.

What the environment is and how it should be treated is at the heart of the moral processes associated with mountaintop removal. Supporters of mountaintop removal and its opponents alike include people as part of the environment. Supporters argue that banning mountaintop removal would put people out of work and into poverty. Opponents of mountaintop removal argue that the coal industry systematically violates their rights and destroys their quality of life. In chapter 8 (among other places) I invoke and critique "environment" as a concept. From social science literature, I draw most heavily on the idea of landscape as a social construct to explain how the meaning of environment can change depending on circumstances. Borrowing from geographers like Henri Lefebvre, David Harvey, Doreen Massey, and Don Mitchell, among many others, I see landscape as an artifact created by the interaction between people and the natural world. Landscape includes both physical features like mountains and forests and the people who live in and on them.

This perspective on community, environment, and conflict in Appalachia is not necessarily new. Historians have explored historical precedents that provide important cultural context for understanding the twenty-first century confrontation over mountaintop removal. Ronald D. Eller profiles Appalachian social and economic structures as they existed in their environment prior to capital-intensive development and exploitation of resources. Mountain settlements before widespread intrusion of capital were neither fully integrated with the formal institutions of post-Civil War United States, but neither were they as isolated from that world as they have often been portrayed. This position gave rise to unique social and cultural institutions including "place," a meaningful amalgamation of land, personal identity, material culture, and economic life. (Place, along with family, underpinned a social order at odds with the rising capitalist model of faceless, impersonal resource exploitation.)[6] Coalfield residents not only know and emulate these cultural values; they have invoked these same claims to buttress arguments about Appalachian culture in the twenty-first century.

David Alan Corbin challenges interpretations of Appalachia's long-conflicted labor relations that try to cast efforts to unionize as being ideologically driven. Rather, he characterizes union activism beginning in the earliest decades of the twentieth century as primarily pragmatic efforts that intertwined notions of work, life, community, the state, and employers, among others.[7]

Chad Montrie's history of activism against surface mining in Appalachia reflects the combination of pragmatism, community, and the importance of land in the negotiation of social relations associated with place.[8] Most recently, Shirley Stewart Burns charted the history, social, political, and environmental impacts of the mountaintop removal conflict through the late 1990s and 2000s.[9]

My approach to understanding Appalachia's coal conflicts stitches together these historical perspectives; theoretical approaches to social action borrowed from geographers, sociologists, and others; and the outlooks forged by the activists encountered in the ethnographic moment. As Eller, Corbin, and Montrie have all noted, specific understandings of the relationships between people, and between people and land, have informed coalfield communities' conceptualizations of their relationship to the coal industry and the world around them. As with these historical episodes, activists in the mountaintop removal conflict continually refine views on history, place, community, economics, politics, and nature. Their views reflect Michael Watts's assertion that nature can be constructed to function both as artifice and artifact. As Watts argues for oil, coal too is both an artifact—black mineral—and an organizing principle for a constellation of social relationships.[10] For contestants in the dispute over mountaintop removal, coal is a concept that bears their contemporary assertions about the relationship between land, community, economy, and justice.

* * *

All anthropology is, in some sense, an anthropology of experience. All of the concepts highlighted above come together and become meaningful in the realm of experience. Many scholars have attempted an anthropology specifically focused on the mundane experience of everyday life. Glenn Hinson argues that ethnography of experience narrated from the distance of objectivity fails because it generalizes experience to the point of obliterating particularity and subjectivity of the individual—the source of "experience" in the first place.[11]

The people at the center of this project, the authors of the comments that appear throughout, are part of an activist network whose primary goals are stopping the practice called mountaintop removal coal mining and building, and asserting the value of healthy, sustainable, and just communities in Appalachia's coalfields. The group at the center of my research is called Coal River Mountain Watch (CRMW), located in West Virginia's Coal River region. CRMW is part of a regional network of activist groups called the Friends of the Mountains. I focused on CRMW because its members are coalfield residents who have taken a stand against the coal industry. A deep tradition of activism in the coalfields includes the United Mine Workers union and long-standing activist groups like Kentuckians for the Commonwealth and Save Our Cumberland Mountains.[12] In the mid-1990s, Coal River Mountain Watch grew out of a region with little local activism with the help of the West Virginia Organizing Project and the Ohio Valley Environmental Coalition. Throughout this project, I have tried to approach the issues related to the coal industry and living in the coalfields through residents' own words and experiences and my own experiences living in and visiting southern West Virginia.

The coal industry and the state dismiss activists' claims by calling them exaggeration, hyperbole, emotional, or radical. Coal and the state dismiss the subjectivity of coalfield residents as "just talk" that does not reflect the real conditions in the region. Industry and government are more likely to use production and employment statistics or some other objective measure to offer their picture of the coalfields. Coalfield history, residents' experiences, and my own research bear witness to Coal's dominance over state politics to marginalize anyone who speaks out against the industry.

The pattern that emerges from the activists' stories and other data gleaned from my research is one of a new kind of struggle to represent people's interests against the powers of industry. In response to changes in politics, governance, and economics that remade life in the coalfields and fostered the growth of mountaintop removal, new forms of activism are needed to represent community interests. In the process of responding to these changes at a local level, activists directly confront questions of culture and society that rarely surface other than in times of collective crisis. Out of these circumstances emerge a social discussion of how economy and environment articulate in a cultural realm. Rather than the zero-sum portrayal of economy and environment as fundamentally opposed, local activists have to confront economic and environmental issues as real and complementary elements of their community. For a community to work, it must have both a healthy economy and a healthy environment. For these reasons, it is helpful to consider environment and economy as components of a commons that includes "those assemblages and ensembles of resources which human beings hold in common or in trust to use on behalf of themselves, other living human beings and past and future generations of human beings, and which are essential to their biological, cultural, and social reproduction."[13] Such a view of commons resources directly contradicts the most basic assumptions of neoliberal theory and lays bare the contours of conflict between economic theories and embodied communities.

The variety of meetings, public hearings, protests, and media publications employed here show that activism is very flexible and capable of operating at many scales from the very local to state, national, and even international arenas. Activists work through networks of organizations that can provide various resources and expertise. In opposition to these flexible networks are well-integrated conglomerates of both industry and government. Corporations involved in mining are often large transnational companies with little local representation. Not only are the corporations vertically integrated from production to corporate offices, they are integrated with government, symbolized in West Virginia by the coal industry's close connections to both state government and the Bush administration.[14] Activists keep track of government agencies on the local level (county commissions, school boards), the state level (Department of Environmental Protection, State Historical Preservation Office, Division of Highways), and the national level (Environmental Protection Agency, Mine Safety and Health Administration, National Labor Relations Board), all of which are, at the very least, deferential to the right of companies to mine. On the international level, "free trade" entities like the World Trade Organization protect the rights of transnational companies from local sentiments such as those expressed by activists.[15]

At all levels of government, activists continually find themselves blocked by the power of industry and government. Activists had some success in federal courts, arguing that mountaintop removal violates the Clean Water Act. In response, the Bush administration rewrote the specific rules in question to make the procedure legal. The combination of this political dominance, systematic dismissal of complaints, and the dismal economy of southern West Virginia creates a situation that almost completely shuts coalfield citizens out of any truly democratic decision-making processes.

So, What Is Neoliberalism Anyway?

Neoliberalism is a set of political, economic, and social ideas that have been incredibly influential in the United States and around the world since the 1970s. Many scholars and cultural observers have tried to describe the changes to societies, economies, and major institutions during that time. Some, like my grandfather, called neoliberalism by one of its earliest labels—Reaganomics. That was the term he used to explain the bizarre new set of priorities that led to his own forced retirement from the mines in the early 1980s. Others, as noted above, have associated neoliberal trends with globalization.

Three decades on, a much clearer picture has developed of these ideas and their effects. Associated in the U.S. with Ronald Reagan and in England

with Margaret Thatcher, neoliberalism refers to an ideology that emphasizes market-based initiatives, competition, and private property rights over
government and social affiliations. Though attention is often focused on
economics, David Harvey marshals extensive empirical evidence to support
his interpretation of neoliberalism as a "*political* project to re-establish the
conditions for capital accumulation and to restore the power of economic
elites."[16] This remaking of society in the image of business necessitated the
elimination of politically and economically powerful "social solidarities,"
most notably labor unions. Reagan's firing of striking air traffic controllers
in 1981 is seen as a clear indicator that neoliberal trends were firmly in place
at the highest level of government. Harvey attributes to Thatcher the saying,
"There is no [society], only individual men and women."[17] Neoliberalism
emphasizes competition both in markets and among individuals, together
with private property and personal responsibility, as the only ways to create
efficiency and stimulate economic growth and prosperity. Along the way,
neoliberal policies reshaped government regulation to facilitate economic
activity and concentrate decision-making in the hands of bureaucratic experts
rather than transparent, democratic processes.

This quick summary of the basic elements of neoliberalism is intended only
to give sufficient background to illustrate how readily apparent those trends
are in the rise of mountaintop removal coal mining in Appalachia and in the
emergence of the activist community to oppose them. As neoliberal ideology spread from business circles to think tanks, government, universities,
and development agencies, it quickly reformed all of those institutions and
altered basic understandings of how society works. We will see how government regulation, unions, economics, and politics have all contributed to the
circumstances surrounding the coal industry in the late twentieth century.

Out of those same circumstances have emerged the community activists
that are at the center of this work. I portray the activists as taking up the
cause of representing the needs of their community against the economistic imperatives of an industry and government reshaped in the neoliberal
mold. In years past, the United Mine Workers of America (UMWA) provided
strong representation for workers and, by extension, coalfield communities.
As the UMWA suffered from the assault on unions, communities needed
a space in which to organize and promote their own interests that were
compromised by business practices that were advancing, quite literally, in
the form of mountaintop removal. In the community activist organizations
portrayed here are many former union members, supporters, and activists.
The legacy of their union past is easily identifiable in their ideas, rhetoric,
and activities. The emergence of community-based activist networks repre-

sents a trend to recreate social solidarities that the neoliberal tide attempted to wash away. Though dominant forces have dramatically weakened social solidarities (especially politically potent ones) for nearly three decades, the (re)emergence of community-based activism as an organizational form and the reassertion of community relationships, values, and needs indicate that society does indeed exist; community does indeed have a value that is not properly accounted for under neoliberal logic.[18]

The difficulties encountered by activists described in this book illustrate the results of all of the neoliberal developments introduced above. Inside the mines, on top of mountains, in the union, in communities, in government agencies, and in the activist organizations, the effects of neoliberal reforms are apparent. The controversies surrounding mountaintop removal and the mining industry reflect the shortcomings of neoliberalism to fully provide for communities. Though the scope of this study is limited to the coal industry, similar principles can be seen operating in other industries and societies around the world. Neoliberalism, like globalization, is represented as being politically neutral. In privileging corporate economic efficiency over other institutional forms (community, government, university, and others), neoliberalism rearranges the political landscape. The pursuit of efficiency for its own sake, removing economic activity from any connection to people or place, undermines the ability to represent collective community interests.

More will be added to throughout the text to fill out this briefly sketched argument.

Objectivities and Objectives

Ending mountaintop removal coal mining in Appalachia will cost jobs. It seems like a relatively simple fact that jobs will be lost if the strip mines are shut down. But facts can be slippery things. The coal industry vigorously defends its practices locally by pointing out that no other industry in the region offers as many jobs as the coal industry, and that the average coal mining job pays wages far above others available. The industry regularly criticizes people who do not present its position on mountaintop removal and related issues alongside theirs for not being "balanced."

Of course, it is equally factual to point out that the introduction of mountaintop removal costs jobs too. Coal miners have a good grip on this fact. Seasoned miners know how tenuous their jobs are. They are reminded every day during the ritual trip to work that begins by checking their safety equipment and sliding their brass nametag to "In." Knowing who is "In" lets rescuers know who is down in the mine in case of an explosion, collapse, or other disaster. A vehicle called a "man trip" hauls miners past a sign saying, "The only job security is a safe, low cost, and efficient work place." Beyond the sign and past pneumatic doors, miners enter an eerie, damp netherworld with only enough light to constantly remind visitors how unnatural this space is. These men (and, since 1973, women) know how tenuous their jobs are. They know they can't compete with the efficiency of a dragline—the mammoth machines that follow powerful explosives, together ripping away entire ridges in 100-ton morsels. These miners know that mountaintop removal costs jobs. It cost the jobs of their former co-workers who now manage a Burger King somewhere in North Carolina, or work construction in Florida—those are jobs scooped away by the dragline that runs twenty-four hours a day with no health insurance, no overtime pay, and no union contract.

In divisive contexts like this, there is something deceptive about objectivity. That is what I believe the coal industry portends when they talk of the need for "balance." They want Coal's story to be told with equal attention to "both sides of the story." But something about that is inherently *not* objective. How, for example, can two seemingly contradictory claims both be objectively factual? How can mountaintop removal both cost and provide jobs? As I said, facts can be slippery.

Anthropologist Terre Satterfield described the way opponents used "science" in the controversy over old-growth timber in Oregon.[19] By using different kinds of information framed in different ways, but still advanced under the rubric of "science," preservationists and loggers "talk past" one another. Environmental activists in Oregon were more likely to talk about science as abstract concepts while loggers spoke of science in applied experiential terms. Similar talking past marks the mountaintop removal controversy when the industry and activists frame information in terms of environment and community.

Where is objectivity to be found in a world where perspective means so much? One answer, the answer I prefer, is that objectivity and balance are not to be found at all. On the other hand, *objectives* are everywhere. Coal is full of objectives, and they are easy to see. Concern with balance allows Coal to present "facts" that are, at best, questionable, at worst, deceitful.

Example 1: Mountaintop removal "improves"
the land by leaving it flat for future development.

In a landscape with very little level land, Coal argues, creating new flat land is needed for economic development. Never mind that there is no infrastructure on these sites. Boone County, West Virginia, zoned land for future development based on its distance from the county's three main roads. Only six sites are within five miles of those roads and only three within five miles of the county's only four-lane highway. There are already over 100,000 acres of stripped land in the Coal River basin alone. Meanwhile, development that has occurred on some mine sites includes a prison in Kentucky whose settling foundation made it the most expensive federal prison in the nation, and a high school in West Virginia that has similar problems. An airport in Hazard, Kentucky, and a golf course in Mingo County, West Virginia, are examples of "economic development." But very few people, other than coal executives, fly or play golf in the coalfields.

Example 2: Topsoil substitute is "better" than native topsoil.

One of many scandalous aspects of mountaintop removal is the designation of "fish and wildlife habitat" as a form of postmining land development. Under the 1977 Surface Mine Control and Reclamation Act (SMCRA), strip mines must either be developed for some commercially viable purpose or reclaimed to their "approximate original contour." For years, state and federal regulatory agencies approved permits for fish and wildlife habitat as postmining development. Critics charged that this was a cheap way for companies to get off without reclaiming sites. Typically, companies spread a thin layer of topsoil substitute (crushed shale) over the land and sprayed it with a mixture of nonnative grasses. Where trees were planted, they were often nonnative species like Autumn Olive (an invasive nonnative species, like kudzu) or various pine species. Often, there was no commercial viability to any of the reclamation species. The industry's argument was that these "habitats" attracted animals that attracted hunters who contributed to the economy.

More recently, West Virginia's Department of Environmental Protection (DEP) encouraged planting more diverse and commercially viable hardwood tree species on mine sites. The DEP agreed with industry that topsoil substitute was better than native soils. By "better," they meant that crushed shale has higher mineral contents than does dirt. Mountain soils are thin and nutrient poor, they argued. This view, tantamount to ecological tunnel vision, ignored the fact that the most diverse hardwood forest on the planet grows in this "poor" soil. In addition to hardwoods, the forest grows a culturally and commercially valuable understory that includes ginseng, bloodroot, goldenseal, ramps, and rhododendron. None of these species have been included in postmining reclamation, despite regulations that land be reclaimed to a state "at least as productive" as before mining. Underlying questions that are not considered include for what and for whom is topsoil substitute "better."

Example 3: Weight limits on West Virginia's roads are out of date because a new generation of coal trucks is engineered to safely carry much heavier loads.

This might be true, but the roads beneath the trucks are not new and not engineered to carry heavy loads. Trucking firms invested in bigger trucks in response to decades of ineffective or nonexistent weight limit enforcement. Though public outcry repeatedly drew attention to coal trucks (most recently from 2001 to 2003), trucks continued running with improper equipment and overweight loads. Often paid by the load, truck drivers had an incentive to haul heavy and fast. Overweight trucks cause extensive road damage that the state has to repair. A 1980 federal study of West Virginia's highways calculated the cost of upgrading roads to maintain minimum safety standards with coal truck traffic. As of 2003, no systematic upgrades had occurred and the estimated cost, adjusted for inflation, was $2.8 billion. While the trucks may be new and fancy, the roads are old and decrepit.

*   *   *

These brief examples are meant to illustrate how selective identification of facts can be used to deceive. The coal industry's propaganda machine is very adept at distorting public opinion using disinformation and intimidation. Demands for objectivity or "balance" obscures the industry's objectives, creates confusion, and undermines the search for accuracy. Of course the coal industry wants to continue mining coal. But that is not their objective. For a century, coal supported countless communities across central Appalachia. Though residents consistently describe life in the company town—when they had community resources and infrastructure—with nostalgia, household income was even then among the lowest in the nation. Those same residents now ask why coal cannot be mined in ways that contribute to, rather than dismantle their communities. The industry's objective often appears to be avoiding any appearance of recognition of citizen's claims or any transfer of power to citizens or communities near its operations. The industry does not present much of an argument to support its position. Insomuch as it is an argument, it goes something like this: coal is the economic lifeline of the region. Without coal, there would be no jobs. If you don't let us do what we want, we'll go out of business and then you'll really be in bad shape.

This perspective ignores the fact that the coalfield economy is among the worst in the nation (West Virginia ranked fiftieth in the nation in median household income for the three-year period from 1999 to 2001).[20] It ignores that the coal industry created and vigorously maintains the economic system that keeps the region impoverished. It ignores the fact that the coal industry has, through mechanization (including mountaintop removal), eliminated over 100,000 jobs since 1950 in West Virginia alone. Industry leaders know that many coal miners are also avid outdoorsmen who, given the choice, might choose not to blast away the mountains where they hunt.

So, this book cannot be both "balanced" and faithful to my community consultants. At times, the two versions of reality seem as disparate as night and day. I focus on the activist community that works to abolish mountaintop removal mining for several reasons. Conceptually, activists perform extremely creative and compelling work reimagining the history and culture of the Appalachian coalfields to emphasize values that reinforce their arguments against the coal industry. Their work and its products are a valuable case study in social and cultural practice and the articulation of the local and the global. A second reason for focusing on the activist community is access. The activist community graciously granted me access to their work, their communities, homes, and lives. The coal industry is very guarded in granting access to its mine sites and inner workings. I did interview some coal executives, and interacted with some miners, but I had nowhere near the access to those communities that I had to activists. Finally, I find the activist position to be more honest and convincing than that of industry, which ensconces itself within intellectually questionable arguments about economics, politics, and law. The coal industry commonly decries studies like this one for not being "balanced." Presumably, balance means giving equal attention to Coal's own claims, as if economic logic, property rights law, and arguments about political process are self-evident. Industry's position demands attention, though not in the unquestioned forms in which it is typically delivered.

The story that emerges with striking consistency from my conversations and observations is one about the machinations of power and the principles and practices of democracy in the dynamic, power-laden social fields of community. Since the days of speculators buying mineral rights from unsuspecting homesteaders, the formal language of law and economics has been used to exploit many rural mountain people. In the case of mountaintop removal, however, law has been interpreted against the coal industry. Among several other examples, federal courts have decided four different times that mountaintop removal coal mining violates the Clean Water Act and the Surface Mine Control and Reclamation Act. In 2003, a Boone County, West Virginia, jury decided that Massey Energy was liable for damages caused by coal dust blanketing the town of Sylvester.

Nevertheless, there have been no substantial changes to coal industry practices. Shortly after George W. Bush took office in 2000, his administration revised the rules promulgated under the Clean Water Act specifically to accommodate mountaintop removal. Two years after a judge had ordered Massey Energy to install dust monitors in Sylvester, no monitors had been installed. As residents have become more successful at using laws to curb the intrusive effects of mining, the powerful industry has become more successful at petitioning the government to change those laws and regulations to protect their practices. In the process, the principles of democratic governance have been all but disassembled. The following chapters include numerous examples to illustrate these processes.

* * *

My hope is to convey in this written work, as well as in my fieldwork and my relationship with the people that made it possible, a sense of both "civic professionalism" and "pragmatic solidarity."[21] Civic professionalism challenges academics to "help construct democratic public spheres" to address social and planetary crises. I sympathize with the struggle to stop mountaintop removal and I sympathize with the struggle to overcome and right decades of injustice in the coalfields. That injustice has affected my own family and in many less direct ways shaped my own life. The "pragmatic" part of pragmatic solidarity is a sense of practical engagement with our consultants, working together with them and contributing our skills and energy to their efforts. What skills I do have, I have offered to Coal River Mountain Watch and other collaborators in the broader Friends of the Mountains coalition. I would hope they agree that our relationship goes far beyond what can be described in this or any other written work.

Nevertheless, I have written this work in the spirit of collaboration and engagement with the idea of contributing to CRMW and Friends of the Mountains in at least two ways. First, by including CRMW and other activists in the writing as well as field research phases of the project, my hope is that we have both learned from one another. As a result of reflecting upon and analyzing our shared activities, I hope that the activists derive additional understandings and senses of their activism that are useful to them. Second, this written work is designed to spread awareness of the activism in Coal

River, West Virginia, and Appalachia to broader audiences. This awareness includes the complexity of the issue in the local communities and the systemic forces that connect Coal River to communities and people all across the United States and even across the globe. As such, I have attempted to use terminology that is accessible to a broad audience, while preserving, to the extent possible, the theoretical underpinnings of my research. Readers interested in the theoretical foundations of this project can find them in endnotes and, hopefully, implicit in the text.

Following anthropological custom, I began this project with a plan to use pseudonyms for all people I quote in the text. During my fieldwork, however, it became clear that obscuring some people's identities would be silly if not impossible. People like Julia Bonds and others became public figures through their activist work. I have created a hybrid pseudonym arrangement using some people's real names with their consent. Others I protect with pseudonyms and by changing names of people, places, and other circumstances. For some conversations containing sensitive material, I have used pseudonyms for some of the people whose names I would otherwise have used.

I have tried to confine the overtly polemical portions of the text to these introductory remarks and the conclusions. It is difficult, if not impossible, to do so because the style of anthropology that I pursue is *inherently,* though not *gratuitously*, political. Giving credence and legitimacy to what I believe to be intellectually untenable claims like "mountaintop removal is an improvement" to the natural landscape would mislead readers from the central tenets of my argument, betray the relationship of trust I have built with my consultants, and distort the issues for the reader. My task is to situate an inherently political topic and argument within an intellectual framework sufficient to show that my conclusions are not merely political, but supported by a body of theoretical and methodological concepts.

Also implicit in this text is the idea that the mountaintop removal conflict is representative of structural processes that shape conflicts in other places. The same fundamental neoliberal forces are at work anywhere the demands for economic efficiency become an end unto themselves. In the process, these trends undermine meaningful yet abstract concepts like solidarity and support that West Virginians evoke with community. The commons approach to environmental and economic activism employed by Coal River Mountain Watch, their collaborators, and activists in other conflicts around the United States and the world, is a valuable development in the reconstitution of community interests in the wake of neoliberal demolition of institutions like labor unions and government regulatory agencies.

My West Virginia

The West Virginia I know is a different place from the West Virginia where my parents were born in 1949. It might as well be a different planet from the West Virginia where my grandparents were born in the 1920s. Theirs is rougher around the edges—more akin to the West Virginia where Chester, a character in Breece Pancake's story "The Salvation of Me," didn't find fourth gear on his car until he drove on Interstate 64. Once he found it, he didn't stop until he got to Cleveland. My West Virginia is a four-lane highway that goes to the Walmart in Bluefield, the town where I was born and where my grandparents still live.

My family is from McDowell County, West Virginia, which has produced more coal than any other county in the United States. Yet, since the early 1980s, McDowell County has suffered an extreme, seemingly unending economic depression. Somewhere between the modern shopping centers of Bluefield or Charleston and the crippling poverty of McDowell County is Coal River—where the coal industry is still active and so are communities' struggles to survive. Among the curves and cliffs of WV Route 3 are some of the state's most productive coal mines. Out of this in-betweenness emerges the ongoing drama of the coalfields. A unique industry and way of life have written and overwritten the mountains with stories about mining and living. The story of Coal is the very picture of an unsustainable enterprise. Mountains can't grow new coal, at least not in a time frame relevant to us. Yet our thirst for energy continues to grow. As mines find new methods to increase production, people and towns have to find new tactics to stay out of the way.

The story of the coalfields is as much about how a place lives and dies, about a way of life, history, and memory, as it is about mining. The Coal River region at the dawn of the twenty-first century—a place that, around the edges, is fading into memory—is ground zero for this battle. Coal River and its constituent parts (vertical strata of coal, stone, and forest, and horizontal spaces—rivers, hills and hollows) are sacred to a great number of people, for a variety of reasons. The different faces of this prism give rise to different faces of the community. There are those who believe coal is a lifeline, the only thing keeping Coal River from sinking into nonexistence. There are those who believe that coal is a noose choking off the life that thousands once lived in the mountains. There are those who are confused, those (like my parents) who jumped on the "hillbilly highway" to North Carolina long ago, and those who are fighting—for either side—to claim the future they imagine for Coal River.

PART I

The Worst Goddamn
Thing I've Ever Seen

The Coal River Valley winds from its headwaters in Boone and Raleigh Counties north through some of West Virginia's richest coal deposits to the Kanawha River near Charleston. The physical and social landscapes along the way are a study in contrasts: at times cold and hard, at others lush and vibrant; sometimes warm and communal, sometimes divided and confrontational; sometimes organic and renewable, sometimes mechanical and destructive. The coexistence of a distinctive way of life profoundly shaped by the mountain landscape and a nonrenewable fossil fuel resource has created these contrasts.

Mountaintop removal coal mining (MTR) is strip mining on an incredible scale that is both intensive and extensive. The method removes several hundred vertical feet of a mountain to extract four or more seams of coal. Many mine sites have come to encompass thousands of contiguous acres, creating vast featureless plateaus. Mining companies have used strip mining techniques in Appalachia since at least the 1920s. MTR differs from earlier forms of strip mining in both scale and procedure. Until the 1970s, most strip mines were so-called contour strips that followed one coal outcrop around a contour of the mountain. Miners would strip the outer edge of the mountain away from the coal seam to create a "bench." Then machines called augurs would drill into the seam beneath the newly created cliff to extract as much coal as possible. Following the contour around the mountain, this process resembled peeling an apple. Some strip mines resembled

MTR in that they removed the top of a mountain from the highest coal seam, but they did not simultaneously extract multiple
seams, nor were they as expansive as MTR mines.

Several advances in technology facilitated the rise of MTR,
among them computer engineering capabilities, large machinery
(including draglines—$100 million machines that can move one
hundred tons of material with each scoop), and powerful explosives (ammonium nitrate and fuel oil—similar to the Oklahoma
City bomb). The process is methodical, rational, and efficient.

The people of Coal River are coal mining people, as Sylvester
resident Pauline Canterberry said, but the relationship between
the industry and residents has become one that many people
describe as abusive. Activist Judy Bonds compared the position
of coalfield communities to that of a battered wife: they know
they are being mistreated but they are unable to break their bond
with Coal.[1]

In the late 1990s and into the 2000s, communities faced
wide-ranging problems attributed to the coal industry: coal
dust blanketing homes; overloaded coal trucks barreling down
narrow, winding mountain roads; floods caused by increased
runoff from strip mines; acid water contamination; and subsidence from abandoned mines.[2] Along with the physical effects of
mountaintop removal, the accompanying social disintegration of
communities was perhaps the most painful effect for many coalfield residents. Within the complex array of social, economic, and
political pathogens, mountaintop removal coal mining became
the poster child for the abusive relationship between coal and the
people who live around it. Homes shake for miles around under
the force of the explosive blasts. Well water becomes tainted,
brown, and smelly, or disappears altogether. In September 2004 a
boulder sent careening off a mountaintop removal site in western
Virginia smashed through a mobile home, killing a three-year-old
boy in his sleep.

Beyond these direct physical effects of mountaintop removal,
its graphic violence—literally blowing up a mountain and dumping it into a valley—offends the most basic moral understandings of the world held by people whose identities and senses of
self and place were formed in the forested mountain landscape.
Standing on what used to be his own grouse-hunting spot in
the woods, it is hard for a coal miner to imagine how the rocky,

Active mountaintop removal site on Kayford Mountain, West Virginia, 2003.

grass-covered plateau that is left after mountaintop removal is an "improvement." Yet, industry officials often described it as such. Hand-drawn football players (presumably from West Virginia University, the "Mountaineers") on a child's poster at an activist demonstration asked their coach what they were supposed to be called when all the mountains were flattened. The coach in the drawing suggested "flatlanders."

For decades, the coal industry and the communities that it supported lived in a kind of embattled harmony. Power always rested with the coal operators, but between 1935 and the 1980s the United Mine Workers union mediated that power. The devolution of communities some people compared to Camelot required nothing short of a perfect storm of changes in economy, technology, and labor relations. This storm remade the relationships between the coal industry and coalfield communities from embattled harmony to what some described as outright war.

The coal industry has always had a powerful lobbying and public relations machine. One of the many ways the coal industry tried to diminish the impact of mountaintop removal was to say that the total acreage affected in West Virginia makes up only 1 percent of the state's total land. The claim is deceptive because mountaintop removal is concentrated in a few counties in the southern part of the state. Informal surveys (including my own based on official permit data) of mine sites in Boone, Logan, and parts of Raleigh and Kanawha Counties have consistently found that around 20 percent of the surface area has been disturbed by strip mining in those areas. Even without this perspective, mountaintop removal is still a gross violation to many people. Responding to the industry's 1 percent argument, longtime activist and Boone County native Julian Martin once exclaimed, "It's still the worst goddamn thing I've ever seen."

Nevertheless, the coalfield communities are divided. People whose identities were formed in the mountains and forests also came of age in the coal industry. Coal has been the economic engine for the region for generations. Some see mountaintop removal with resignation, as if it is a natural progression in the industry that has historically given life to the region. "Coal is all we got," is the working man's version of industry's chorus about the jobs that coal provides.

In this section, I describe the rise of mountaintop removal coal mining and the uproar that accompanied it both in West Virginia and in Coal River.[3] The conditions that facilitated MTR in the late 1990s included trends in industry stimulated by neoliberal corporate restructuring, labor relations, politics, government, and regulation. Manifestations of these conditions on multiple scales from federal regulations to local businesses have shaped the battle lines in Coal River. Out of these conditions, I chronicle the emergence of a fresh round of activism against strip mining and the emergence of Coal River Mountain Watch within that activism. I describe the physical and social landscapes of Coal River in order to situate the reader in the particular place that is crucial for grasping local understandings of Coal and community. I trace the history of Whitesville and Sylvester, two towns that sit side by side in the heart of Coal River. I describe the creation of Coal River Mountain Watch and its style of activism. I introduce the idea of the commons to describe the relationship between the social and physical landscapes of the mountains. I conclude by discussing the difficulties of understanding activism within a community that is deeply divided over coal. I frame this final discussion in the context of prayer, faith, and the moral questions that shape people's responses to mountaintop removal.

1. Welcome to Coal River

A Hard Winter

Snow is pretty on the mountains, a white blanket that throws the jagged contours into relief. Sheets of ice pour down the cliffs along the road, like frozen cascades reaching toward the ground. Ice clogs the river where it bends and behind the rubble dams the coal companies use. Where it is unobstructed, sheets of ice swell at the edges, leaving a narrow sliver flowing down the middle.

Just as the snow made the features of the mountains more apparent, so did it make the features of the town more apparent. My street was not scraped or treated for the snow. To avoid sliding, I crept slowly around the curve and up the little hill to the main road. At the top of the hill, the pristine appearance of my neighborhood disappeared into black slush. As plows cleared the snow and ice, small mounds of snow coated with the black undercoat-turned-overcoat of coal dust and dirt lined the road. Around the mounds and other puddles, a black stew of water and coal dust waited to be splattered over the ground's white coat. The dirt followed me inside. No matter how hard I stamped my feet, kicked and wiped the snow from my boots, the black soup followed me. On the floor, I got my own streaked version of the mess on the streets.

Coal River seemed more isolated, more downtrodden, more hopeless in the dirty snow. What color the town had was muted into gray. The white ground only emphasized grit and grime. The disrepair and disuse of the many abandoned buildings stood out more sharply. Streets usually infused the town with swaths of color from passing cars, but they were all whitewashed with a thick, briny coat.

In winter, the backdrop for town was the gray sieve of naked tree branches. If not for the snow, the mountains would blend into a foggy day. In the dust-splattered relief of winter the feeling crept in that this place might just disappear. Maybe slowly, with buildings, streets, and people fading to gray; maybe in one destructive blast, this entire town might succumb to the gray blight that spread down from the mountains and up from the street gutters and be gone.

Misty Valley

April redbuds trumpet the rolling explosion of color and life that is a Coal River spring. Forsythia and wisteria take over in May, honeysuckle and rhododendron in June, wild lilies line the roads in July, and black-eyed Susan leads the wildflowers into summer. The intense life of the mountains works hard during the summer to reclaim itself from the hard gray of winter and people respond with life of their own. Four-wheelers come from every driveway and hollow. People sit on porches all waking hours. Shirtless men mow lawns. Children splash in the pool.

Riding down Clear Fork on a cool, humid June evening was a treat for the senses. At dusk, mist crept into the valley from above and below, hanging down from the treetops and wafting up from the river. Cicadas sang in the tunnel of trees and flora growing from the rocky mountains out into and over the road. Only a sliver of dusky light penetrated, blurring the colors into a dark green, blue, and black canvas. Fresh cut grass hung heavy on the moist air like sweet anise. The gurgle of the river soothed away the sounds of the day. A man and woman waved from their front porch.

Mountains that were hard, rocky, gray, and dead were now thick with the vitality of summer. The living blanket crept down the hills in the summer heat. Jungle-thick trees, vines, and brush claimed every shard of sunlight. Weeds crept up through the cracks in an abandoned patio to reclaim this space for the forest. A canopy grew over the roads. Keeping land cleared is a constant battle against the vibrant growth of the mountains. In the summer, the feeling rises that this place could be nursed back to health by the natural forces that created it.

The Constants

In the soupy mush of winter or the soupy air of summer, some things did not change. Coal poured from conveyor belts and stacker tubes. Stockpiles swelled and receded as empty trains clanged their way into Coal River and loaded trains crept out. Preparation plants at Sylvester, Marfork, Montcoal, and Sundial ran continuously, pumping their tainted stew of liquid waste into enormous lagoons or old underground mines.

On the surface, drills prepared holes for explosive shots to fell another section of what some called a mountain, others called overburden. The dozers and draglines worked behind, scraping away what had already fallen.

Changing seasons do not affect valley fills. They feed off the rhythmic backup beepers from trucks that send overburden (formerly mountain) careening down their steep slopes. The mechanical growth of valley fills obliterates organic growth in shady hollows. Steadily shrinking mountains and ever-filling valleys replace steep slopes with expansive plateaus.

The burdens of life in Coal River did not fluctuate with the seasons. Coal trucks sent lucky cars to the side of the road. Some weren't so lucky. Truck drivers said it wasn't their fault. Maybe so, but Route 3 was built long before 60-to-80 ton trucks started running the flume from Coal River to barge terminals on the Kanawha River near Charleston.

"If you put coal dust in a Ziploc bag, it'll find a way out," said one Sylvester resident as he showed me coal dust built up in his windowsills.[1] Coal dust came in clouds from the preparation plant over the town of Sylvester regardless of the season. Mary and Pauline collected dust samples rain or shine, sleet or snow, to show accumulation of dust in town. Coal dust accumulated in Whitesville too, but there was no uproar there. The mayor was a mine foreman.

Mr. Brown had replaced five doors—three front and two back. Blasting warped the frames so they wouldn't open and close any more. His neighbor drilled three wells, all tainted by mining around or beneath them. The community of Dorothy looked up at a cracked mountain above. Mine cracks are common, but they usually don't hover above people's homes. Dorothy residents knew if the mountain slides they wouldn't have a chance of escaping. Meanwhile, the state approved a new strip mine permit for the area around the cracks.

Regulatory agencies monitored blasting, investigated mine cracks, monitored dust levels. State police fined overweight trucks. But the problems didn't go away. "They're within regulations." "There's no immediate threat." "I found no violations." "We don't know where they're hauling from."

Outrage stayed year-round also.

The Perfect Storm

The first permits for mountaintop removal (MTR) coal mining in Coal River were issued in the late 1970s.[2] Eastern Associated and Addington Brothers ran a few mountaintop removal sites that were rather small and isolated compared to the mammoth sites that dominated the region by the end of the century.³ As MTR became a preferred mining method, the sites grew. Regulations that were designed for small, remote mine sites proved unsuitable for larger sites that eventually encroached on populated areas. The intent of regulations (described below) didn't really matter, however, because in many cases regulatory bodies simply did not enforce them. A 1997 lawsuit brought by Logan County citizen James Weekley became a watershed event in the emergence of a new generation of activism over strip mining. According to longtime mine regulator Jack Spadaro, "By 1998, there wasn't a legal operation in the state of West Virginia. All of the operations, particularly the mountaintop jobs, were completely out of compliance with federal law—with the intent of the federal law."⁴

In Coal River, most people had some idea that strip mining was happening back in the hills. They might encounter it while out hunting or riding four-wheelers, but few if any residents had a grasp on how intensive and widespread the problem was. Coal River Mountain Watch (CRMW) co-founder Randy Jarrold, a laid-off union coal miner, described how mountaintop removal snuck up on him. Only when science journalist and Coal River native John Flynn returned to the area to retire did Jarrold notice what had happened around him.

> I first started noticing—it'd been around a long time—but John Flynn . . . needed someone to haul people around in four-wheel drive and I had one. I got to hauling [people] around out in the mountains and . . . everything is pretty well hid now and unless you got back out in the mountains you didn't see it. I didn't know how big it was until I got to riding around the mountains with them and John got to pointing things out to me. 'Cause he had been gone for like thirty years and he noticed the change where I'd been living here and it didn't . . . it just crept up on me and I didn't notice. . . . When John got to talking about how it changed I got to looking at pictures of how it was when I was running the mountains when I was back in school. All us boys used to go up and camp out on these mountains and now they're all blocked off and there's nothing there but bare rock. And that was when I got to hit the impact of it how big it was and how much destruction they'd done.⁵

In 2003, eight years after CRMW began working to publicize coal industry practices, some Coal River residents still did not fully appreciate the scale of the destruction around them. While living in Coal River, I showed my neighbor an aerial photo I had taken of an MTR site separated from our houses by a single ridge. He looked at the picture in disbelief and said (as so many people do) that it looked like the moon. Most people knew that floods had become more

Dragline operating on a mountaintop removal site on Kayford Mountain in 2003, surrounded by the landscape often described as a "moonscape."

frequent and more intense in the region. They suspected that strip mining had something to do with it. But many had never seen mountaintop removal. Of all the services that Coal River Mountain Watch provided, showing people the extent of the destruction was one of the most effective.

As graphic and destructive as mountaintop removal is, it is only part of the storm that hit Coal River. A local businessman described Whitesville in 1950 as "the hub of ten thousand miners." Whitesville was a regional center between the cities of Beckley and Charleston. Coal River had been a strong union area since the early 1900s and remained so into the 1990s. Part of the antagonism that inflects the fight over mountaintop removal stems from the rise of fiercely nonunion Massey Energy in the heart of Coal River.[6]

Other mine operators had tried to break with the union in the 1970s with mixed results. The United Mine Workers still held considerable power in the coal industry and in coalfield politics. On the federal level, changes in the National Labor Relations Board (NLRB) that began with board appointments during the Nixon administration tipped the balance of labor policy in favor of employers. The NLRB was able to alter labor policy by changing the way employers could influence union organizing campaigns, forcing unions to organize larger bargaining units, and requiring unions to show a majority through an election rather than signing cards. In 1978, a coalition of business and industry interests from around the country lobbied furiously to defeat a broad labor reform bill. During the 1970s, an industry of labor relations consultants arose that specialized in union busting.[7] The coal industry latched onto these national trends and, using a variety of tactics, Massey became the industry leader in operating nonunion mines.

In 1980, Massey began construction of its first Coal River mine near the town of Sylvester. Many union miners say that pickets at the Elk Run mine had been fairly successful and the union stood a good chance of getting a contract until one violent episode in which union miners stormed the guard shack on Massey's property. That confrontation marked a turning point in the relationship between Massey, the union, and local communities.[8] The fallout of the violent rampage has marked the history of Coal River ever since. Union miners, union officials, and many local people assign blame differently, but most agree that breaking the union became a personal mission for Don Blankenship, a Massey executive who became CEO in the early 1990s.

Even though union miners and sympathizers in Coal River resented Massey's presence at nearby Elk Run, the relationship remained fairly benign for a decade. Massey opened its second Coal River mine at Marfork in the early 1990s. Marfork is a long winding hollow with many branches that was once a popular recreation area and home to several communities and many people. Massey bought out all remaining residents and moved them out of the hollow. The last to go was Judy Bonds, who had lived in Marfork nearly all her life. Living near the mouth of the hollow, she and her family shared a well with their neighbor. Bonds and her family had lived for several years with the trucks, dust, noise, trains, and toxic black-water spills. But when the neighbor sold out giving Massey control over her water source, Bonds no longer felt safe.

The brewing storm over MTR grew quickly after Marfork opened. Bethlehem Steel and Peabody Energy sold most of their mines in Coal River to Massey. Several of the miners I interviewed worked for Peabody at the time. By the mid-1990s, Massey owned the majority of the mines in Coal River and operated them without union contracts. Union sympathy remained high, but economic hardship forced many union miners to accept Massey's nonunion terms. Through several union elections, Massey mines have remained nonunion.[9] Rumors and accusations fly about the tactics Massey uses to win elections. The union organized three votes at one particular mine in the 1990s.

Twice, the union initiative lost by one vote. The third vote was a tie. Labor laws require 50 percent-plus-one vote to force a company to recognize a union.

Meanwhile, the small, isolated mountaintop removal projects of the late 1970s had grown through the 1990s. Companies like Arch Coal, Inc., and Massey had started large MTR projects. The first one operated by Addington Brothers—their Princess Beverly mine on Kayford Mountain—illustrated the pattern most companies would use to exploit mountaintop removal regulations. They began to string together individual mine permits that eventually led to enormous tracts of contiguous mountaintop removal. The Princess Beverly mine began with a 1,000-acre permit issued in 1981. When the mine shut down in summer 2003, it encompassed 2,558 acres under five additional permits. A stone's throw away on Kayford Mountain, Catenary Coal Company (a subsidiary of Arch Coal, Inc.) began its mountaintop removal operation with a 203-acre permit in 1987. By 2003, Catenary had accumulated five additional permits that expanded the site to 4,877 contiguous acres.[10]

Stringing together individual permits to make a contiguous whole exploits the regulatory permit review procedures. Permitting procedures require agencies to evaluate each permit on its own merit, ignoring any cumulative impact the permit might have when combined with other permits even if the boundary between them is indistinguishable on the ground. As one official from the West Virginia Department of Environmental Protection said, each permit "stands on its own."

* * *

Longtime West Virginia politician Ken Hechler served as secretary of state through the renewed uproar over mountaintop removal until 2000. When I asked him about MTR, the eighty-nine-year-old former congressman took a folded sheet of paper from his breast pocket. It was a photocopied page of the *Congressional Record* from July 22, 1974, containing comments he made during debate over federal strip mining legislation.

> Mr. Chairman, mountaintop removal is the most devastating form of mining on steep slopes. Once we scalp off a mountain and the spoil runs down the mountainside and the acid runs into the water supply, there is no way to check it. This is not only esthetically bad as anyone can tell who flies over the State of West Virginia or any places where the mountaintops are scalped off, but also it is devastating to those people who live below the mountain. Some of the worst effects of strip mining in Kentucky, West Virginia, and other mountainous areas result from mountaintop removal. McDowell County in West Virginia, which has mined more coal than any other county in the Nation, is getting ready right now to strip mine off four or five mountaintops.

They are displacing families and moving them out of those areas because everybody down slope from where there is mountaintop mining is threatened.

Through the 1970s, Congress debated several bills to regulate strip mining. Hechler sponsored bills to abolish surface mining nationwide. Though he was no longer a member of Congress when a bill regulating mining finally passed, Hechler was invited to the White House Rose Garden signing ceremony for the Surface Mine Control and Reclamation Act (SMCRA) in 1977. Hechler recalled how, standing in the Rose Garden, he explained to President Jimmy Carter why SMCRA (pronounced "smack-ruh") would fail. "This bill is only going to work if it is strictly administered according to the spirit of the law. Just remember there are going to be tremendous pressures on the people who administer it to cut corners and change and promulgate regulations that negate the spirit of the law."[11]

Jack Spadaro, a mine engineer who spent thirty years in federal regulatory agencies, was among the authors of the first regulations promulgated under SMCRA. Based on his experience, he offered a narrative of changing regulations that confirmed Hechler's Rose Garden predictions.

I was among the first thirty inspectors hired by the Office of Surface Mining in April 1978. And then I got to go to Washington to write the federal regulations on coal waste disposal and reclamation standards for contour mining and valley fill construction. At that time we wrote very rigid rules for valley fill construction. It would have been hard to do the kind of mining that they are doing so haphazardly [now] if they had kept those rules. But those rules were changed after the Jimmy Carter administration. The Reagan-Bush administration came in. In the early '80s all of those rules were weakened so industry could pretty much indiscriminately dump their waste into valleys. And it created some of the most horrendous environmental problems I have ever seen.

The original rules were written so that the sizes of valley fills would be limited to, I think at that time, 250,000 cubic yards of material—small. [Valley fills] usually would be for the initial cut in the mining operation, that would be all. The rest of the material was to be kept on the mine bench or the mountaintop site. And the fill was to be compacted in two-foot layers, with standards for compaction and drainage controls that were very stringent. So you had a stable structure that would not destroy a whole watershed. As soon as the Reagan-Bush people came into office, they weakened those rules and went to something called durable rock fills that could be end-dumped from the top of the mountain all the way into the valley without any compaction, without any standards for construction.[12] Just indiscriminately dumped. Technically, it was supposed to be 80 percent durable rock, but none of these fills that have been constructed are. [They contain] soil, pliable shales, clays. And there was no size limitation so through the '80s and early '90s, even through the Clinton administration . . . operators were allowed to dump large volumes of spoil into valleys. And some of those fills grew to be the largest earth structures east of the Mississippi. They might be as large as 300 million cubic yards of soil and rock indiscriminately dumped into valleys, completely obliterating the streams and the valleys. So . . . by the late 1990s more than 1,500 miles of streams in Appalachia had been destroyed by valley fills.

During his years as an inspector and supervisor, Spadaro worked on a variety of projects that included the governor's report on the 1972 Buffalo Creek disaster,[13] the federal Abandoned Mine Lands program in Kentucky, and the Mine Safety and Health Administration's inspector training school. Over the years, Spadaro participated in several activist efforts against specific mining activities in his native Raleigh County and his home in Lincoln County, West Virginia. At the same time, he developed a reputation as a whistle-blower within the regulatory agencies. In 2003, Spadaro was fired from his position as director of the mine inspector training school. He eventually reached a settlement with the Mine Safety and Health Administration and resigned.

"We did the best we could through the 70s trying to raise awareness about the destructiveness of strip mining," he reflected.

At that time there weren't a lot of mountaintop removal jobs. But as the federal rules were weakened, and therefore the state rules were weakened in the '80s,[14] larger equipment was brought into Appalachia—larger earth moving equipment. And the need for the large valley fills increased and made it economically feasible for big equipment to be used and for the larger mining corporations to conduct these operations on a massive scale.

In the late '80s I became concerned. And even though I was still employed by the Office of Surface Mining, I got up in a helicopter one day in September 1988 and flew over about twenty-four mine sites and took photographs and videotape. And that videotape and photos were used as part of a lawsuit by the [West Virginia] Highlands Conservancy in 1988–89 . . . trying to get control of a program that was completely out of control. The West Virginia regulatory program was completely out of control. It was understaffed; there was no enforcement going on. And in Kentucky the same thing was going on. So, vast areas were being destroyed at a rapid pace with large equipment with almost no control.

The Highlands Conservancy lawsuit was settled in 1992, Spadaro said, with no effective results. Prior to the next significant action against strip mining, James Weekley's 1997 lawsuit, mountaintop removal grew on an incredible scale. In 1996, U.S. Secretary of the Interior Bruce Babbitt spoke at Arch Coal, Inc.'s Hobet 21 mountaintop removal mine in Logan County, West Virginia.

Babbitt called the reclaimed landscape "a miracle," and added that it was "a better landscape than it was before."[15]

The combination of these attitudes at the highest levels of the Clinton administration and state regulations that, Spadaro suggests, were ineffective, if not nonexistent, facilitated massive expansion of mine permits during the late 1980s and early 1990s. Permits issued for surface mines on Williams Mountain and Kayford Mountain in Coal River offer evidence of this explosion. Of twenty-eight permits issued for the two mountains between 1976 and 2003 totaling 15,577 acres, only five permits totaling 2,147 acres (about 14 percent of the total acreage) were issued before 1987.[16]

Not coincidentally, in 1985 then West Virginia governor Arch Moore pushed through the legislature an early indicator of neoliberal policy in the form of tax incentives, ostensibly to promote job creation in West Virginia.[17] Called the Business Investment and Jobs Expansion Credit Act, the tax incentives were to be given at the governor's discretion and the recipients of the incentives were not disclosed. In 1990, Charleston *Gazette* investigative reporter Paul Nyden wrote that millions of dollars of tax incentives had gone to coal companies that had cut their workforce under the logic that, without the credits, the companies would have cut even more jobs. Essentially, the state subsidized Coal's payroll as companies cut jobs.[18]

These so-called super tax credits occurred as the sulfur restriction amendments to the federal Clean Air Act, which took effect in 1990, were on the horizon. Some coal companies used West Virginia's tax windfall to move enormous mining equipment from the high-sulfur coalfields of Indiana, Illinois, and Ohio to Appalachia's low-sulfur coalfields. These draglines and shovels, along with rising demand for low-sulfur coal, lax regulation, and law enforcement were the principal architects of the explosion of mountaintop removal mining in the 1990s.

Back in Coal River, residents felt the effects of mountaintop removal on a daily basis. Residents of Clear Fork beneath the Princess Beverly mine on Kayford Mountain called the state Department of Environmental Protection (DEP) every day to complain about the explosive blasts that shook their homes. One resident from the town of Dorothy described his own experience dealing with Princess Beverly:

> They shook us from about 1996 up until 2000, maybe 2001, I'm not really sure. And, uh, they shook us and shook us with their blasts, and every time they put off a blast, we called the DEP office. They'd say, well, we'll check in on it. They wanted to know the time and everything. And then, within a week we'd get a paper from them saying the coal company was within their blasting . . . specifications, within their legal limits. And you know, when you shake somebody's house, slam doors, shake stuff off the walls, you know, crack your

[foundation] blocks, and stuff like that, even some people had the sills broken in their windows, and they say they're within blasting limits . . . we need to lower their limits.[19]

Randy Jarrold had been laid off in 1995 when Peabody sold the union mine where he worked to Massey. He began working with John Flynn on mountaintop removal issues in 1996. In a 2000 interview, Jarrold narrated the changes in the coal industry, including the rise of mountaintop removal, through changes to the communities in Coal River. Most notable are his comments about the union local in the town of Sundial that had over eight hundred members when he was laid off. He estimated the local had shrunk to about twenty-three members.

> JARROLD: Now Sundial is a perfect example of all the towns on the river. What's happened to Sundial has happened to all of them—they's probably at least twenty-five houses that's gone that used to be here that's all been torn down in the past fifteen [to] twenty years. They's this one tavern here that's still in operation; down below the tavern here there was a service station and a grocery store. Right below it was another service station and a grocery store. Right below it was the post office—they had their own post office. Right across the road from it was J&L Machinery—J&L Steel out of Cleveland had a big machinery plant there. . . . And right beside it was another grocery store—just a small grocery—and right below it was the local hall. . . . And then this little yellow building down here years and years ago used to be a grocery store but them people died off and they closed down, but the other ones still operated. They was one, two, three, four, five—five businesses, a post office, a union hall in this one little town.
>
> McNEIL: Now the union hall is still standing—that's the only union hall still around. How many other union halls were there say thirty years ago, forty years ago?
>
> JARROLD: Gosh, I don't know to tell you the truth. Each community had it's own local hall because it was so many people employed. Just about every—if you can name the communities you can name the local halls.
>
> McNEIL: Okay, and now the only one between here and Beckley is right here?
>
> JARROLD: Is Sundial—local 6608. It was two locals in that 2271 and 6608 used the same building. 2271 was Sundial up on the hill here and 6608 was Montcoal and us down there. Less than ten years ago there was eight hundred and some people belonged to that local hall and now it's twenty-three people left.

Whitesville, Dog Patch, and Sylvester

The effects that Jarrold narrated for the small community of Sundial are apparent throughout Coal River and rest of the coalfields. Kayford Mountain rises between the Coal River Valley and Cabin Creek Hollow. Bernie Stanley lived as a child on the Stanley family property atop Kayford Mountain. Stanley worked in several underground mines inside the mountain and watched the communities disintegrate as strip mining spread across Kayford's ridges.

> You can see, Cabin Creek is gone. Now, Coal River, they're just getting it little by little. Over at Marfork, that hollow used to be full of houses . . . right here in Kayford there was enough people at one time they had three voting districts. That's the way they do, they just keep pinching the community out. That's the same way they do it in Logan [County]. . . . They keep pinching you out and your property ain't worth nothing, so they come up and have an appraisal. . . . Over at Logan, they put them people back on that strip job [after] the flooding. I took a load of food over there that the Union Mission got. [They] said they was gonna put them up there out of the flood prone zone. They moved them up on the [old strip mine], you know. And now they told them, "If you don't buy the property, you gonna have to get off." So, like one man said, "I can't afford to buy the land, the trailer and the land both." He said, "They took my home and I don't know what I'm going to do."
>
> See, now they're wanting to do away with Northfork, Falls Branch . . . Kimball [in McDowell County] . . . see they're just pinching them out. Then they can do what they want.[20]

The pattern Stanley described has played out generation after generation as technology advanced across Appalachia's coalfields. My efforts focus on Coal River, an area that runs through Boone and Raleigh Counties in West Virginia. Coal River is a locally recognized social distinction that generally follows portions of the Coal River watershed. My focus begins in the headwaters of the Big Coal River's Marsh and Clear Forks around the Raleigh County communities of Dorothy, Rock Creek, and Naoma.[21] At the town of Whitesville, the forks meet and form the Big Coal River. My focus extends downriver to Lens Creek Mountain and Drawdy Mountains and the communities of Racine, Peytona, and Drawdy. Between these symbolic bookends, perhaps thirty miles apart, the Coal River Valley is narrow and winding, with countless hollows and tributaries. On the east, the valley is bounded by Coal River Mountain and Kayford Mountain, on the west by Montcoal Mountain (also called Cherry Pond Mountain) and Williams Mountain.

The Hub of Ten Thousand Miners

Arriving in Whitesville in 2000, a place best described as a ghost town, it was impossible for me to imagine the Whitesville that lifelong residents described. Prior to construction of the West Virginia Turnpike in the early 1970s, Route 3 was the primary north-south artery between the cities of

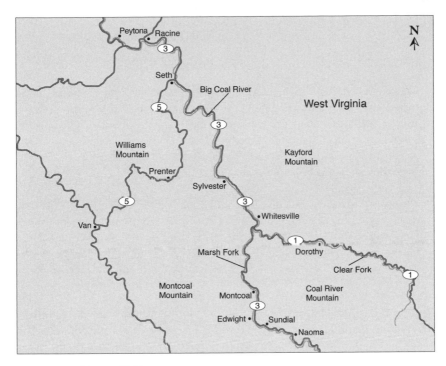

The Big Coal River Valley

Beckley and Charleston. Exactly halfway between the two, Whitesville was the largest town, and regional hub, along the route. Older residents described streets full of cars, sidewalks full of people, grocery stores, department stores, furniture stores, and either twenty-six restaurants or twenty-six beer joints, depending on whom you asked. In the Whitesville I know, the only grocery store left was the Fas-Check, a West Virginia chain store.

Pauline Canterberry grew up in Whitesville Coal Camp, the company town just across the river from Whitesville, where her father worked for Anchor Coal Company. Canterberry described boomtown Whitesville and the development of the nearby town of Sylvester, where she moved in 1948.

> Business in Whitesville was booming, literally booming. On Saturday night, you couldn't pass on the street the town was so full. Because all your small communities around, all your coal camps, small communities, bled into Whitesville. They had buses that ran out to them, brought them into town. Whitesville had two theaters. It had a bowling alley. It had about four furniture stores. It had twenty-six restaurants. It had about four clothing stores—good clothing stores. It had a Haddad's, Cannon's, and Taylor [department stores] too—the better

line of clothing. Beside your Ben Franklin, five-and-ten. You didn't have to go
to Charleston to buy anything. You could buy it in Whitesville.[22]

Freda Williams also recalled the good times in Whitesville.

I can remember when we had several furniture stores, department stores that
carried the best brands of clothing, we had theaters, we had bowling alleys,
an ice-skating rink, you name it and we pretty much had it in this little town.
Several restaurants. At one time there was three to four grocery stores. And the
people from the outlying coal camps would come into Whitesville on pay day
to do their shopping because they could get what they needed and the prices
were better than at the company store.

   Gosh, I'd say the population [in 2000] is one-sixth, to a tenth, of what it
used to be. I can remember coming to a movie, walking from Ferndale—you
know where Ferndale is, up Seng Creek—walking from there to Whitesville
to come to a movie and there'd be so many people in town that there wasn't
enough room on the sidewalks. You'd have to walk out into the street where
the traffic was.[23]

Even subsequent generations enjoyed a vibrant community in the hub of
Coal River. Ernie Harless described the Whitesville of his childhood in the
1960s and 1970s: "When I was a kid, there was a Big Star, a Foodland, a Fas-
Check, [all grocery stores] probably, I'm guessing two or three local grocers,
as far as local guys, not counting the Dollar General store, the Family Dollar,
we had a Haddad's retail store, a Ben Franklin's, all those stores operated in
Whitesville. Not counting the hardwares . . . now they're gone."[24]
   Neighboring Sylvester is unique among towns in Coal River because it
was never a coal camp. In fact, prior to the construction of Massey's Elk Run
mine just north of town, Sylvester was never associated with any particular
mine. Prior to 1950, the bottomland that now makes up most of Sylvester
had been used as a golf course and a small landing strip for airplanes. On the
hill overlooking the bottom were some residential homes, and a little hollow
with a bus stop known as Dog Patch. In 1997, Sylvester began hosting a town
homecoming around their July 4th celebration. Called the Dog Patch Re-
union, the festivities feature a parade, games, watermelon and hotdog eating
contests, singing, and entertainment. In 2003, just about everyone in town
attended, along with many former Sylvester residents. Pauline Canterberry
recalled the historical development of Sylvester:

Up Dorothy Hollow you had Dorothy, Ameagle and Colcord, all three of them
[mines] working up there. Farther up the river you had Eunice and Birchton
and Montcoal and Stickney and on up that way that were working. And then
up Hazy Hollow and Edwight. You had around seventeen to twenty mines in

operation and each one had a little town, a little coal camp town around it. You know, you went in and rented from them. They owned your home, they owned everything. You worked for them, you paid a little bit of rent with them, most of the time around ten or twelve dollars a month. They paid your power bill. . . . The only thing you had was a string down the wall that you strung a light on. But it was livable. And, it got to the point then that things picked up around here so much that you couldn't find no place to live. So then the Branhams and the Porterfields built [Sylvester] up.

Up until [the early 1980s, when Canterberry moved to Sylvester], you couldn't buy a house in Sylvester. People moved to Sylvester and they didn't move out. Cause this was away from the . . . coal camps. It was a treat to get to move to Sylvester. Everybody but the foremen wanted to move to Sylvester. This was the elite section of Coal River. This was the place everybody wanted to go to. Once they moved here, they never did move away.[25]

At her home a couple of streets away, Canterberry's sister, Elizabeth "Punky" Casto, also described living in Sylvester.

We lived in Whitesville Coal Camp. I was married and had one child and we moved to Sylvester in nineteen and forty-eight. Most everybody was moving out of the coal camps at that time and getting individual homes. . . . Sylvester was just starting. There was probably fifteen or twenty houses here in the bottom. . . . the Methodist Church was built. [The Branhams] owned the mines up Garrison or Ferndale, whichever you want to call it, in Seng Creek. They owned that mines up there and they owned all of this [land that is now Sylvester]. . . . Back when I was going to school it was a golf course. . . . Mostly the mine officials played golf.

When the town of Sylvester was formed, Elk Run Coal was not in existence. We moved down here in 1948 and it steadily went to building up down through here. It was one of the nicest communities to live in. Our kids has often made the remark that they grew up in a Camelot environment. And that was just about true. We used to come down, quick as [Casto's husband] come in from work at High Coal—he worked at Anchor Coal Company's mines at High Coal at that time—I'd have supper on the table and we'd come down to the ball field. [The principal of the school] would have the playground open after school and . . . we'd play softball all evening. Cause I know one time my two kids and my husband got on one side and I was on the other side and I got up to bat and my youngest son said, "Let's get 'er daddy." And this was the type of community that Sylvester was. You couldn't have lived in a more perfect community.[26]

Around 1980, Massey began construction of the Elk Run mine complex just north of Sylvester. After a climactic confrontation between union miners and Elk Run in 1981, relations between the mine and the town were generally unremarkable until 1997. In that year, Elk Run obtained a permit to build a new stoker plant and expand their loading facility by adding two new railroad tracks. There was no direct conversation between the mine and the town about the changes to their plant. Sylvester's mayor was the first person to notice the plans in an official advertisement in the local newspaper.

Conveyor belts running through the mountains feed raw coal into the stoker plant, mostly from surface mines. The stoker plant crushes dry coal to a powder consistency and then stockpiles it before it is loaded onto trains. Elk Run blasted away a natural bluff that had previously shielded the town from the mine operation. The DEP issued the stoker plant permit over the objections of fifty-one of Sylvester's two hundred residents. Town residents then contended that the actual plant was built three hundred feet closer to the town than the permit specified, but the mine was not penalized.

The stoker plant was built where the bluff had hovered above town. Immediately after it began operating, prevailing winds in the valley swept dry coal dust away from the plant and into town, blanketing everything with a grimy black coat.

After her husband retired, he and Casto lived in Florida during the winter. Returning to Sylvester one summer, Casto's husband, who suffered from black lung disease, found that he could not live there because of the coal dust in town. Casto recalled:

> We'd go down [to Florida] five months and we come back seven months up here. Until . . . when all this coal dust started here, we came in and every time he got out the door he coughed his head off. And he hadn't been doing that; he didn't have a cough, he was just short of breath. When we came back that summer, he absolutely could not stay outside. So we stayed here probably about three weeks and it got so bad we just turned around and went back to Florida. [When he went to the doctors] he was still coughing real bad and they wanted to know what started that. So, we told them and they said, "You can't go back up there no more."
>
> The hard part about that was . . . it wasn't living in Florida. I don't have nothing against Florida; I loved it going down there in the winter time, that was great. I don't care too much about it in the summer, it gets too hot . . . but, I don't know, this was home to us. And Perry felt the same way I did. And he couldn't hardly stand it when spring would come and he couldn't come home. . . . And the hardest part was when he got critically ill. We brought him back in 2002 for two weeks. He just kept begging to come home so bad. The doctor said, "Bring him home, at this time it doesn't really matter."

After he died in spring 2003, Casto brought her husband to be buried in Coal River.

What a Ghost is Like

ATTENTION BUSINESSES:

In an effort to spruce up our town, American Flags will be placed on all of the lighted utility poles along Coal River Rd. and Raleigh St. Eighty flags will be needed, however, and the city does not currently have the funding to be able to incur this expense. Businesses and local citizens are being asked to purchase the flags for $37.43 each, which includes the flag, shipping and mounting of the flags on the poles. Flags may also be purchased in memory or in honor of someone at no additional cost. A wall of the city building will be used to display a smaller version of all of the flags that have been purchased in someone's name. All businesses are being encouraged to purchase at least one flag as that would put us halfway to our goal of eighty flags. However, you may purchase as many flags as you like.[27]

The decline of Coal River communities since 1980 has, for the most part, been a slow progression punctuated by a few key events. The 1981 violent confrontation between the union and Massey at the Elk Run mine was a major event that signaled Massey's arrival in Coal River and the first major defeat of the United Mine Workers in the area. Peabody Energy's sale of several area mines to Massey in the mid-1990s was a second major event, making Massey the major employer in the area and making nonunion jobs more plentiful than union ones. A slow and steady decline in population, traffic, and business accelerated after Peabody sold to Massey, as Massey laid off virtually all of the union miners employed at the operations.

Changes to the Coal River landscape are profound. Enormous architecture that dominated the built landscape like tipples, rail yards, gob (waste) piles, and even entire towns—have disappeared, torn down and reclaimed by weeds and saplings.[28] Gradually, Whitesville came to resemble a ghost town. A feeling of loss marked people's comments as they listed the stores that Whitesville once had. "You just have a feeling that it's barren and desolate," Freda Williams said of the experience, watching the once-vibrant town recede into a dilapidated state. "You can think back to when there was people active there in that area. And it's sort of like what a ghost is like. You know what used to be there and what it is now. And it's deserted, but you couldn't buy a piece of that land from the land companies or the coal companies, no matter how much money you'd have. And it will continue like that unless [the companies] come up with a use for it."[29]

In fact, rather than coming up with a use for the land, as Williams suggested, land companies and coal companies have, in many cases, taken land out of use. Any expanse of flat land in the coalfields tells this story. Flat land is not plentiful and it is a safe assumption that vacant flat land was once used for something. The wide space along the "straight stretch" near Stickney *was* home to a tipple. The flat land in Sundial *used to* house a machine and fabricating shop. The broad expanses just across the bridge in Edwight *were* home to The Coffee Pot, a coffee shop and restaurant, and what *was* once the largest open-air sawmill in the world. The grassy bottom known as Twin Poplars *was* once home to a drive-in theater. Concrete abutments that supported the screen rise above the grass to indicate that something once happened there.

For these and countless other spaces the story is the same. The land companies own the land. Shadowy power brokers whose existence is simultaneously everywhere and nowhere, land companies own vast tracts of land across southern West Virginia, yet as corporations they can be nearly impossible to find. Pocahontas Land Company, a subsidiary of Norfolk and Southern Railroad, is headquartered in Bluefield, West Virginia. By chance I stumbled upon the offices of Shonk Land Company while searching for a parking space in Charleston. Other land companies that own large portions of Coal River, Pritchard Land Company, Federal Land Company, and Rowland Land Company, are virtually invisible in state records or on the Internet.

Perhaps the best example of land taken out of use in Coal River is a park near the community of Montcoal that Freda Williams described as "a neat little place . . . it was clean and neat and a lot of people took advantage of it and they enjoyed it." Montcoal has been home to mines for as long as anyone can remember. In 1995, Massey acquired all of the operations in and around Montcoal. Shortly thereafter, the park was closed and dismantled.

Randy Jarrold tried to reopen the park.

[It was] a beautiful park. It had like three or four big long shelters, bathrooms, all kinda playground stuff for the kids. I mean . . . Saturdays and Sundays this park would be full of people picnicking. Over yonder it used to be good, nice fishing down through there. They've dumped all kinda big rock and screwed it up. But I mean this was the center point of outdoor recreation for Coal River right here in this general vicinity. Everybody used to meet everyone there. You'd see one and pull in, then one more would pull in. . . . I tried my best to get the land company to lease it to me and they wouldn't lease it. They said that, they claimed something about insurance, they wouldn't really come out right and say. They just kept mentioning insurance, which we was willing to get the insurance and cover it, you know. I tell you Massey has the land leased around here now and it's just like buying the people out, they don't want anybody around a place. . . . See, Armco [Steel company, the former owner of the mines at Montcoal] had a big picnic [shelter] built on the top of Montcoal Mountain here. It was open to the public, they had a big shelter, big cement barbeque pits and everything for the public to use anytime they wanted to.

Situating oneself within the bewildering history of Coal River is difficult for lifelong residents. I asked many people what would become of Coal River in ten years. Responses ranged from, it will be "pretty much the same" to it will be "one big mud hole." A mother with two children in college wanted more opportunities so her kids could move back to work in Coal River. Her husband worked for Massey and she vocally supported the company as offering one of very few opportunities in the area. In a 2003 debate with longtime activist Cindy Rank, Massey CEO Don Blankenship referred to Boone County as "one of the more prosperous counties," and attributed the "prosperity" to the more than fifteen million tons of coal his mines produced in Coal River. A common theme in Blankenship's statements is that increased mining is the key to increasing prosperity in West Virginia. Whether you see Massey and coal mining as a blessing or a curse, it is hard to compare Coal River today to the community that Punky Casto likened to Camelot.

A common reaction among people who encounter Coal River and the issue of mountaintop removal for the first time is a sense of disbelief that people (homeowners, residents, coal miners, citizens) encounter such circumstances in the United States. This sense is made all the more ironic by the patriotic image of Whitesville's streets lined with fresh American flags.

2. Fighting Back . . . Again

The outrage that greeted mountaintop removal coal mining in the late 1990s was by no means new to the Appalachian region. Time and again conditions of social relations and political and economic domination have given rise to reform movements. In comments about the lessons learned from the volume *Fighting Back in Appalachia,* Stephen Fisher argued that for an enduring social movement to achieve substantive change in Appalachia it must transcend single issues in ongoing, democratic, membership-driven organizations.[1] He cited groups like Save Our Cumberland Mountains in Tennessee, Kentuckians for the Commonwealth, and the Ohio Valley Environmental Coalition as existing examples of the activism he described.

A critical discussion of Coal River Mountain Watch, their network partners, and their brand of activism follows in a later section. Here, however, I introduce CRMW as an organization and describe its formation, organization and growth over the first five to seven years of its existence.

A Community Organization

When John Flynn died suddenly in 1996, Randy Jarrold, Freda Williams, and a few others combined their individual efforts to draw attention to the adverse affects of the coal industry. Together, with the help of two notable academics working in the region, Harvard Ayers and Mary Hufford, they created Coal River Mountain Watch.[2] Working with other regional environmental activist groups (most notably the Ohio Valley Environmental Coalition, the West Virginia Organizing Project, and the West Virginia Highlands Conservancy),

CRMW grew in size and importance. By 2003, CRMW had several dozen active members (plus a much larger base of support from sympathetic, if not active, local residents), funding from several foundations, tax status as a nonprofit organization, and an office in Whitesville. The group addressed issues that affected several communities along the Coal River and participated in networks with other groups to address state and regional issues.

"Well, it started with me in my back room of my house and it's growed now to where we have our own office and about everybody in every community knows about us," Jarrold recalled. "And . . . it's not just an organization against mountaintop removal," he continues, "it's a community organization. That's what we've turned it into."

> In '97, I went to Kentucky, and they had a Lucy Braun meeting down there.[3] And I took a slide show. Mary Hufford went and a couple other friends of mine went and we talked to them people down there and they was West Virginia organizations there that didn't really know that this was going on in their back yard. . . . With the help of Mary Hufford, you know, we started to get the word out to people and these groups started coming up here to me and I started taking them up on the mountain. Showing them what was going on and then one thing led to another, these groups started getting involved and finding out more information about what was going on. And, Mary come up, we'd knocked names around for our organization for a long time, and [pause] and the name Coal River Mountain Watch come about and that's the name we stuck with. But that was, in '96 July of '96 . . . or July of '98 was when we had our really formal rally.[4]

The "formal" rally was a public coming out for Coal River Mountain Watch. Several of the key figures in CRMW joined at the event, including Julia Bonds and executive director Janice Nease. Representatives from those West Virginia groups that Jarrold met at the Lucy Braun meeting, including the Ohio Valley Environmental Coalition and the West Virginia Highlands Conservancy, attended. Together, these new members and partners became the heart of a coalition focused on ending mountaintop removal.

While mountaintop removal has continued around them, that Coal River Mountain Watch sustained itself for a decade was a success in and of itself. As Jarrold, among others, described, one of the CRMW's services was to show people in the coalfields that they can stand up to the industry:

> I think one reason it's important is a lot of people is scared right now of the coal companies because the coal companies has crapped on the people of Coal River for so long . . . you've got to work getting them involved with smaller projects first that they can accomplish to show them that your group is sticking together and

something can be done. And, you know, once they get involved in little projects and get them done, then they'll, most of them will follow up and get involved in mountaintop removal because they see they can beat the coal company.

While Jarrold and other members frequently talked about community participation, organizing, and the variety of issues they tackled, CRMW members indicated that mountaintop removal epitomizes the problems facing their region. The issues that people address in their own communities—highway dangers, fugitive coal dust, flooding, blasting, restricted land access, pollution of streams and drinking water—have been longtime concerns for the coalfields. Outside of the occasional, often politically motivated discovery or rediscovery of Appalachian poverty, the social conditions that mark life in the coalfields have endured with relatively little outside attention. Mountaintop removal is an exception. It has attracted much attention from national and international media in recent years, beginning with a 1997 article in *U.S. News and World Report* by journalist Penny Loeb. Media attention was influential in initially framing mountaintop removal as an environmental issue, breaking with the longstanding company-union dynamic.

Despite the barrage of attention, particularly after Judy Bonds won the Goldman Environmental Award in 2003, media coverage did not result in sustained scrutiny of the industry or outrage at mountaintop removal. Virtually all of the reporters who wrote about mountaintop removal contacted attorney Joe Lovett, the architect of a series of successful federal lawsuits against MTR.

> There hasn't been a single media outlet come down here to write a story that wasn't completely favorable to us. And a lot of them come down with this, you know, kind of fair-minded bullshit. They called me and, you know, "well, there's two sides to the story, right?" And I said, "No. This isn't the McNeill News Hour, there is one side here and I'm going to tell you what it is." And they all laugh at me and then they call back [and say,] "Oh my God, you were right." And that's happened . . . you know, *Wall Street Journal, Business Week,* has been down here and written [stories]. There hasn't been a single story written by any media, except for the West Virginia media, that was positive [toward the coal industry].[5]

Nevertheless, CRMW and its friends continued to respond to as many media requests as they could schedule to portray mountaintop removal as the ultimate symbol of corporate disrespect for the landscape and populations of the mountains, and symbolic of the coal industry's overwhelming power to impose its will on the region. Locally, the issue of disrespect was the fundamental target of organizing activities as CRMW worked to build its base and coax more coalfield residents to transform their quiet disgust into activism.

Two events from 2000 illustrate some of the growing movement's multiple facets, and show the kinds of activities CRMW participated in, their tactics and motivations, and their relationships with the broader Friends of the Mountains coalition. The ideas and issues that CRMW advanced, and the activities that they participated in reveal that their activism is not limited to environmental or ecological issues as generally conceived in stereotypical portrayals of the environmental movement. Apparent in these vignettes is an incorporation of mountaintop removal, as well as issues of environmentalism and landscape, into a broader political project focused on social and economic justice based on a common understanding of community needs.

Sylvester

Around the same time that the Elk Run mine installed their stoker plant, the mine and railroad worked to add new tracks to existing rails that ran along the river and against the mountain. Workers blasted into the mountain cliff and used the material as fill to expand the bank out into the river. Punky Casto and her neighbor James Simon live directly across the river and watched the rocks they dumped into the river. According to Simon, their permit specified that rock used as fill material could be no larger than a certain size, which he estimated with a gesture of his hands. He exclaimed, "There's rocks over there bigger than my truck!"

During the same time period, Elk Run built a rubble dam called a weir in the Coal River in front of their plant. Mines use the weirs to create a pool of water to draw from to operate their preparation plants. Not only did Elk Run not have a permit to construct the dam, their DEP inspector told them not build it. Elk Run built the dam over a weekend when no inspectors were working.

This pattern of behavior generated widespread outrage in Sylvester and other Coal River communities. Sylvester residents tried to work with Elk Run and the DEP to stop the coal dust blowing into town from the new stoker plant. (One of the contentious meetings held to discuss the issue is described below). Eventually, 151 of the town's 200 residents joined a class-action lawsuit against the mine. Among the sanctions against the company that resulted from the lawsuit was a requirement that Elk Run enclose the stoker plant in a large fabric dome.

Sylvester residents complained about the dust as a nuisance that prevented them from being outdoors. Their barbecues, picnic areas, and swimming pools were ruined or rendered useless by the dust plague. Parked vehicles were coated with dust. The nuisance crept indoors into heat pumps and

The town of Sylvester sits downwind of the Elk Run coal processing plant (foreground). The controversial stoker plant was contained within a fabric dome in response to a court order.

attics. Cafeteria workers at Sylvester Elementary School, directly beneath the stoker plant, reported having to wash coal dust off their pots and pans when they arrived at school in the morning. The life-threatening coughing fits that exiled Casto and her husband to Florida are a powerful reminder of coal dust's ominous health implications.

After two years of complaints by town residents, the DEP conducted a yearlong investigation of the coal dust problem in Sylvester. Over the course of that year, DEP officers cited Elk Run three times for allowing so-called fugitive dust to escape its operating area. According to DEP guidelines, three violations constitute a pattern of violation. After receiving three violations, a company must ask for a "show cause" hearing at which they must show cause why their mining permit should not be suspended.

In June 2000, then DEP director Michael Castle decided that Elk Run had not shown sufficient cause, and issued an order to suspend their permit for seventy-two hours.[6] In his report, he ordered the company to make necessary changes to stop dust from escaping the complex and to establish a formal communication with the town to monitor the progress of dust suppression. Castle added another unusual provision to the suspension order. To "avoid hardship" on Elk Run's employees, he would allow the company to continue operating during the suspension period if Elk Run contributed $100,000 to fund community improvement projects.

Sylvester residents were puzzled. They were not really interested in suspending the company's permit or in collecting $100,000. While some government and media representatives questioned the legal authority of the DEP director to make up a condition not provided for by state law, the primary concern expressed by local residents was that the dust stop blowing through town. Public sentiment showed distrust of Castle's ruling. Rather than avoiding hardship, many saw Castle's provision as a way for the company to buy its way out of a work stoppage.

The town of Sylvester invited Castle and representatives from Elk Run to explain the order at a town council meeting. On a muggy July evening, more than one hundred people crowded into the Sylvester community center for the meeting. All of the seats in the one large room were filled, and more residents stood along the walls. At the front of the room was a panel of twelve people. On the right were four town councilmen and the mayor. On the left were various public relations and legal representatives from the DEP. At the center of the panel was DEP director Michael Castle.

From my seat in the back of the room, I watched as everyone focused intently on the panel when the mayor called the meeting to order. A pastor prayed over the meeting, asking for guidance not only for Sylvester, but also the surrounding community. After opening the meeting, the mayor invited Chris Knight III, president of Elk Run Coal Company, to address the assembled group of people. Not a part of the panel, the casually dressed Knight spoke from the middle of the room about the improvements made within the mining complex to address the dust problem. He pointed out that the company had paved roads, installed steam-cleaning truck washes, fogger sprays, and windscreens around coal stockpiles. These measures, he admitted, had not been as effective as he hoped in controlling fugitive dust. In what Knight referred to as an "unprecedented measure," the company had installed a sophisticated, centrally controlled sprinkler system on their coal piles. He then introduced a meteorologist sent by the company that designed the system.

The meteorologist, an instructor at the University of Virginia, came forward with a presentation in the format of an academic lecture. As he put his first slide on an overhead projector, the crowd revealed that they were not attentive students, but a group of unhappy and very skeptical people who did not trust the mining company, the government officials, or him. Before he could begin speaking, members of the audience responded to the opening caption, "What is fugitive dust?"

"We know what it is," one resident exclaimed in a contentious voice. "I've got it on my house," shouted another.

Upon learning that the system had been operational for a month prior to the meeting, one resident asked why there was still dust coming into town. The meteorologist explained that the sprinkler system could only control dust from the coal stockpiles. Any number of other areas within the mine complex could produce fugitive dust.

Seeing that the assembled crowd was not satisfied with the professional scholarly presentation, the Elk Run president interrupted the meteorologist. "It is our intention to do right," said Knight. "Nothing irritates me more than being accused of wrongdoing. I'm just a regular guy. I care about your problems and I'm working hard."

James Simon stood and challenged Knight. "You want to do right? You want to help us? If that's the case, you'll be gone in two months." In a later conversation, Simon claimed that officials from Elk Run and other local mines had been replaced by their parent company, Massey Energy, for trying to work with local people to solve problems.[7]

The mayor then introduced DEP director Castle, who read aloud his formal decision regarding Elk Run and invited questions about the ruling. Because it was unprecedented and, according to some, not provided for under state law, the final condition in Castle's order—the provision for $100,000 in community improvements—caused heated debate. The first question regarded the distribution of the community projects called for in the ruling. Residents from outlying areas were concerned that they might not benefit from community improvements if they were conducted only within town limits, despite the fact that they outnumber the in-town population. Castle and the mayor said that there was no provision or intent to restrict the projects to the town limits, but could include residents outside town. Castle reassured the crowd that the ruling was a suspension order that resulted from citizen complaints.

As Castle spoke, a woman stood and showed him a white rag caked with black dust. The rag, she said, was used to wipe off the siding on her house earlier that day. Another woman came forward carrying a zip-lock bag filled with black dust. "I swept that off of my porch," she said. She laid the bag on the table in front of Castle and pointed at it as she backed away.

The tone of the meeting grew increasingly contentious. These two women displayed explicit evidence that, in spite of the improvements made inside the mining complex, the sprinkler systems, and Knight's good intentions, they still had coal dust in town. Residents attending the meeting did not try to hide their distrust of Castle and Knight, challenging them on nearly every point they made. Though the purpose of the meeting was to discuss Castle's proposal for funding community improvements, residents raised many diverse issues that related to Elk Run Coal Company and the DEP.

One resident asked if there were any DEP enforcement officers at the meeting. A DEP attorney introduced several who were scattered through the crowd, including one who monitored activities at Elk Run. James Simon, the local resident who had earlier confronted the company president, stood and shook hands with the Elk Run inspector. "You're a good man," he said. "You're trying to help us." Other people asked about the incessant noise from locomotives since an extra track had been installed. "I haven't had a decent night's sleep in three years" due to trains loading at night, one man claimed. Another man questioned the Elk Run inspector about the dam that the company built without a permit. The man asked if they had a permit and if the inspector had told them it was okay to build the dam. The inspector indicated that he had advised the company not to build the dam, but they did it anyway. The crowd then turned to Castle for a response, but he declined to comment.

As I observed the tense exchange between residents and officials from the state and the company, residents gave the impression that they did not expect comments from Castle about these issues. Rather, they used their list of grievances against Elk Run and the DEP to illustrate their awareness of the mine's unwillingness to change its way of conducting business. Residents pointed to repeated violations, citations, and citizens' complaints, yet as the woman's dust-caked cloth indicated, the problems remained. Residents accused Elk Run and the DEP of not addressing their problems in good faith. They implied that the company simply acted as if it were addressing problems while going about its business as usual.

During my interview with James Simon, he showed me the coal dust on his house in a residential area downwind of the coal loading area. It was fairly clean, he said, because the incidents of dust escaping had been less frequent in recent months. He opened windows to show thick accumulations of black dust inside the sills. Despite reduced frequency of dust escaping the plant, Simon didn't think the problem had been adequately solved. If you put coal dust in a Ziploc bag, he said, "it'll find a way out."

Simon's attitude toward Elk Run and Massey was a common one among Sylvester residents. The company's mining activities, he alleged, sunk his well, cracked the foundation of his house, and severely eroded his riverbank—all in addition to the fugitive dust. "Not one person [from Elk Run] has ever said 'I'm sorry that it's happening,'" he said. "If [Knight] cared, he'd come out here and ask what they can do."

Thinking of his future in the area, Simon said his only option was to leave. He didn't want his grandchildren to be exposed to the damaging coal dust. "The environmental protection won't help us," he said, "the law won't help us.[8] Nobody on earth wants to help us. My only solution is to get out of here."

Many people within the greater Coal River area shared James Simon's attitude. Others, however, do not feel they should have to leave. Coal River Mountain Watch appeals to people whose lives, like Simon's, have been adversely affected by mining practices, but who are nevertheless not willing to leave. They want to change the way companies and state regulators treat residents. While mountaintop removal mining is the poster child for this mistreatment, the events in Sylvester illustrate that the problems attributed to the coal industry go far beyond the single issue of mountaintop removal. The stories told throughout Coal River establish a pattern. Coal companies engage in activities that benefit their business while disregarding or denying their adverse effects on local populations. More perverse to many residents is a feeling that the regulatory agencies apparently fail to provide adequate protection to the public—and sometimes seemed to defend the industry.

The Funeral for the Mountains

Many members of CRMW attended and spoke out at the Sylvester town meeting. While the meeting was a contentious exchange in which residents openly displayed their distrust of coal companies and the DEP, other events staged by concerned citizens' groups took on very different tones. On October 28, 2000, a group of several hundred activists participated in a "Funeral for the Mountains" held on the state capitol grounds in Charleston. In contrast to the open hostility and political awareness of the Sylvester meeting, the funeral took a traditional cultural form to convey the emotional feeling of loss associated with mountaintop removal.

Several months of planning went into the elaborate event. Props for the ceremony and one-mile parade included large green fabric puppets that represented healthy mountains. Marchers carried cardboard caskets in the funeral procession, each representing a part of the landscape that has been lost to surface mining. One casket contained mountain peaks; others carried animals, birds, fish, soil, plants, and streams. Finally, a casket represented the community of Blair, one of the mountain communities that had been decimated by mountaintop removal. The scripted funeral ceremony included prayers, songs, and eulogies for each of the artifacts represented in the caskets. The event began with a one-mile funeral march from the Office of Surface Mining to the capitol grounds. About one hundred people assembled for the funeral march—most dressed in black, some in garish Halloween outfits, some wearing simple black veils. A bagpipe played and drums kept cadence as the group marched.

At the capitol, a stage was set up with a podium, tables, flowers, and a backdrop depicting mountain peaks. On a grassy area to the side of the stage and seating area, the participants in the funeral set up a large cemetery with cardboard monuments, each bearing the name of a mountain, community, or stream that had been destroyed or damaged by surface mining.

The activities were a collage of cultural forms mobilized for the purpose of framing outrage in terms of local and regional identity associated with life in the mountains. Throughout the parade and funeral participants sang and prayed, incorporating their religious sensitivities into their speeches. Under the appropriate backdrop of a cold, gray autumn day, the black-clad marchers kept a solemn mood to illustrate their sense of loss.

Each of the activities that made up the funeral was part of the protesters' struggle to claim a position of moral authority in the political negotiation with industry and government. Using the language of religion and emotion, activists juxtaposed the moral rectitude they associate with their cause to the callous greed they associate with the coal industry.

Among the most controversial issues addressed at the funeral was the "act of God" defense that is now infamous in the coalfields. When unable to pinpoint an exact cause of a mining-related event, the DEP can officially determine that the event was an act of God, thus absolving the state or any company of legal responsibility. Mourners spoke out against the act of God stipulation as both a catchall excuse for government and industry and an affront to their religious beliefs.

Participants concluded their funeral by remembering the 125 men, women, and children killed in the deadly flood at Buffalo Creek, West Virginia, in

1972. In perhaps the most well-known application of the act of God ruling, a wastewater impoundment collapsed in a narrow hollow, sending forth a wall of black water that swept away an entire community. Mourners at the funeral in October 2000 remembered the dead from Buffalo Creek and offered a plea that regulatory and industry agencies act to prevent future disasters.[9]

Industry opponents, like those participating in the funeral for the mountains, conflate many themes of loss under the icon of mountaintop removal. The degradation of the physical landscape has many repercussions throughout the mountain communities. Mourners at the funeral highlighted the connection between the rugged landscape that has influenced the lives of generations of mountain dwellers and that has fashioned the practices of mountain life and the mountaineer identity that has grown alongside them. Destroying the landscape, mourners argued, destroys an important element of mountain culture. It is in these mountains, after all, that residents and their ancestors have crafted lives in which they take pride. At the same time, mining opponents lamented their increasing inability to control or influence the political and corporate forces that influence their lives. This lack of control stems from declining political representation, participation, and access—all of which residents associate with consolidated corporate power, declining strength of the union, and collusion of government and industry.

Judy Bonds spoke to these issues when she addressed the audience at the funeral to eulogize plant life lost to surface mining. Bonds wove together the themes of access to mountain land and the cultural politics of citizenship in local communities. She spoke of plants through personal interaction with the natural world of the Appalachian Mountains, recalling berry picking and other favorite childhood experiences. She described ramps—the strong, wild mountain leeks—as "nature's own spring tonic."

While scientific issues are often incorporated into environmental and political activism, in the context of this cultural celebration, Bonds focused instead on her personal experiences with the flora of the mountains. She spoke in terms of experiences common to mountain communities rather than the value of ecosystems or biodiversity. Her sentiments conveyed that the physical landscape has inherent cultural value for which scientists and coal executives cannot account.

* * *

In contrast to the tense exchanges and political overtones of the Sylvester meeting, the Funeral for the Mountains was an event that engaged emotions of loss and, at the same time, hope. At the funeral, participants expressed sorrow, disgust, and anger associated with the experience of loss that accompanies mountaintop removal. At the same time, the funeral was a celebration. Remarks like Bonds's illustrate that the people who came together on that gray October afternoon shared a mountain heritage. When she mentioned ramps, everyone in the crowd chuckled. Everyone knew that ramps were "nature's own spring tonic," and that ramp dinners were fun times of fellowship that are specific to an Appalachian cultural context. The participants in the funeral spoke fondly of their mountain roots and expressed hope that, through their activism, they would be able to reinforce the wisdom and beauty they see in the mountains and preserve it for future generations.

The movement against mountaintop removal draws strength from the combination of political savvy, emotional fervor, religious sentiment, and the ability to speak to people's hearts and to their minds. By combining these aspects of activism, CRMW and others in the mountaintop removal network are able to convey their messages to a broad spectrum of supporters.

3. What Are We Fighting For?

"We considered it public land," is a common refrain used to describe community relationships with the surrounding forests and mountains. Documented by historians to preindustrial Appalachian farmsteads, this tradition of common use is the basis for a local understanding of mountains as having an intrinsic value of their own.[1] Just as it did when the formal national economy first made inroads into the mountains, trying to include this value in a formal financial accounting scheme has proven to be like fitting a square peg into a round hole. West Virginians value the mountains as a place to *be*, where all of the experiences of mountain life play out on their natural stage: the hole where you caught a trophy smallmouth; your own secret ginseng patch; the opening where your father stood by as you shot your first deer; the old family cemetery that you clean and tend every spring; the garden from which you coax exuberant life every summer. All of these are sacred places, the places where the soul of the mountains and mountain people reside.[2]

Nearly all of these places are on private land, but for generations no one really knew or cared who owned the hilly acres. Everyone assumed that most of the mountains were "land company land," but whether any particular spot was owned by Rowland, Shonk, Federal, Pocahontas or any other corporation was of less importance. For practical purposes, generations of coalfield residents thought of the mountains as a de facto commons.[3] The mountains and their constituent streams, forests, peaks, coves, and caves were considered public space in what Mary Hufford describes as the social imaginary of "the mountains."[4]

Generations of family interactions on and in this social imaginary forged identity and a sense of place in both material and immaterial ways.[5] Coal has always been king in southern West Virginia. Most communities would not exist—nor would ever have existed—if not for the mines that built them. But around the mines, in the hills and hollows between the seams of coal and the stars above, a unique way of life emerged that is rooted deep in the mountain environment.

This mountain life is characterized by knowledge: knowing what stand of trees will be busy with squirrels during the fall hunting season; knowing how to leave young ginseng starts in the ground so there will be a crop next season; knowing how to prepare Molly Moochers, ramps, and creasy greens. The knowledge that seasons mountain life is something that many coalfield residents have taken for granted, as all culture is taken for granted by those who practice it. To many people it was just getting along. Getting along required these knowledges and practices in the era before the union and before social welfare programs. Taking advantage of the land's resources was essential for survival in the 1930s and before, when work was unpredictable. As work in the mines became more stable, people continued the activities they learned from previous generations; many of them survive today as recreational activities that nourish the soul more so than the body.

Knowledge of the mountains and getting along in them has taken on renewed importance with the advance of mountaintop removal coal mining and restructuring in the coal industry. For generations, living in the mountains and mining the coal beneath them combined to become the distinctive markers of life in the Appalachian coalfields. The relentless expansion of mountaintop removal mining across the landscape since the late 1980s disrupted this symbiotic relationship between life inside and outside the mines. Mountaintop removal destroyed hunting grounds and plowed up million-dollar ginseng patches. Mountaintop removal silted the streams, filling swimming and fishing holes. The spread of mountaintop removal brought a dilemma to dinner tables and living rooms across the region: are we coal people or are we mountain people? For the first time, many people felt compelled to choose because the two sources of identity, intertwined for so long, now seemed to be in stark opposition. The process through which this happens is a dialogic, dialectical, *moral* social process.[6] Negotiating answers to these questions is nothing less than the process of constructing a sense of right and wrong in an impossibly complicated scenario.

The Commons: Indian Creek

"Indian Creek was almost like a public place," says Tommy Jarrold, who grew up near it. Tucked between the small towns of Racine and Peytona, Indian

Creek is not far from where John Peter Salley first discovered coal in West Virginia in 1742. The hollow winds about ten miles from the Coal River back through mountains rich in forests, coal seams, and stories.

At a house near the mouth of Indian Creek, Mother Jones warned marching miners that danger awaited them at Blair Mountain. In Indian Creek, whose water reportedly made some of the world's best whiskey, moonshiners painted their jugs white and set diversion fires to fool the revenue men. A man named Uncle Tom fed possums to "clean 'em out good" and make them ready to eat. Joe Cantley, the barber, walked the neighborhoods charging 35 cents to cut hair during the Depression. If you had 35 cents, you got a haircut. If you didn't, you got a haircut anyway.

The story of Indian Creek was heated between 2000 and 2003. Massey Energy received a permit in 2003 for a mountaintop removal mine that would strip mountains around Indian Creek and run a haul road along the ridge above the hollow. Across the ridge, Massey wanted to build a new preparation plant, the size of which would rival the Elk Run plant in Sylvester. The combination of the mine, the haul road, and the prep plant raised the concern of many residents in the Racine, Peytona, and Drawdy communities. Many people became active in opposing the permits. Out of their activism, the stories of Indian Creek as a place were revived. The story of Indian Creek provides a striking example of how a once-vibrant community can fade away in the mountains, often without leaving a trace.

Indian Creek Today

Riding up Indian Creek Road on a warm sunny April afternoon in 2003 with my guide Paul Nelson, the hollow struck me, a first-time visitor, as a newly wild place. At first glance, a forest of young saplings seemed to have reclaimed the hollow. You have to look close through the thick undergrowth to see evidence that Indian Creek was once inhabited. Stones from an old foundation poked through the leaves. A hand-dug well stood open; stone masonry covered with thick moss lined the inside.

If you missed these subtle reminders of the past, you cannot miss "the stack." Rising from the valley floor is a giant brick smokestack. Built in the 1910s as part of the power plant that served Indian Creek's mines and homes, the stack is all that remains of the town of Sterling. Despite the disappearance of their original surroundings and the graffiti and garbage of their new surroundings, the stack, the stone foundation, and the well all have an elegance about them that testifies to the craftsmanship that went into building them.

As the forest works hard to reclaim the area, these fragments testify to Indian Creek's inhabited past.

The rich forest is what brings many people back to Indian Creek nearly thirty years after the last human residents moved out. On that April afternoon, Indian Creek native George Buffington gathered shawnee greens and creasy greens. If it rained over the weekend, he said, he'll come back for Molly Moochers (morel mushrooms) on Monday.

I showed Buffington a hand-drawn map of Indian Creek made by a locally recognized authority on Indian Creek, Bobby Kirk. Sitting on his four-wheeler, with a grocery bag on each handlebar keeping the greens separate, Buffington studied the map. His finger came to rest on a square marked "Buffington." He said it sits on the part of Indian Creek called the "straight stretch." Buffington looked up and pointed into the thicket across the road to the left. "Right over there is where I lived when I was a boy."

Getting to the Indian Creek straight stretch is anything but straight. These days, it takes four-wheel drive to get there on the best of days, an all-terrain vehicle in bad weather. Indian Creek Road (State Route 119/19 and County Route 79/A) begins near West Virginia Route 3 at Racine. Across the bridge, Indian Creek Road follows the railroad to the right. Houses line the road for a few hundred yards. The pavement ends and the road descends to the riverbed. The left turn into the mouth of Indian Creek goes through the creek itself and under the railroad trestle. The road is rough with deep ruts. The hollow was lined with gas wells and lines. Piles of cut brush, rusting appliances, and household garbage pointed to one of the clandestine uses of Indian Creek today. Kirk, Buffington, and Nelson were all outraged at the illegal dumping that scars the hollow. They also spoke out against Indian Creek's other illegal activity, marijuana cultivation. They relayed stories about drug growers and users camping and partying in the hollow.

As I spoke with Buffington and Nelson, three men drove up on four-wheelers. Buffington showed them the map and chatted with them before they roared away. Four-wheelers make up most of the traffic in Indian Creek. People in them come to the hollow seeking the forest and mountains, but no particular part of them. But the people I met and interviewed valued Indian Creek as a place to simply *be* in the mountains.

In 2003, several mine permit applications in the area piqued attention to Indian Creek. At the head of Indian Creek, Independence Coal Company, a subsidiary of Massey Energy, obtained a permit for its 1,534-acre Laxare East mountaintop removal mine. Across the ridge on Drawdy Creek near Peytona, Massey applied to build a new processing plant called Homer III on

an old tipple site. The West Virginia Department of Environmental Protection initially denied the Homer III permit due to concerns over air quality
near the plant. Between the sprawling Laxare East site and the Homer III
site is Indian Creek. Massey decided that Indian Creek's western ridge was
the ideal route to haul coal from the strip mine to the plant.

Residents from the town of Racine who live near and use Indian Creek
reacted angrily to the proposal. At a hearing regarding the haul road permit,
Dorothy resident Bill Price expressed disgust with the permitting procedure
by pointing out how the piecemeal process denies public knowledge of the
larger complex of which the road is to be part. In his comments, Price described the project as "the road to nowhere." "The road connects a mine that
doesn't exist [Laxare East, whose permit had not yet been issued] to a plant
whose permit has been denied. My question is," Price concluded, "why do
you need the road?"

Of the forty people at the hearing, a dozen rose to speak against the proposed road. One woman raised horses and taught riding near her home at
the mouth of Indian Creek. She used water from Indian Creek for her horses
and feared losing access to the hollow.

Another common fear had to do with access to Indian Creek's two cemeteries. On my April trip to Indian Creek, graves were adorned with fresh flowers
and faded American flags. Several people had been buried in the cemetery
within the past five years. Several people still intended to be buried there—
their names and dates of birth appeared alongside their deceased spouses.

The right to use the hollow for all of these activities, however, centered on
access to the public road, County Route 79/A. Residents of West Virginia's
coalfields were already familiar with the disappearance of public roads. A few
miles from Indian Creek, public roads connecting the towns of Orgas and
Chelyan, West Virginia, were ceded to Eastern Associated Coal Company
years ago. Though the roads still appear on state maps, they are gated and
residents are not allowed access.

Racine resident Buddy Hunter spearheaded resistance to an earlier at-
tempt to close off Indian Creek Road in 1993. Hunter argued adamantly that
residents of West Virginia have the right to travel the road. That right would
be denied, he contended, if Massey's plans were permitted.

At a Surface Mine Board hearing considering an appeal of the haul road
permit, Massey lawyers presented a formal legal brief with the condescending title, *Why 79/A is not a Public Road*. Attorneys established, to the board's
satisfaction, that counties in West Virginia have no authority over so-called
county roads. If a road, like 79/A, was not incorporated into the West Vir-

ginia State Roads Commission when it was established in 1933, then it was not a "public" road. According to the brief and cited legal precedents, 79/A belonged to the landowner. All of those Sunday afternoon picnickers were actually trespassers, and the hunters and ginseng diggers thieves.

The controversy highlighted a common dilemma in southern West Virginia. In the nearly one hundred years since the town of Sterling was built in the Indian Creek area, major changes occurred in the coalfields. The ancestors of current residents were brought to the coalfields to mine coal. Companies, all of which depended on a large labor force, built company towns to provide services for their workers. Around mid-twentieth century, the company town system broke down and companies sold off workers' houses but retained the land beneath them. With the expansion of surface mining, more and more people were forced to move off of company land. In many ways, the relationship between coal mines and communities had completely reversed. The struggle over Indian Creek exemplifies how communities had become an obstacle to mining.

Conflicts like that over Indian Creek raise the question, do occupants of land, who create and maintain vibrant communities, have any claim to land that they do not own? Absentee corporations called land companies own most of the land in southern West Virginia.[7] Indian Creek's owner is a good example. The Pritchard Land Company owns five thousand acres that make up most of the hollow. At the top of the mountain, the Pritchard tract abuts a tract held by the Federal Land Company. Both companies appear on maps for the new mine proposals, but both are nearly impossible to find anywhere else. Neither appears on the Internet. Neither is easily identifiable in the West Virginia secretary of state's online business records. With virtually no public face or local representation, local people have little opportunity to address the companies that hold enormous power over life in the coalfields.

By incorporating both the physical landscape and the social and political processes inherent in its governance, questions over Indian Creek resound the multifaceted definition of the commons. Donald Nonini defines the "commons" as "those assemblages and ensembles of resources which human beings hold in common or in trust to use on behalf of themselves, other living human beings and past and future generations of human beings, and which are essential to their biological, cultural, and social reproduction."[8] Within this more expansive definition, the activist community came to embody a crucial role as a social resource in the reproduction of a civic commons. The importance of this role will be discussed in subsequent sections. Negotiating ideas and agendas within this social commons, however, can be a difficult process.

Prayer Circle

"I pray for the development of alternative energy sources," said a woman from Ohio, holding aloft in front of her the sacred eagle feather. By the time this woman spoke, about three-fourths of the seventy people in the Indian prayer circle had already offered their prayers. Some prayed for respect and protection for sacred Mother Earth. Some prayed to Jesus Christ for guidance and wisdom. Others took the feather and bowed their head in silence. One woman recited the Lord's Prayer. The circle itself was a strange-enough juxtaposition, occurring, as it did, in the very shadow of a mountaintop removal operation, with background music provided by heavy earth-moving machinery. But the question of what to pray for reflected the multiple interests and agendas within the coal activist community.

The event was designed to build solidarity with the American Indian Movement and increase community awareness and participation. Throughout the day, drums reverberated off the mountains behind the elementary school where the event was held. Unfazed, trucks and other machinery continued to run at the neighboring Massey coal complex.

Participating in the circle was an array of activists from across the coalfields. The leader, an American Indian elder from Morgantown, West Virginia, told of his local fight to prevent Walmart from building on an Indian burial ground. In addition to the core of CRMW activists, there were many local residents (including less active CRMW members), and activists from OVEC, KFTC, and other coal, energy, and environmental activist groups.[9]

I noticed around the circle at least three current or former coal miners, several wives or widows of miners, and many miners' children. I had to wonder what the coal miners and their families thought as the woman prayed for alternative energy. On a large scale, alternative energy would certainly help stop mountaintop removal. If left to its devices, though, the coal industry would likely first eliminate underground mining jobs and continue mountaintop removal. The woman who prayed for alternative energy lived in a region of Ohio where a concentration of coal-burning power plants caused a host of environmental and health problems. Arguably, it would make no difference to her where the coal comes from, mountaintop or underground. CRMW organizers long held that they could not organize locally on a stop-all-coal-mining message. What was an organizer or a coal miner to pray for?

Activists discussed the same issue at a strategy meeting in January 2004 sponsored by Citizens Coal Council (CCC) that brought together leaders from many different organizations. This exchange illustrates organizers' sensitivity to and aggravation with the "jobs issue."[10]

BEVERLY BRAVERMAN (MWA): Room and pillar mining [sometimes called conventional mining] causes almost as much damage as longwalling, just not as fast.[11] So people thinking that that is an acceptable alternative is a problem.

TERI BLANTON (KFTC): Until we get in people's mind that coal is not a cheap source of energy . . . we pay the price everyday . . .

JULIA BONDS (CRMW): I agree with that, but also, I have to say this. Living in the coalfields, you have to realize that that is our only source of income. Okay? . . . If you tell the people in the coalfields we're going to cut out coal mining altogether, you're going to lose those people. You're absolutely positively going to lose those people. . . . There's a spectrum. . . . We're in the middle, and we have the spectrum of the extreme power-hungry, profit-hungry people, which is the coal companies. We have the people who [are] working in the coalfields, and people that's affected by this. And the other extreme is . . . radical environmentalists that want to end coal mining. . . .

The closest we came to stopping strip mining and mountaintop removal was when we got deep miners in the late '60s and '70s to go and say, "you're taking our jobs." And that's the closest we came. . . . I understand that coal is bad for the environment, but I can't organize in Boone County, West Virginia, and say we're going to end coal mining. I can't do that.

BRAVERMAN: Pennsylvania, like a lot of other states, had a lot of underground mining, which turned into longwall mining. [It] has lost 80 percent of the mining jobs from the change in technology. . . . I have to give it to the UMWA. . . . They set up job centers, and they started educating people to do something else. I've actually heard some coal miners say, "There's life after coal." And I think that that's something that we need to have on our radar screen. . . .

I understand there's a jobs issue. And I'm sympathetic to somebody who is losing their job. But you know, there's a point where I really just don't care anymore. If they're blasting [at surface mines], and they're breaking our homes up, and they're longwall mining, and everybody's losing their water, . . . that's why I have a real reluctance or problem, I guess, with "Well, we could do this type of coal, that would be OK, or we could do that type of coal." I think we need to look at what's the damage, and we need to say, we can't have this damage. . . .

Barry Stout is a senator, in the coalfields, very powerful. When the machine was chugging in his direction, they would not go around an historic registry home, they destroyed it. But damn, you know, they stopped right before [Senator Stout's] property and jogged around it. So, you know, if they want to do it, they can do it. They can be more responsible and more responsive. They just are choosing not to.

BONDS: I agree with that too. . . . The only problem is, like I said, on the other end of the spectrum. We have to get the message out, there is life after coal. But you're not going to get them to listen to you . . . you know, you lose people, they block that off in the coalfields.

Vivian Stockman, an organizer for the Ohio Valley Environmental Coalition (OVEC) who is also more attuned to broader activist and progressive organizations, offered a different approach to combining alternative energy and jobs.

> STOCKMAN: A major new study on global warming [suggested that] two years from now one-fourth of land species or more could go extinct. That's not just coal, but it's a giant coal issue. . . . [Referring to the Apollo Alliance],[12] alternative energy [could create] three million jobs . . . and that report, the global warming thing, said we have to move to alternative energy now . . . I mean you know, United Mine and Alternative Energy Workers of America.[13] There's jobs, that's the future, . . . outside forces [are] going to be dictating that we use less coal, and whether or not we pay attention or whether or not we careen into greater mass extinction.

The comments reflect activists' awareness that all coal issues exist in broader social, economic, and political contexts. Bonds, Braverman, and Stockman's comments in particular reflect both a need to address the issue of jobs in Appalachia and the coalition's partnership with organized labor. All three indicate an interest in luring the union into a more solid partnership.

Miners themselves are split on the issue of jobs. Of course, union members who work on MTR sites support the practice that employs them, but several other points of view emerge from conversations with miners.

An outspoken disabled miner, CRMW member, and avid union supporter argued that the United Mine Workers of America (UMWA) should work to abolish mountaintop removal altogether. Mountaintop removal, he said, cost the union thousands of members. The mine where he worked at the time he was injured employed three hundred miners. "You can run a strip [mine] with forty, fifty men," he said.[14]

Another union miner tried to strike a middle ground by distinguishing jobs from the environment. "I'm not talking about jobs," he said. "They should at least have to put back what they destroy." He went on to suggest that the companies—including the one he worked for—wouldn't comply with regulations. Ultimately, he stated a firm opposition to MTR on the grounds that coal companies cannot be trusted to abide by regulations.[15]

A nonunion Massey worker said, "They've torn our mountain all to pieces" [referring to the MTR site where he worked]. "It's awful, what they're doing," he added, his voice indicating an attitude of resignation.[16]

A Moral Question

The jobs issue stems from an absurd economic circumstance that, in effect, glorifies the criminal for committing the crime. The state and industry applaud Coal for providing needed jobs—even though Coal has cut over 100,000 jobs since 1950, with roughly 37,000 of those cuts between 1979 and 2000. The problems related to West Virginia's dismal economy raise critical questions about how people locate themselves in a community where deciding right from wrong can be so badly distorted. In the case of Coal's take-it-or-leave-it offer of jobs with the accompanying price of dismantling community and landscape, both options are unacceptable.

The lack of real choices over economic circumstances leads directly to questions about the function of democracy and the validity of a moral system. Not a moral system in the sense of religious beliefs about behavior, but morality as a *social process* people use to decide right from wrong in a complicated social world. In both democratic and moral systems, people must choose the circumstances by which they make a living, interact with one another, and negotiate right from wrong. As the "choices" here stand—coal jobs or no jobs—fulfilling one community need will directly undermine the other. It does not matter what communities in southern West Virginia decide, the outcome is not going to satisfy the needs of the community for both good jobs and a healthy environment. This inability to choose fundamentally undermines the concept of democratic governance. Nevertheless, creating and understanding a personal position within the bitterly divided conflict is difficult for many people.

A pro-coal caller to a Beckley talk radio program illustrated the problem. Rebutting activist arguments with the need to provide for his family, he said, "You can't eat a mountain."

"That's true," Judy Bonds responded on the program the following evening. "But neither can you drink or breathe money."

The coal industry's domination of central Appalachia traps residents in a system that prevents them from developing community resources in ways outside the state's agenda—an agenda that systematically protects coal.[17] Closure of public spaces intensified with the advance of mountaintop removal: some public parks fell into disrepair, others disappeared altogether like the one at Montcoal; the twenty-six restaurants in Whitesville became two or three that struggled to stay in business; the population of Whitesville dwindled to pre-1920 levels; many schools closed; a region that was once home to thousands of union miners had only two local halls with fewer than two hundred members.

An environmental reform agenda that advocates an end to coal as a source of energy denies the fact that coal provides the only well-paid jobs (with benefits) in the region. (Beyond paychecks, very few people in the Coal River region have health insurance outside of the coal industry, Medicare, and a state-sponsored program for children.)

In the absence of an alternative to coal employment, community activists could not advocate an end to mining. As attractive as a United Mine and Alternative Energy Workers union may be to activists, without support from the state or the union, no significant source of jobs is likely to emerge. Support for underground mining with a focus on the health of the community became a strategic decision aimed at winning local support for mining reforms, including the abolition of mountaintop removal. Nevertheless, the activist position reflected a form of commons environmentalism that breaks free from the zero-sum logic of jobs or environment. An environmentalism that incorporates a comprehensive view of the communities' needs, both economic and environmental, is a valuable development in the trajectory of coalfield debate activism.

PART II

Banana Republic, Neoliberal Style

banana republic *n.* A small country that is
economically dependent on a single product
or crop, such as bananas, and often governed
by the armed forces or a dictator.
—*American Heritage College Dictionary,*
Third Edition

"I sure would like to see it," said Roger, an elderly retired coal
miner, of rumors that Massey Energy would build a new tipple
in the Sycamore community.

"Why?" I asked.

"'Cause things might pick up 'round here," he replied.

Judy looked at him cockeyed, wondering why anyone would
want to see a new coal processing plant near their home, much
less one run by Massey. "Do you really want that up there?" she
asked.

"No," Roger backpedaled, "I don't want to see none of it, when
it comes right down to it."[1]

Roger was new to the activist community. Thinking that more
coal means more jobs and more prosperity is something of a
rookie mistake in coalfield activism. In the late 1990s and early
2000s, mines in Coal River and all across southern West Virginia
produced enormous amounts of coal. No period in state history
rivals the fifteen years from 1988 through 2002 for tons mined.
The state produced an average of over 165 million tons per year
during that time. Prior to this late-century surge, only in 1947 and
1948 did West Virginia produce over 165 million tons in any single
year. At the same time, mines in 2000 employed fewer people
than ever before. The effect of mechanization is all too apparent

when the all-time employment low of 14,281 miners in 2000 is compared to the boom-year high of 125,669 miners in 1948.

Roger's instinct that more mining should help the local economy seems like a perfectly logical notion. The reasons why it is inaccurate are as old as Appalachian coal mining itself.

According to legend, John Peter Salley was the first European to discover coal on an escarpment near the small Coal River community of Peytona in 1742. Seemingly ever since, economic development has been a peculiar endeavor in West Virginia. Coal has always been at the center of the state's economy and remains there despite indications from around the globe that coal is an industry in its twilight. More recently, West Virginia has gone to great lengths to nurture a tourist economy. In the Monongahela National Forest in the northeastern part of the state, West Virginia has gone as far as imposing mandatory buffer zones between plowed fields and streams. These restrictions are intended to protect streams from runoff and protect the aesthetic beauty of streams for boaters.[2]

Coal production vs. coal employment, 1910–2000. Source: West Virginia Coal Association, www.wvcoal.com.

The coal industry in West Virginia and elsewhere often frames its argument for strip mining in terms of private property rights.[3] On the surface, there appears to be a contradiction between protecting Coal's sacred property rights and infringing on farmers' rights to plow their land. An analysis of the rhetoric, policies, practices, and politics of development reveals a thread of consistency between these two positions. In these examples and many others, the capability of people—local people—to make use of local resources is compromised for the benefit of a centralized, industrial model of development.

An analysis from the Caribbean banana industry shows similarities between coal and other industries that have been restructured according to neoliberal principles. Anthropologist Karla Slocum illustrates how neoliberal trade policies created a paradoxical circumstance in the banana industry that also applies to the coal industry. Combined dependence on fixed resource production and integration with global markets creates an inflexible economy that effectively prevents economic diversification.[4]

It is apparent that economic development in West Virginia, especially southern West Virginia, is still guided by a coal-first philosophy. Beyond actual mining, Coal's extractive industry model profoundly influences economic development in general. West Virginia's economic development policies follow a pattern in which the state systematically favors industries over citizens, regardless of consequences—including restricting people's access to resources, reducing citizens to working in service jobs that cater to out-of-state travelers, and reducing citizens' ability to create economic opportunities for themselves.

The chapters in this section illustrate in detail how the controversies surrounding coal mining in Appalachia have been shaped by neoliberal trends in politics, economics, and society. Chapter 4 describes dramatic changes within the United Mine Workers of America (UMWA)—once the most powerful force in American organized labor. At the end of the twentieth century, the UMWA seemed incapable of organizing nonunion mines, even in the region that once provided its strongest support. Chapter 5 details the bureaucratic maze of state regulations that community activists face. It quickly becomes clear that procedures within the state Department of Environmental Protection funnel citizen input away from critical decision making. Only in the state legislature, activists are told, can they argue that mountaintop removal should not be allowed. That same legislature is awash in political campaign contributions from coal companies, and in fact populated with many members who are themselves tied to the industry. Chapter 6 analyzes how West Virginia's economic development policies as well as practices built on neoliberal influences systematically favor the coal industry and fail to create a diverse economy or reduce poverty .

4. Strained Solidarities

Over its lifetime, the United Mine Workers of America (UMWA) has moved through three distinct eras that I label confrontational organizing, labor brokerage, and crisis management. John L. Lewis's legacy as iconic union president transformed the union from a fractured organizing body to a streamlined labor broker, negotiating contracts and winning the best possible wages and benefits—one that brokered the best deals possible with industry. However, the wildcat tradition of the 1970s directly confronted union leadership in its labor-broker role. In Coal River, I argue, the community and environmental activism of the late 1990s emerged as a challenge, only somewhat veiled, to the leadership of the UMWA, this time demanding a strong stance against mountaintop removal. To frame this argument, I set a 1977 strike in two important historical contexts—the UMWA as an institution, and the history of the relationship between union leadership and the rank-and-file miners and coalfield citizens who made up the union.

* * *

It was an unwritten rule, but one everybody understood: you don't cross picket lines in West Virginia. The United Mine Workers' District 17 is one of the most storied divisions of one of the most storied unions in American labor history. Miners from District 17 marched across southern West Virginia in 1921 to organize mines in Logan County when they met a militia backed by U.S. troops atop Blair Mountain. The Battle of Blair Mountain was the first instance of the U.S. military attacking its own citizens.

In the 1970s, District 17 comprised the heart of the West Virginia coalfields in Kanawha, Boone, Raleigh, Logan, and Mingo counties. Roving pickets and daily wildcat strikes earned District 17 a reputation for miners being fierce and brash in confrontations with coal operators. At that time, my grandfather was a coal miner in McDowell County, West Virginia, part of District 29. A group of striking District 17 workers he met while deer hunting stopped speaking to him when they heard District 29 was working.

A new generation of miners entered the mines in the 1970s. Virtually all of them had grown up with the union. Many of the young faces in District 17 became union leaders, including current UMWA international president, Cecil E. Roberts. While they participated in, and in some cases led, the pickets, many miners of this generation now say they took the union for granted.

As the contentious 1970s gave way to the depressed 1980s, no one can identify one single factor that caused the wildcat strikes to end. According to some, President Ronald Reagan's message to labor was loud and clear when he fired striking air traffic controllers—the old rules no longer applied. Others say that the brash young miners of the 1970s grew up into more reserved family men in the 1980s. Some point to the booming coal market of the 1970s that collapsed into depression in the early 1980s. Whatever the reasons, the labor climate changed in West Virginia.

A History of Gains

What I call the confrontational organizing period of the United Mine Workers encompasses the period prior to the Wagner Act that established the right to organize labor unions in 1935. The so-called mine wars, the tent colonies, and the infamous Baldwin-Felts mine thugs that characterized what Mary Harris "Mother" Jones called "medieval West Virginia," all fall into this period. The idea of organizing the coalfields was a radical concept. The politics and geography of southern West Virginia made it particularly hard to organize. The railroad was the only way into and out of many company towns. Often union organizers were met at the depot by armed guards who forbade them to get off the train.

In his biography of Mother Jones, Elliott J. Gorn suggests that in the first decade of the twentieth century the miners themselves were often not eager to organize. In many places, he argues, coal was plentiful and the structure of the company towns allowed miners and their families to carve out a decent living. Changes in the industry and workforce, notably an influx of African Americans from the South and a wave of immigrants from eastern and southern Europe, eventually forged a class consciousness across racial and ethnic boundaries that aided the union.[1] Coal production in West Virginia soared through the century's first two decades. As operators demanded more of their workers in the way of ten- and twelve-hour days, interest in the union grew. Although the 1921 Battle of Blair Mountain is cited across West Virginia as the birth of the UMWA, the union did not succeed in organizing many parts of southern West Virginia until after the Wagner Act passed as part of the New Deal.

John L. Lewis became president of the UMWA in 1919 and remained in office for forty years, leaving a mark on the United Mine Workers, on American organized labor, and on the coalfields that cannot be overstated. Coalfield residents recall having three pictures on the wall: Jesus Christ, Franklin Roosevelt (or John F. Kennedy, depending on the generation), and John L. Lewis. During his first decade as president, Lewis embarked on a fierce effort to unite disparate factions within the union and solidify the union's bargaining power with industry. By most measures, Lewis actually failed to achieve the consolidation he wanted during the 1920s. The Great Depression and New Deal legislation, however, enabled Lewis to complete his transformation of the UMWA. Lewis, more than any other individual, transformed the union into a labor broker—a process that intended to reform the union as much as industry.[2]

While he was known for his fiery and uncompromising rhetoric, Lewis made one compromise in the 1949 contract negotiations that, in retrospect, seems like a deal with the devil. The health care program in the 1947 contract was nothing short of revolutionary. Lewis got the Bituminous Coal Operators Association (BCOA) to pay a per-ton royalty into a fund controlled and administered by the union.[3] Before the 1947 contract expired, however, many operators stopped paying into the fund. In response, Lewis pulled miners out for short strikes and implemented a three-day workweek to improve his bargaining position for the 1949 contract. After the contract expired in 1949, miners nationwide struck for fifty-two days—a mark that stood until 1977 as the longest strike in the coal industry.

The 1949 contract embodied Lewis's commitment to protecting the quality of mine workers' jobs—with health and welfare benefits—while sacrificing the quantity of those jobs. With Lewis's approval, widespread mechanization of the coal mines started in 1950. (By 1960, the number of miners employed in West Virginia had been cut in half.) When the 1949 contract was finalized, Lewis focused attention on the fact that he had saved the health and welfare fund—the industry financed "health card" that union miners would carry until 1977. Though Lewis's major concession on mechanization drew less attention at the time, it probably reshaped the coalfields more than any other decision of any other individual.

The legacy of the 1947 and 1949 contracts was revisited during the 1977 wildcat strike. The wildcat tradition bore the mark of Lewis's militant and confrontational style, but 1970s rank-and-file militancy was often directed at the union's own leaders. During the late 1960s and early 1970s, a generational turnover brought new young men into the mines. Many of these men had returned from service in Vietnam—a collective experience that was very influential on the coalfields. Though much smaller in number, educated young people—some idealistic, some radical—came to Appalachia under the Volunteers in Service to America program (VISTA). Out of this cauldron emerged a confrontational rank-and-file group marked by a take-no-shit attitude from Vietnam veterans spiced with a dash of 1960s radical politics.

Many miners promoted the "right to strike"—a concept that never had support from the union leadership, but was very popular among many of the rank-and-file members. While the union contract bound miners to a grievance arbitration procedure, some rank-and-file groups asserted that local unions should have the right to call a strike. Former UMWA attorney John Taylor described frustration with the grievance procedure that, in 1976, culminated in a series of wildcat strikes aimed at the federal judiciary. Miners asserted that mine operators were breaking the contract by not upholding the grievance procedure in good faith. Rather than process a grievance, an operator could delay and provoke the inevitable wildcat strike. When miners walked out, the operator could go to court, get a temporary restraining order followed by an injunction, and then sue the union for damages resulting from breech of contract. Across southern West Virginia, miners struck to protest the ease with which operators got restraining orders, arguing that the courts were not holding the companies to the terms of the contract. As they did several times during the mid-1970s, West Virginia miners traveled to distant places like Alabama's UMWA District 20 to picket mines.[4]

* * *

After the UMWA solidified its place in the coalfields following the New Deal, union solidarity grew into a powerful tradition in West Virginia. Attitudes that gave rise to the saying, "You don't cross picket lines in West Virginia," made the United Mine Workers a strong advocate for workers' and community rights.

What District 17 was for the United Mine Workers, Coal River and Boone County were for District 17. The hurt caused by the rise of Massey and the decline of the UMWA runs deep for many Coal River residents.

"Oh, Jesus," John Taylor says of Boone County's role in the union. "It's just like an ocean of gas and coal underneath the county. Some of your really big big-time capitalists like Eastern Associates, Koppers, and those people [operated there]. A lot of the main day-to-day leadership of District 17 came out of

Boone County. Boone County was sort of the political center as well as being the geographic center. The subdistrict office that was busiest was by far the one in Danville. They struck more over there. They were just more militant."[5]

While the tradition of solidarity made the union a powerful organization, solidarity could also be abused. Industry, as is often the case, accused miners of striking for no reason. Some miners admit that they abused their own power by walking out for reasons that now seem silly. Paul Nelson, an ardent union supporter, suggested the strain caused by a few people made solidarity work against the union. Ultimately, he linked walkouts to the decline of the union through the 1990s.

> I blame a lot of it on the union itself for supporting men who didn't want to work. A lot of times, it was what you called a wildcat strike, for a man that wasn't worth the salt in his bread. And that made it hard on everybody. . . . The union is a good thing, but they still supported men that was not worthy to be there. They kept everybody from working because they didn't want to work. You might go to work, and a man throws his water out. You didn't know why. Sometimes I start across the hill and here they come. "Boys . . . midnight didn't work." Everybody went back home. But the other mines around would be working.[6]

Taylor arrives at a different conclusion than Nelson about the wildcats. Taylor's grandfather was a UMWA organizer and Taylor himself organized a radical workers' movement that challenged the authority of the United Auto Workers in Detroit. As an attorney in the District 17 office from 1975 to 1979, Taylor handled the legal work pertaining to the wildcat strikes.

"[The wildcat strike] was so irritating to the business forces, to the capitalist side," Taylor said. "Just the idea of these hillbillies—*these hillbillies*—running around shutting down *our* coal mines. I mean, it's just sort of an affront . . . some of them would take it serious—personally. 'What do you mean you're not working?' 'You guys strike all the time.' . . . I remember a couple of editorial cartoons that portrayed an angry-faced coal miner running out with a strike sign because he didn't like the way the sun looked when it came up. . . . I honestly can't say," he concluded, "that I saw any grievances that I thought were silly."

* * *

Strictly speaking, wildcat strikes were illegal. The union contract bound miners to work under agreed-upon conditions. Walking out while under contract, without first getting a court injunction, violated the agreement. Companies could and did sue for damages from lost work due to wildcat strikes. Negotiating the legalities of the strikes fell to Taylor.

After calling the local office and district offices, Taylor would appear before a judge and file "canned" motions to dismiss the company's "canned" grievances and "put as much shit on management" as he could. He described this formality as his "hands up" defense—throwing up his hands before to judge to say that he didn't know why the men were striking. These appearances became so routine that one judge referred to them as "the morning orders."

Depending on circumstances, Taylor sometimes had to meet with the striking workers at the local hall.

> It was a whole dynamic because I come out, I'm the lawyer, I got a suit on, I got these damn papers—paperwork is intimidating—and I got to get up and talk . . . I got to make sure . . . to make these fellas understand. But it was easy for me because I'm just talking to my uncles—they were all coal miners and factory men. . . . There would be times when people would be drunked up or whatever and challenge you. . . . What I learned in Detroit was, you can never let yourself be physically intimidated. If you're physically intimidated, then that's it. You might as well leave, cause they ain't going to pay attention to you.
>
> There was one incident up Cabin Creek, one of the Carbon Fuel mines, they were striking. . . . They had the strike meeting in a hall up above a restaurant there. I came to the up and I was telling them what the legal realities was and so forth and [that] they better go back to work. And of course, their local official was telling them that and [it] was very unpopular. . . . He took the initiative. I don't think anyone from the district came up to that meeting. They didn't like to come to those meetings because they could get beat up. But, um, they threw shit on him [the local official] and of course, some of it splattered on me. . . . A young man . . . got up and said "You're paid off," "You're just one of the company people," "You're a company suck," or some damn thing like that. It was wintertime and I threw off my coat, threw off my suit coat and went back after him. And he ran from me. He ran . . . later I found out he was high on something.

Judge K. K. Hall of the U.S. district court in Charleston interrupted one hearing to observe, on the record, the regular appearances of the UMWA and coal operators in his court.

> I've just about reached the conclusion that the Court—this Court is being used in a manner that was not anticipated at all, that the way to settle strikes has just come to be by going to the Federal Court and getting him to issue a temporary restraining order without the parties doing something about it. . . . The Court finds it distasteful being placed in the position of being the policeman or disciplinarian for the coal companies all the time. . . . If it continues this way, every coal company will come in every morning for their morning orders from the Court, and we just can't let things get out of hand like they have.[7]

After the coal company attorney responded to the judge's remarks with descriptions of pending lawsuits that would have changed the legal procedures for handling wildcat strikes in the companies' favor, Taylor also responded. "We recognize [wildcat strikes] as a very serious problem for everyone involved, including the Union, the miners, the total economy, the state, everybody. It often seems that many of the coal operators have attempted to use the courts to conduct their labor relations. That may sound like a harsh statement, but that's the way it has seemed."[8]

Solidarity Abused?

Perhaps the strongest display of solidarity also gave rise among many miners to the thought that they had been manipulated by the community. George and Mary Snodgrass recall the so-called Textbook Strike of 1974.

GEORGE: When I was working over Cabin Creek, miners wouldn't cross a picket line. Here was these women sitting there [on a picket line] with the textbook controversy, when they started putting this trash in school books.

MARY: Sex education in Kanawha County.

GEORGE: Well, . . . I hadn't drawn a check in a month or two. I was out cutting weeds for everbody, working like a dog, you know. Me and her went hungry so [our daughter] could eat. This one woman [on the picket line] said, "Well, I got to go." One said, "Where you got to go, Betty?" Said, "I got to go get my husband off to work, he works down at Carbide." That done it. [I] said, "Hey, you all gonna pull us out you better pull [the chemical workers] out too." We 'bout throwed their butts in the creek and went back to work.

MARY: A lot of the women, their husbands worked at Du Pont and [Union] Carbide and different places, but their check never stopped.[9]

GEORGE: One guy was raising Cain, getting everbody stirred up, he owned a store but he didn't shut the doors. Everbody's money kept coming except the miners. What it boiled down to, ever time a beef come up, go get the miners, they'll strike for anything. They won't cross a picket line for nothing. But when the miners needed them, they wouldn't be there. And that's what's wrong today.[10]

Miners consistently pointed to the Textbook Strike as an example of the union supporting issues that affected the community beyond the mines. From the point of view of shifting notions of solidarity, a telling characteristic of the strike is the amount of discrepancy in recollections of the underlying issue. Many rank-and-file miners who took part don't recall clearly what the problem was with the books. If they say anything, most will say, like the Snodgrasses, that sex education caused the uproar.

Another member of the mountaintop removal activist community told the story of the 1974 strike from another side. Jimmy Jackson, who was a teacher in Kanawha County at the time, began his story of the Textbook Strike by talking about the Black Panthers and the Black Power movement. Jackson testified on behalf of the American Civil Liberties Union about the need for "multicultural education." According to Jackson, the county school board adopted textbooks that reflected a multicultural perspective, including stories about African American children and depictions of white children and black children playing together.[11]

The textbook controversy highlighted several social fractures in Kanawha County. The strike pitted urban, racially and socioeconomically diverse Charleston against rural, predominantly white, and working class mining areas on the periphery. As news spread, the textbook controversy attracted attention from conservative groups across the country, including the John Birch Society and the Ku Klux Klan.

Using the Textbook Strike to build solidarity with other union shops in the area proved to be unsuccessful. George Snodgrass referred to miners' frustration with workers from DuPont and Union Carbide, large chemical plants of the Kanawha Valley, some of which were union, some nonunion. Others recalled coal miners attempting to picket union shops in other industries in the region, including some instances of physical violence. But a unified effort that combined different unions never coalesced.

The history of union organizing and the wildcat tradition built coalfield solidarity into a deeply valued concept. Solidarity like that shown by the UMWA in the Textbook Strike brought the union power that miners and community members now long for in their confrontations with industry. Nevertheless, Snodgrass's comments indicate that solidarity could be abused. In this case, people outside the union pulled miners out of work, but other members of the community did not make similar sacrifices.

* * *

The decade of wildcat strikes and the underlying right-to-strike ideology reflected a confrontational style that clashed with the union's role as labor broker—the role that had been firmly entrenched at least since Lewis's tenure as UMWA president. Labor-broker unions fit into an institutionalized relationship between labor, capital, and the state. The union's role, strictly regulated by labor laws, was to bargain for a bigger piece of the pie. Taylor described the friction between the leadership and the rank and file by saying that unions did not exercise what political power they did have because they were no longer set up to challenge capitalists' interests. He summarized the contrasting attitudes as this: whereas the union leadership's collective bargaining position said, "We want our piece of the pie," the miners' attitude was, "Fuck that! We make the pie—let us have it."

Perhaps the best example of rank-and-file miners challenging the union leadership is a walkout that immediately preceded the 1977 contract negotiations. Prior to talks, serious problems surfaced in the union's health and welfare fund. The fund's trustees suggested that, for the first time since 1947, miners might have to pay significant portions of their health care costs. (Since John L. Lewis won the so-called health card in the 1947 contract, union health benefits had been sacred to miners.)

With wildcat strikes shutting down mines throughout Appalachia in the summer of 1977, the United Mine Workers officially struck when their contract expired. The 1977 contract strike lasted 110 days—the longest strike in UMWA history. While the lengthy contract strike is the stuff of history, little is written about the wildcat walkouts that preceded it, or about the fate of the health card. The card itself symbolized to many the very meaning of union solidarity. Health benefits, which expanded over the years to include black lung and other forms of disability protection, were won in hard-fought battles that chronicled the history of the union. That all union members held the same card with the same benefits reflected the solidarity that miners took so seriously.

Historical accounts describe the UMWA international leadership as in a chaotic state of disarray as it entered collective bargaining for the 1977 contract.[12] A survey of the rank and file showed that miner's top priority for the negotiations was to secure the right to strike at the local level—in effect formalizing and legitimizing the wildcat strike. The industry bargaining team would not entertain that option. The first of three agreements that were voted down (two by the union's bargaining committee and one by the rank and file) included a wage increase and a large deductible for fund-administered health care. The right-to-strike provision was not included, and industry won what it called "labor stability" measures—the right to fine or fire miners who participated in wildcat strikes, including those who honored picket lines.

A second agreement included the wage increase and the deductible. It changed the "labor stability" language, but retained management's right to discipline workers for wildcat strikes. The rank and file soundly rejected the agreement, despite an extensive advertising campaign by union leadership.

After the rank and file ignored President Jimmy Carter's invocation of the Taft-Hartley Act ordering them to return to work, negotiators reached a third agreement. The pact included the same wage agreement, muted the industry's rights to discipline miners, and substantially reduced the health care deductible miners would have to pay. However, the agreement allowed each company to negotiate its own health care provisions rather than pay into the health and welfare fund, thus permitting companies to establish their own health care programs with private insurance companies. For the first time since 1947, miners would not all enjoy the same health coverage. The union's concession also affected retirement benefits. Miners who retired before 1977 have a different set of benefits than those who retired under the new contract.

The Battle of Elk Run

Many coal operators tried to open nonunion mines during the 1970s. While some were successful, the UMWA still held great power throughout the coalfields. Outside the region, trends in government and industry refigured relations between capital, labor, and government on all levels throughout the 1970s. These trends accelerated in the 1980s under the Reagan administration's deregulation programs and its approach to labor symbolized by the dismissal of striking air traffic controllers in 1981. At the same time, policies and practices that gave industry the upper hand were creeping into West Virginia. The late '70s and early '80s were turbulent times in the coalfields, as the profitable coal market of the 1970s collapsed and multinational energy companies consolidated and restructured the coal industry. With the legacy of the wildcat strikes still fresh, several coal companies broke away from the Bituminous Coal Operators Association, the industry bargaining conglomerate.

Throughout Coal River, people point to a violent protest by about two thousand United Mine Workers at Massey's Elk Run mine as the watershed event in relations between the UMWA, Massey Energy, and the communities of Coal River. Massey, whose operations were still concentrated in Mingo County, West Virginia, and in eastern Kentucky, already had a reputation for antagonism toward the union based on years of preventing it from organizing Massey mines.

Local union miners familiar with Massey's reputation reacted with hostility to news that Massey would open a mine near Sylvester, in the heart of Coal River. Antagonism brewed between the community and Massey as construction proceeded on the Elk Run complex. Massey had fanned the union flames locally by not hiring UMWA workers to build their facility. On May 14, 1981, striking miners held a rally about a quarter mile from the entrance to Elk Run. By all accounts, then–District 17 president Cecil Roberts gave the kind of fiery speech for which he is well known. Most attribute the violence that followed to the miners' drinking at the rally. As many as two thousand miners marched down the road and across the bridge, ransacking the guard shack and other buildings on Massey's property. News articles quoted a miner's wife who said, "We're 100 percent union here. They might as well work UMW[A] or leave the state."[13] Elk Run's president called the events "sheer acts of terrorism."[14] Nearly everyone in Coal River has an opinion of what happened that day:

* * *

That's the reason I had a $62 million lawsuit handed to me one day on my front porch by a federal marshal about seven foot tall. Right below Elk Run there's a place called Boone Hydraulics, on the left in that curve. Everybody met there in that building and had a big rally. Well, Cecil Roberts got up there and got everybody all fired up, pumped up, and everybody was ready to go, you know, kick ass. Everybody marched up there and ripped the gates off the bridge and went across the bridge. And I mean they was going up the hollow backwards in them pickups over there across the bridge. Trucks, they wasn't even turned around. And that's when it all happened. . . . They was a hell of a crowd down there . . . I mean it was jam packed . . . everybody couldn't even get across the bridge—they was so many of them they was just trying to pile up.[15]

* * *

I was the only local person working over there. I was in college and working for a construction company over the summer. My job was to haul water from my mother's house in town up to the construction site. I made $14 an hour. All the other workers worked for a contractor out of Tennessee. . . . They were with the United Steel Workers. . . . I guess the union's beef was that they hadn't hired local UMWA contractors. After making a delivery to the site, I looked down and saw 5,000 union men on the bridge. I didn't want to be seen because I lived in town. I saw one man toss a bottle of gasoline that exploded. . . . I quit the next day.[16]

* * *

You know, everything here was union; this was union country. And [Elk Run] moved in and . . . they wouldn't go union. And then they had the big conflict, you know, when [the union] decided to go over there and tear them up. But that was whiskey talking that day. They didn't have no business doing that. . . . I think they hurt the area and the community when they done that.[17]

* * *

This all started at Elk Run in, I think, 1984.[18] They had a big rally up at Elk Run when they first opened up. Thousands of miners marched, it was a big riot. A big riot went on. And basically, we got sued. It's personal for [Massey CEO Don] Blankenship. He's an asshole.[19]

* * *

The so-called Battle of Elk Run became a watershed for many reasons. Video surveillance equipment at the site made it possible to identify many of the participants. The courts severely wounded the union with a multimillion-dollar fine for the incident. Perhaps equally significant, Massey won an injunction against the UMWA at Elk Run. Many say that Don Blankenship, who ascended to Massey's leadership shortly after the conflict, already held a grudge against the union that was only strengthened by the actions at Elk Run. Some go as far as to say that Elk Run provoked something of a vendetta between Blankenship and the United Mine Workers.

Whatever the cause, in the aftermath of the Elk Run confrontation, Massey became the industry leader in operating nonunion mines. Their sphere of influence spread beyond Elk Run up and down Coal River to Marfork, Montcoal, Sundial, Uneeda, Cazy, and Drawdy. Other companies operating in the region followed suit and opened nonunion mines. In an area where every miner was a union member, locals can now count union operations on one hand.

* * *

In the 1983 contract negotiations, then–UMWA president Richard Trumka established what has become known as selective striking.[20] Rather than striking all union mines at the same time, the union would select certain mines to strike while others would continue operating. Union sympathizers in Coal River almost uniformly point to selective striking as the downfall of the union.

The idea behind selective striking came from corporate changes in the coal industry. The rail and transportation companies that dominated the Appalachian coal industry at its inception had long since yielded to steel and automotive companies as Coal's major corporate owners. The names of largest employers in Coal River reflected the trend: Bethlehem Steel, Armco Steel, and U.S. Steel. Paralleling global economic shifts, the 1970s and 1980s saw a similar shift from steel and auto to large transnational energy conglomerates.[21] Among today's largest coal producers, Peabody Energy, Massey Energy, and Arch Coal, Inc., took control of mines in Coal River through the 1980s and 1990s.

Massey Energy, the largest coal producer in West Virginia and fourth largest in the United States, began as A.T. Massey Coal Company, a small local operation along the West Virginia–Kentucky border. In 1981, A.T. Massey became part of Fluor Corp., a transnational construction and energy empire whose holdings also included Royal Dutch Shell.

When steel and automakers owned their own mines, the UMWA had immense power not only over coal, but also over the industries that depended on it. Large energy conglomerates, however, could survive strikes because of their diverse business holdings. The larger the corporate owners, the fewer direct connections companies were likely to have to local sites of production. Former UMWA attorney John Taylor said unions used the selective strike model successfully in the auto industry. The theory behind the selective strike was that by striking only the biggest producers the union would set a precedent for the rest of the industry. Compared to the auto industry, however, Taylor described the institutional control of the UMWA as "anarchy," a sentiment borne out in descriptions of the wildcat strikes.

No matter how it sounds in theory, coalfield residents blame Trumka for breaking the tradition of solidarity on strikes and the mantra of "United we stand, divided we fall; A wrong to one is a wrong to all." Coal River residents recalled the most recent contract strike in 1993, when they experienced the full implications of the selective strike.

"When they give up the right to strike for a couple more bucks, they gave it all away," said retired miner Paul Nelson. Nelson's mine was selected to strike in 1993, while his neighbor's mine worked. "When they gave [solidarity] up, they give up their voice. United we stand, divided we fall—a lot of them forgot about that."[22]

Coal River resident Kathy Jarrell accuses Trumka of the same kind of nepotism that characterized Tony Boyle's infamously corrupt UMWA administration (1963–72). Jarrell draws a direct connection between the UMWA International's selective strike policy and the decline of the UMWA in Coal River. By going to the selective strike, she says, "[Trumka] more or less gave it to Massey—he gave [Coal] River to Massey."

"I was working at Stockton No. 5 mines," David Jarrell, Kathy's husband, says of the 1993 strike.

> It was a selective strike, and they struck Peabody. The tipple [at Stockton] was on strike. The tipple had picket lines. I worked at the . . . union contract mines on top of the mountain and had to cross that picket line to go to work, 'cause they didn't choose to strike our mines. . . . So for about a week or so, we had to cross that picket line. . . . When I crossed that bridge with guys I worked with

for twenty years standing there on a picket line and I go by 'em going to work, I got sick. You know, like a big rock in the pit of your stomach. My mother—love her to death—called me a scab . . . I like to died.[23]

Union Proud

"When I went into the mines at Robin Hood No. 9 [in 1974], they told me when I started that I'd have nothing to worry about, that I'd be able to retire there. I was laid off three times from there. I actually went to work for a little subcontractor. Then came back. My mines shut down and I had to go to [the mine at] Prenter. . . . I still haven't retired."[24]

There are many stories of how the changing world of work in the coalfields has affected individual lives. Miners told of longtime friends who left the area and lost touch. Some stayed in the area but went to work in other jobs. One man traveled extensively servicing ATMs. One, who was lucky enough to work thirty years in the mines and retire with benefits, worked for the Division of Highways. Others stayed and continued to work in union mines when work was available. These men told stories of on-again, off-again work in the mines, combined with the other jobs to make ends meet.

Clyde McKnight

"The union at that time was kinda handed to me on a platter," said Clyde McKnight, a father of two in his early fifties. McKnight began working in the mines after he dropped out of college in 1976. His father and grandfather were both coal miners in Coal River. A former union local president, McKnight continued to be active in the UMWA and ran for state legislature twice.

> I didn't have to do anything but pay an initiation fee and swear an oath at the local hall. . . . I kinda took it for granted, just what my dad and my grandfather had told me and what they had fought to get . . . it was handed to me. And it took me a few years to actually see what the benefits of the union was and really learn to appreciate it. 'Cause when you're young, you're getting a payday, all you're looking for is, "I got a payday now, I got gas money, beer money, or whatever, I can go . . . take a girlfriend out." You didn't look at the health care, pensions, retirement that you need to look at down the road.

McKnight was active in the union pickets against Massey's nonunion operations at Elk Run and later at Marfork. He was president of the local hall when Peabody Energy sold several area mines to Massey. He worked to get Massey to abide by language in the union contract that held successive owners to the contract for its duration, but Massey subverted his efforts by laying off all the workers and reopening the mines "union free" a year later.

> I had a gold and black Chevy club cab truck . . . bug shield had "Union Proud" on the front of it. I would ride it around everywhere. I'd just go around Marfork, Elk Run, I'd just go near security guards, out real quick. I wouldn't . . . cross the bridge, as far as Elk Run was concerned.[25] And I went to . . . their meetings. And if I felt we had a grievance . . . they wasn't doing something right, I was quick to call their hand at it. I'm blowing my own horn, but I stood up for the union and what I believed in—workers' rights and the community.

McKnight was laid off in 1991 and called back once for about six months. While he was out of work, he went to college with financial support from the union. With his degree, he worked as an auditor for a hotel in Beckley until he was called back to a union mine in 2001. I asked why he went back after several years working as an auditor. "Well, I like coal mines. I love the union. And it's because of the union that I've had everything I've ever had, and everything I ever will have . . . The union recall, through the language in the contracts, give me the right to recall to other mines. It gives me benefits, job security when I'm at work. I got a health and retirement to look forward to when I get older for me and my family. It's raised my two good kids. And I like working this type of work."[26]

Danny Howell

"I guess I basically worked for Mister Massey for a very short period of time," Danny Howell began, "and then they laid me off." Howell and McKnight worked for the same mine when Peabody sold it to Massey in 1991. As Howell began to tell the story of supporting his wife and two children after he was laid off, his wife, Kay, interrupted him to tell it her way.

> DANNY: I have been called to Massey mines. But, uh . . .
> KAY: He chose to run a newspaper route instead of working nonunion. He ran a newspaper route for three years. Up at three o'clock in the morning, seven days a week, in order to put food on the table.
> DANNY: I said at the time, and I still say it: I will not say I will never work for Mister Massey. I won't say that because if it comes to feeding my kids and stuff, I'll do what I have to do. But, if I've got a choice of feeding them and clothing them by doing something else, I'll do it.[27]

* * *

Often the only noncoal employment in southern West Virginia is in the service sector. McKnight the auditor, Howell the newspaper deliverer, the Division of Highways worker, the ATM technician, and countless other examples suggest a trend in coalfield employment. For former coal miners, especially those who started in the 1970s anticipating lifetime work with union benefits, service employment can be socially as well as financially demeaning. Job retraining programs exist, but there are no jobs that offer the financial stability and social status of coal mining.

For men of McKnight and Howell's generation, as with their fathers' generation before, coal mining has been as much a way of life as a job. The union provided not only the financial benefits and security McKnight described, but also a measure of power and respect both inside the mine and in the community. Miners exercised this power more in the 1970s than ever before in the form of wildcat strikes. Being a union miner had cachet, illustrated by McKnight taunting Massey with his "Union Proud" truck. More than any other institution, the union shaped what it meant to be a working man in Coal River in the 1970s.

Since then, the shifting sands of coal employment have shaken the foundations of the region's working class and their communities. McKnight estimated half of Coal River's population had left, he said, on the "hillbilly highway" to North Carolina. One of Howell's friends followed that well-traveled path. The last Danny heard of the man, he managed a Burger King near Hickory, North Carolina. Graffiti scrawled on an abandoned building in 2000 supported the story: "Coal River has relocated to Hickory, NC (JOBS)."

In the 1970s, coal miners with a high school education could reasonably expect reliable employment and good wages. By effectively breaking the union, the coal industry (under Massey's leadership) reshaped the expectations of workers. Coal has always experienced booms and busts, with layoffs being common. But nonunion jobs have removed the assurances of union work, exposing workers to a fickle workplace over which they have little, if any, control.

On top of the fact that southern West Virginia's economy has been depressed since the early 1980s, economic development efforts in West Virginia are geared toward service sector jobs, primarily in tourism, gaming, and retail sales. Outside the mine, there is no work for a laid-off miner that has comparable wages and benefits, not to mention the social status and respect union miners once enjoyed.

Compromising Compromises

While all wildcat strikes challenged the union hierarchy in some way, certain wildcat strikes directly targeted the union leadership. John Taylor's stories about the number of walkouts and the work he did to mediate them reflects the effort and expense the union went to in order to quell wildcats. The union also incurred financial penalties when its workers violated the contract.

The 1977 contract, along with the "official" strike and the wildcat strikes related to it, exemplify the seemingly constant struggle between rank-and-file miners and the union leadership. After John L. Lewis's iron-fisted intolerance of dissent, it is nearly impossible to find a harmonious relationship between miners and the leadership. The Miners for Democracy movement attacked corruption within the union in the late 1960s. Their eventual toppling of the notoriously corrupt administration of union president Tony Boyle was a watershed event for the United Mine Workers and all of organized labor.[28] The UMWA has prized its internal democracy ever since the MFD movement. While the rank and file valued democracy, many miners in the 1970s looked to the union to take a more radical stand against the coal operators. Most commentary focuses on specific grievances as the immediate cause of any one wildcat strike. Taken together as a whole, the overall tone of the wildcats can be seen as a rank-and-file challenge urging union leadership to be more confrontational with industry. Confrontation was common among the rank and file, but the union as an institution had long since moved away from its confrontational days.

* * *

Mountaintop removal is mechanized job loss on an enormous scale. What I have called the union's period of crisis management began in 1980, when the election of Ronald Reagan coincided with a sharp downturn in the coal market. The union suffered and restructured as the industry restructured. Among the many features to emerge from the union restructuring was Richard Trumka's "selective strike" policy, which undermined the rank-and-file tradition of solidarity.

The union's narrow focus on jobs and the workplace was increasingly compromised by political and economic conditions through the beginning of the twenty-first century. While the coal industry argued that mountaintop removal provided jobs, at the same time the massive strip mines cost the region thousands of jobs that would have been provided by underground mines. It might seem logical for the union to oppose mountaintop removal.

Prior to 1997, the UMWA walked a fine line in trying not to take a clear side in the growing clamor over mountaintop removal. Union president Cecil Roberts published an op-ed column in 1998 that exemplified the union stance. Mountaintop removal, he wrote, should not be done in certain important places, citing the location of the famous 1921 union march on Blair Mountain and the Stanley Heirs land tended by Larry Gibson on Kayford Mountain.[29] On the other hand, Roberts defended the concept that MTR could be done "responsibly."[30]

By unfortunate circumstance, the 1997 lawsuit against mountaintop removal mining specifically targeted a mountaintop removal site that employed three hundred union members. As a result, Roberts led the charge to defend those jobs. Union leadership—apparently compliant with industry rhetoric about jobs—drove a wedge between themselves and coalfield citizens who opposed mountaintop removal when they literally sided with the coal company against the community and local sentiment.

Divisions between the union and community activists persisted until the two joined forces, beginning in 2001, to fight the coal truck weight increase. The union's impossible position—trying to balance dwindling jobs and increasingly hostile politics while maintaining and growing grassroots support—resurfaced in 2003 during the formal comment hearing on the environmental impact statement on mountaintop removal. A union representative from the Charleston office was among the first to speak and left immediately after delivering a conspicuously vague statement that mirrored language from Roberts's op-ed, including the need to balance jobs against protecting special places like Kayford Mountain and Blair Mountain. The union statement offered no substantial comment on the environmental impact statement itself.

While it has proven ineffective at confronting mountaintop removal, and more importantly at organizing new mines, the UMWA has led the charge on some social issues that resonate in the coalfields. In 2003, the union went to New York to protest Viacom corporation's plans to create a "Real Beverly Hillbillies" reality television program. Viacom's ABC division was scouring Appalachia looking for a family who was stereotypically "backward" enough for their plans to move them to a Beverly Hills mansion. The union also led the fight against Bush administration efforts to roll back health and safety regulations inside the mines. As the industry continued to restructure, the union went to court to fight companies that tried to renege on their pension and retirement obligations as a condition of their sale.

All of these positions were popular in the coalfields and showed innovative leadership on behalf of the labor union. But, the union's inability to take strong stands on critical issues like mountaintop removal and its inability to organize mines, especially those run by Massey, has consistently drawn criticism from the rank and file and coalfield communities more generally.

The union's difficulties showed in their campaign to extend the federal Abandoned Mine Lands (AML) program in 2004. The AML fund, created as part of the Surface Mine Control and Reclamation Act in 1977, provides money to clean up old mines left by now-defunct companies before the law was created; a condition of the program allows the union to take interest generated from the fund to provide health benefits to its retirees. The union fought hard to get the program renewed before it expired in 2004. With the help of West Virginia's congressional delegation, the AML program was temporarily extended for one year—not a bad option considering that some proposals would have eviscerated the program.

On the other hand, during the 2004 election season, the union endorsed incumbent Republican congresswoman Shelley Moore Capito. Capito, a conservative Republican and the daughter of former governor Arch Moore, had been shouted down by miners and coalfield residents at the UMWA Labor Day celebration less than two months before the endorsement occurred. In an official statement, the union said that Capito had been a "conduit to the Republican leadership," particularly on the AML campaign. Nevertheless, endorsing Capito looked like a quid pro quo deal that enraged many grassroots union supporters who saw it as a sellout.

5. The Chase

In the nineteenth century, railroaders and other industrial scouts developed plans and infrastructure for harvesting Appalachia's rich natural resources.[1] Created alongside the company towns and steel rails was an economic system whose distinctive relationships shape the region still. Land company agents took control of land and mineral rights using a variety of techniques that included paying delinquent property taxes for or paying paltry sums to subsistence farmers who had no idea how these actions would reshape their lives, their communities, and the land itself.[2] Initially, these efforts were affiliated with railroads that came to own enormous tracts of surface land and mineral deposits. The benchmark Appalachian Land Ownership Study published in 1983 documented continuing absentee ownership of surface land and mineral rights throughout Appalachia. In the fifteen West Virginia counties surveyed, absentee interests owned 69 percent of the surface acres and 74 percent of mineral acres.[3]

In the mid-twentieth century, Helen Lewis and Harry Caudill led the effort to describe Appalachia's economy as a colonial regime.[4] While changes have been made to the conceptual model of internal colonialism, only superficial changes have occurred in the economic circumstances of central Appalachia's coalfields.[5] The colonial relationship remains intact in the sense that poverty in Appalachia stems from the region's integration with, rather than isolation from, mainstream America.[6] In fact, many features of West Virginia's twenty-first-century economy lend even more credence to the arguments made by Lewis and others thirty years earlier.

In 1981, Charleston *Gazette* reporter John G. Morgan published a series of stories based on the Appalachian Land Ownership Study, one of which focused on the growing trend of coal producers coming under the ownership of transnational energy companies like Gulf, Esso, and Royal Dutch Shell.[7] In retrospect, this trend occurred alongside growing neoliberal trends in politics and economics associated in the United States with the Reagan administration. Together, these changes affected the structure of the coal industry and the role of organized labor in the coalfields and throughout the United States.

In 1990, investigative reporter Paul Nyden exposed a political tax scandal associated with former Governor Arch Moore. Known as the "super tax credits,"[8] incentives given in the name of job creation amounted to a giveaway to the coal industry that cost West Virginia tens of thousands of coal mining jobs. With no transparency or accountability, no one knew where this money was going for five years.

From the shady dealings of land companies in the nineteenth century to the shady dealings of Governor Moore, West Virginians are accustomed to Coal's institutional dominance over their politics and economics. Today's activists encounter barriers put in place by powerful forces seemingly at every turn, yet they rarely get to confront power directly. The venues for citizens to comment on and participate in the processes that influence their lives are constructed to give the illusion of democracy. Ultimately, layers of bureaucracy make it difficult to hold politicians or the industry accountable. Following activists through the maze of confusing information, disinformation, public hearings, and political meetings resembles a chase in which they are always one step behind the power they seek to confront.

The Chase

The first time coalfield a resident is likely to learn about a mining permit is when a permit appears in the newspaper, *if* (a) the resident reads a newspaper; (b) happens to read it during the time that the permit is advertised (once a week for four consecutive weeks, under permit regulations); and (c) can understand the technical and legal language and read the map.

Mine permit advertisements typically have a small map, perhaps two inches square, noting, perhaps, a few features, unnamed creeks, and a small section of road. A singular point labeled by longitude and latitude presumably represents a point somewhere in the proposed mine site. A mountaintop removal map offers a "blasting schedule" that might simply denote a year's time or more. These advertisements are small, difficult to understand, and make no mention of residents' rights under law to contest the permit. And, by the time a permit appears in the newspaper, it has already been given an initial review by the Department of Environmental Protection (DEP).

Citizens' only opportunity to comment on a permit during the review process is by requesting an "informal conference." At the informal conference, the DEP cannot answer questions on the record. Coal companies are not required to attend nor are they obliged to respond to residents' concerns. After the conference, speakers who raise issues on the record will receive written confirmation of their comments and explanation of how their issue has been resolved in the permit through revisions, if needed.

Sometimes, issues raised by citizens in an informal conference lead to revisions of the permit. Rarely, if ever, does a conference lead to a permit being denied. Once a permit is issued, citizens can appeal to the West Virginia Surface Mine Board (SMB).[9] The SMB is a governor-appointed group that meets regularly to hear mining appeals. The board operates on the principles of civil procedure and rules of evidence modified to accommodate pro se cases brought by citizens.[10]

Citizens (or companies) can appeal an SMB decision to the state circuit court. There, citizens face technical and legal obstacles similar to those they face at the SMB. Finally, circuit court decisions can be appealed to the West Virginia Supreme Court.

Informally Formal

Colloquially, informal conferences are known as public hearings. The distinction is important: the meetings are public, but the DEP controls the procedure. Arcane and intimidating procedures create bureaucratic distance from actual decision making. Though citizens often expect to have their questions answered, the conference is not a situation in which government or company officials respond. The process is designed to allow citizens to express their interests, concerns, and questions, but only in a formal on-the-record format. The official procedures prevent DEP representatives from responding to questions during the conference. Though not required to attend, at least one representative of the coal company usually does. Even so, they are not required to respond to questions. At one conference, a coal company engineer tried to address some people's concerns in informal conversations after the meeting. When one woman became confrontational, the engineer informed her that he was there "out of the goodness of [his] heart."

A DEP official presides over the informal conference. The official reads a formal introduction that lays out the format of the meeting. From this point on, the meeting is recorded. The recording becomes part of the permit application. People who speak on the record are informed by mail that their comments have been received. If they asked questions, they are informed of steps made in the permit application to address their concerns.

The following summary comes from an informal conference held in April 2004 in the Coal River community of Peytona. In question was the renewal of a permit for a coal slurry impoundment known as Jack's Branch that had been inactive for several years. It was uncommon for people to request a hearing for a permit renewal. This permit was unique, however, because many people in the community knew that the impoundment would be part of a large, new coal processing facility.[11] The complex would include a large surface mine (over fifteen hundred acres), a haul road, a processing plant, and the impoundment. The DEP treats these components as four separate permits, with four separate hearings and appeals, even though all of the permits would be physically and operationally contiguous. Residents saw the complex as one whole fitting into what they perceived as a pattern of inadequate regulation allowing widespread destruction in and around their communities.

* * *

About twenty people affiliated with the activist community attended the meeting. Joe Bowden, the head of the DEP's Logan office, and two female administrative assistants were the only representatives from the DEP.[12] No DEP inspectors attended the meeting. One engineer represented Elk Run Coal Company. The engineer and the two women from the DEP sat together far from the discussion on the opposite side of the school gymnasium. Prior to the meeting, the permit in question was available for scrutiny on the main table with the recording equipment.

Before beginning the formal recorded comment period, Bowden (who apparently was not sure why citizens had requested a hearing for the renewal of an inactive mine structure) informally introduced the permit and the process. Whether or not he intended to, Bowden opened the door to a flood of questions that were not recorded because he had not formally opened the meeting. He started out by explaining that every permitted mining structure, active or inactive, must come up for permit renewal every five years—this is a standard procedure that the DEP requires of the companies.

Tommy Jarrold began a barrage of questions by asking Bowden if the dam in question was leaking. Bowden responded by commenting on the distinction between a dam and an impoundment, explaining the technical terms and how they apply. All of the structures are called impoundments, but if they are over a certain number of acres, they qualify as a dam. (Jack's Branch qualifies as a dam.) The two men then turned to discussing what could be causing the creek at Drawdy Falls (just downstream of the impoundment) to turn orange. Bowden mentioned several possibilities, including iron. He said that only a change in pH would cause damage to aquatic life. Bowden also addressed people's concerns about expansion of the impoundment, saying that, according to the permit in question at this meeting, nothing new would be done at the site—contradicting what residents already knew about future plans for the impoundment.

Bill Price pointed out that Bowden hadn't answered the question about leaking. Bowden said he didn't know the answer. Someone asked how often it [the dam] is inspected. Bowden responded, "They follow up when they can get there."

The meeting then became more contentious. Jerry Dillon declared, "The pond is leaking. That's a fact." Bowden replied, "I'm here to help you guys." Several people in the room were talking, but those who heard this comment grunted in disgust. Price then asked, "Why is the leaking not showing up in the inspection reports?"

Dillon pulled photos of the fissures in the dam out from under his note pad and said, "Here, I wasn't planning on showing these puppies, but look at these." He flipped two of the pictures to the other end of the table for Bowden to see. After looking at them as conversation continued, Bowden said that residents should call in a complaint. "We'll send someone out to look at it and see if it's leaking bad water." Janice Nease responded, "It's not a question of bad water, it's a question of stability."

Dillon then asked about the proposal for the permit, which included a 149-acre impoundment. Dillon said he was under the impression that there would be a surface mine around the impoundment. Bowden explained that the pond itself is permitted to be up to 149 acres. He discussed how dams are built and how they are made taller. Bill Price walked around, looked at the map again, and then consulted with a group of activists. He noted that the existing pond was currently forty-one acres below capacity. Meanwhile, the group had erupted into a debate about increasing the height of the dam and depth of the pond. Dillon, shaking his finger, said to Bowden, "I'm going to hold you personally responsible" if the dam breaks.

Larry Martin spoke up after this confrontation had quieted the room, asking, "If leaking is found, would the permit be denied?" Bowden hedged on that question. James Young chuckled to himself.

Nanette Nelson asked for the impoundment's capacity in gallons. Bowden responded that it would have to be calculated. Dillon interjected, "Every impoundment has a capacity." Bowden replied that the pond has a capacity, he just didn't know it. At this point, the crowd became irritated that Bowden did not have answers to their questions, nor did he have inspectors who could provide information to the citizens.

James Young asked for the dam's hazard rating, A, B, or C. He was familiar with this system because the dam being built near his home in Delbarton was a "class C high hazard dam." Bowden indicated that the Mine Safety and Health Administration (MSHA), a federal agency, rates dams in this manner, but the DEP, a state agency, does not.

Bowden then moved to get the official part of the meeting started. (One of the assistants from the DEP was visibly upset that this was taking so long and she fiddled with the recording equipment to hint that they needed to get going.) Bowden said, "A lot of people hold hearings, they don't talk to you. I try to help . . . if there is anything I know." He made another appeal for people to call in complaints, saying "Don't give up on complaints." Jarrold responded, "I call to complain and they counter me and defend the coal company." Jarrold went on a bit longer before Bowden cut him off to start the official part of the meeting.

After Bowden read the opening protocol, Jerry Dillon was the first speaker. He raised concerns about why a leaking dam received clean inspection reports. He described a recent trip up the face of the dam where he found the leaks—fissures as wide as a body that went all the way through and occurred all the way across the face of the dam. He found a drum of material labeled "caustic" that he knew was used to treat water discharged from the dam, but noted that the drum sat in a place where there was no water and dripped onto dry ground. Dillon also asked a question common among those in attendance: Why is an enlargement of the pond being considered in a renewal permit and not a separate new permit?

Nanette Nelson, the second speaker, addressed the piecemeal accumulation of permits. She said that it didn't show up on this permit, but local citizens knew that the pond in question would be used at the proposed Homer III processing plant Massey intended to build and that the existing pond isn't big enough to hold all the slurry from that operation. She presented Bowden with a letter from Coal River Mountain Watch requesting a citizen's inspection of the dam to be conducted before the permit renewal is granted. She addressed the crowd, saying that anyone who lived there and is affected by this dam could come on the inspection. She added, "That's our right. Don't pass your rights away." (West Virginia law allows citizens to accompany inspectors onto mine sites.)

Bowden reacted visibly to the idea of a citizen inspection as if he were caught off guard. He interrupted Nelson's speech when she mentioned the inspection, telling her that would have to be done through an inspector by calling in a complaint. This comment upset people in the room because Bowden was the head of the office and the supervisor of the inspectors who would be called to document a complaint. Nelson insisted that he keep the letter, and Bowden agreed.

Dillon tried to raise a question between speakers, but Bowden cut him off.

Larry Martin was the third speaker. This was the first time he had ever spoken at such an event, so this was a public coming out of sorts. He introduced himself as being from Delbarton, in Mingo County. (Even though the Peytona meeting was far from Delbarton, the Logan office was overseeing construction of an impoundment in the Mingo County community.) The substance of his remarks was that if the impoundment hurts the health and well-being of the citizens of the community it should not be permitted—a veiled protest of the Delbarton dam. People from the activist community who had been nurturing Larry Martin and James Young as leaders in Delbarton applauded his simple but significant contribution.

Judy Bonds spoke briefly, reiterating the points made by Nanette Nelson and Larry Martin. She addressed the lack of communication between MSHA and DEP. She asked Bowden whether the community would be notified if Massey wanted to reactivate the dam, and if so, how. Bonds was also uneasy because Bowden didn't know which field inspector was responsible for the dam or capacity details of the permit in question at the hearing. She raised the issue of the Martin County, Kentucky, disaster,[13] and advocated new core drillings at the Jack's Branch pond since the facility was so old and "obviously failing," according to firsthand accounts. Bonds argued that someone who inspects this dam should be at the meeting to answer people's questions. Further, she noted that forty acres of the permitted capacity of the impoundment in question was still unused, close to 30 percent of the total. She emphasized that 30 percent could legally be added to a dam that is already leaking and that this should be sufficient to deny the permit renewal.

Freda Williams, the fifth speaker, asked why Peytona was the only place where inspectors failed to show up at the hearings. She said she knew that the DEP only considered technical information, but pointed out that people came to the meeting to give valid reasons why this permit should not be approved. "People don't come here because they have nothing else to do," she concluded. "They know danger exists."

Janice Nease spoke last. "There is something dreadfully wrong with this whole process," she began. "No one came to this meeting to answer questions" (a point of procedure, but also a lack of preparedness in this particular case). "The entire burden is put on the citizens." Nease repeated a common complaint that citizens need early input into the process. She noted that much critical information about dams is not made available to the public and pointed out that regulations require companies to create an evacuation plan for an impoundment, but not to publish or disseminate that plan in the community, or to test its effectiveness. Nease then changed her tone to that of an organizer appealing to the crowd, saying, "Coal River Mountain Watch needs your help."

After Bowden read the closing protocol and stopped the recording, Paul Nelson asked to make another comment. Bowden hesitated and while he did, Nelson said he would request an appeal if the permit is renewed for the pond. Bowden stated there was a process for that, and repeated, "I'm trying to help you guys . . ." The conversation once more became quite confrontational. Jerry Dillon again singled out Bowden, saying "You are the inspector here." Someone else wondered, "Are we going to have another Buffalo Creek?" referring to the 1972 impoundment failure that killed 125 people and still looms large in the collective memory of southern West Virginia.

* * *

The Jack's Branch impoundment meeting illustrates how frustrating the informal conference is for citizens. At another conference, someone asked how they could get a "formal conference," meaning one where questions would be answered. There is no such provision under West Virginia's mining regulations.[14] The informal conference is the first and only opportunity for citizen input in the permit process. The purpose of the meetings for the industry and DEP is to accommodate any critical issues that may arise in the conference by revising the permit. Citizens like those at the Jack's Branch hearing often bring issues that they believe should prohibit proposed mining altogether. But the structure of the informal conference, like the permit procedure in general, shields the DEP and industry from this kind of protest.

The Jack's Branch hearing also shows how activists make use of the conferences. After years of such meetings, CRMW veterans knew that they were not going to get a permit revoked at an informal conference. Yet the conferences served other important functions. For people who were just beginning to speak out against Coal, requesting and speaking at an informal conference was a valuable and empowering experience. It allowed frustrated citizens to "blow off steam" in an organized format (approved by both DEP and CRMW). Nanette Nelson, Judy Bonds, and Janice Nease all made comments at the Jack's Branch conference that were not intended for the DEP, but for the citizens in attendance. They used the informal conference as an organizing tool to reach out to frustrated people who had yet to take action.

As the meeting broke up, several men cornered Bowden to ask about different issues related to the dam. An older man came up to Judy Bonds, who was standing with me, and asked about CRMW—about meetings and whether they were open, because he wanted to come to meetings. He had tried to find CRMW's office in Whitesville, but didn't know where it was.

They spoke for several minutes. Bonds said CRWM would probably have a meeting in June; she also told him where the office was and invited him to come by any time.

After the Jack's Branch conference, Joe Bowden and the Elk Run engineer left together and drove to the impoundment. By the time the Nelsons had their citizens' inspection several weeks later, the dam had been extensively repaired, though the company was not cited for any violations.

Kangaroo Court

On July 8, 2001, the community of Dorothy suffered one of the most destructive floods ever to occur around a mountaintop removal site. A heavy rainstorm dumped 5.4 inches of rain on the area, including the Princess Beverly mine site on Kayford Mountain. A valley fill in Booger Hollow, at the upstream end of Dorothy, failed, causing the face of the fill to slide into sediment ponds at its base.[15] Most people, including the first DEP inspectors to visit the site, associated the valley fill failure with the flooding in Dorothy. Thick mud, rock, and even fine coal particles filled people's yards. One man's home took in 29 inches of water. Residents were without electricity and water for over a week.

The DEP inspectors issued an order to shut down the mine until the fill was repaired. According to Dorothy residents, Princess Beverly began paying settlements to some people in town. One resident reported,

> They started paying these people . . . [and] the insurance man for the coal company [told me] . . ."You'll make a mistake if you get a lawyer." I said, "Well, I haven't got a lawyer." "Well, I'm just telling you, it's our problem, and we're going to take care of it and we're going to make things right." I said, "Okay."[16]

The Surface Mine Board, however, reversed the DEP's shut down order, which it found to be "unreasonable and unfounded." Based on an appeal by Princess Beverly, the board found that "the rainfall event exceeded the design standards required for sediment control structures of the types constructed by Princess Beverly. West Virginia's surface mining regulations require that a sediment structure such as that constructed in Booger Hollow safely pass a 10-year/24-hour storm. . . . The rainfall event of July 8, 2001 exceeded the 100-year storm for 3-hour, 6-hour and 24-hour increments."

Further, the board agreed with testimony from a geomorphologist and hydrogeologist provided by Princess Beverly that "mining-related debris did not move from the Princess Beverly mine site into the community of Dorothy and that the flood-related damage in Dorothy would have occurred even if the mine had not been present."

The same Dorothy resident described how, after the SMB ruling, Princess Beverly stopped paying settlements:

> When [the SMB] made the decision that they didn't think the coal companies were fully responsible, they quit paying. I called the insurance man, and he told me, "How can you prove what got you wasn't the river and it was our pond?" I said, "Well, if you live next to a river and . . . you get flooded, and the water goes down," I said, "what do you got in your yard?" He said, "Sand." I said, "I got about 6 or 8 inches of coal muck in my yard out of your pond." He said, "My advice . . . if you want something from us, you better get you an attorney."

*   *   *

As indicated by the informal conference procedure, the entire process of citizen involvement in the permit process is carefully engineered to keep a safe distance between citizens and the decision-making process. The informal conference and the SMB each give the appearance of encouraging citizen involvement, but the effect is far from democratic participation.

Appointed by the governor, the 2003 Surface Mine Board consisted of six men. The chair, Thomas Michael, had expertise in law and saw to it that the hearings ran according to a modified version of legal procedure used in state courts. Other board members had expertise in geology, engineering, and other relevant areas. They were also described as representing various constituencies. For instance, the SMB web page described Michael as representing "advocacy of environmental protection." One member supposedly represented the mining industry, though at least one other member was a coal company executive and another an executive for a company that manufactures coal trucks.[1] Citizens were not reassured of the board's impartiality when the members left for lunch in an SUV sporting stickers that said "Friends of Coal."

SMB appeals are intimidatingly formal procedures for citizens with no legal training and often no experience with courts or lawyers. Janice Nease, who presented citizens' cases coordinated through CRMW pro se, recalled that they were all shocked on their first trip before the SMB. They had come ready to testify, but not to actually present a case themselves.

Subsequently, SMB rules have required CRMW, because of its status as an organization, to be represented by an attorney. Attorneys familiar with the board and with CRMW questioned the legality of this requirement. Not having the funds to hire an attorney, CRMW members took to listing themselves individually as appellants while continuing to represent themselves pro se.

SMB operated in a formal, legalistic manner, with an official record and a court reporter, but it was less formal than a court of law. Rules of evidence and discovery applied, though less rigidly than in a court. The board was obligated, under law governing the SMB, to help citizens present their case. As such, pro se cases were generally given more latitude than they would in a court proceeding.

Appeal No. 1: Laxare East

Tommy Jarrold was only vaguely aware of the details for a new mountaintop removal mine behind his house on Drawdy Creek, but he was all too aware of the blasting that already shook his house. His testimony at the informal conference took the form of an irate rant about blasting and Massey's behavior toward residents. "They put off such a blast the other day, I'm tellin' you, it rattled the dishes out of the dish rack in my house. My neighbor, his wife goes in for knickknacks and stuff like that. When he came home he thought his house had been vandalized. He came over and asked me if they had put off a shot and I told him about it. That shot knocked all his wife's knickknacks off the shelves and across the floor." Jarrold said that the blasts shaking him and his neighbors were coming from a mine about six miles away. Regardless of their provenance, the blasting would get a lot worse if the Laxare East mine were permitted. Plans called for the mine to encompass over fifteen hundred acres, including the ridge right behind Jarrold's home.

CRMW members worked for weeks preparing an appeal for Laxare East after the original permit was issued. Their case focused on several points, including the existence of abandoned underground mine works in the vicinity of two proposed valley fills, the mine's authority to close a "public" road that ran through the permit area, and species diversity of trees to be planted in the postmining land use plans.

Retired miner and CRMW member Paul Nelson used to work in underground mines at Morgan's Branch where a valley fill would be constructed. When called to testify, he walked directly to the permit map displayed on an easel in the middle of the room and began pointing out locations of mine portals that were not shown. He described the mines he worked in and how they were shut down because they kept filling with water. He produced a map of even older mine works in the hollow that showed mining continuing for an "unknown distance" in the direction of the proposed valley fill. Residents asserted that the omission of these mines from the permit was an oversight that called the entire permit into question. Old mines filled with water caused fear throughout the flood-prone region. It is easy for residents to imagine a blast fracturing geological strata and releasing accumulated water into residential areas. It is also easy to imagine an undocumented underground mine collapsing under the weight of a valley fill, causing it to fail and leading to a catastrophic landslide.

Several residents testified about what they called County Road 79/A. The road runs from the town of Racine up a hollow known as Indian Creek.[18] Indian Creek formerly housed a mine, one of the earliest power plants in the area, a train depot, and a town called Sterling. The last residents moved out of Indian Creek in the mid-1970s when the ridges around the hollow were contour-stripped. Before and after strip mining, Indian Creek has been a popular recreation place for hunters, picnickers, four-wheelers, and anyone who just wants to be in the mountains.

In the early 1990s, a coal company petitioned to have 79/A abandoned by the state. Local residents fought the abandonment and had it overturned on grounds that the coal company didn't own the land. A lessee, the court ruled, could not petition to have a road abandoned. In 2003, residents again fought the potential loss of 79/A. They argued that the earlier court decision gave authority over the so called county road to the county commission. Looking ahead, CRMW had already spearheaded a successful effort to have the county commission sign a resolution opposing any closures of public roads.

Appellants also argued that the postmining land use plan was insufficient in that it did not provide for the land to be returned to a condition "at least as" productive as it was prior to mining, as required by SMCRA. They asked why the permit allowed for something called "topsoil substitute" rather than stockpiling and reusing native topsoils. They also challenged the tree planting plans, arguing that other reclamation projects had allowed nonnative invasive species to be planted.

At several points during the hearing, Chairman Michael seemed to be arguing on behalf of the citizens. Testimony during the hearing revealed that Massey Energy had merely "checked off" the form indicating there was no endangered species habitat within the mine site, but did not actually investigate the possible presence of the most likely such species, the Indiana bat. When the board members and lawyers for DEP and Massey decided that the regulations merely required an "inquiry" from the Department of Natural Resources, but not necessarily an investigation, Chairman Michael shook his head and declared, "I think it's absolutely ridiculous, but it seems to be what the rules set up." He quickly added, "I mean, that's my personal opinion."[19]

After more than eight hours of testimony, the Surface Mine Board unanimously upheld the permit, despite the many points on which they seemed to find justification for the appeal. From my perspective as an observer, I wasn't surprised that they upheld the permit. Based on the tenor of some of the board members' questions, however, I was surprised that the board did not ask the company to make specific modifications to the permit.

As we left the DEP offices, board members, DEP inspectors, and permit reviewers all congratulated Nease and other CRMW members for presenting a good case. Joe Bowden said that CRMW had obviously put in a lot of preparation time, but so had the DEP. This scene in the parking lot reminded me of the ritualized handshaking at the end of a Little League baseball game. People from CRMW were frustrated and defeated. They were in no mood to cordially acknowledge the odd sort of congeniality extended by their opponents.

In a discussion several days later, Janice Nease put the Laxare appeal in the context of the other appeals CRMW has organized. The SMB is not friendly, she suggested, "but it is friendlier than it has ever been."

> I think that Coal River Mountain Watch has to take a lot of credit for that because we have tried to be very credible when we go there. We have . . . witnesses and . . . we have attacked crucial things. . . . [We don't] just come in and say "This is ruining our homes and our communities." . . . [We give] valid reasons why this is wrong and this should not be.
>
> We [have been] able to get some things changed, but they were baby steps. . . . you have to remember that this has never been done before. On the flood study . . . we were able to get laws passed in the legislature to prevent future floods.

"We're really tired of studies," she concluded, "[but] they are a way to get our foot in the door and make them see that we are going to have change."[20]

Appeal No. 2: Edwight

The next SMB appeal that CRMW coordinated confronted the massive eighteen hundred-acre Edwight Surface Mine permit issued to Independence Coal Company, another Massey Energy subsidiary. Citizens focused on fewer key points, including a study on the effects of blasting on cliffs near the mine site that hovered over Route 3, the main road in the region.

CRMW had hired a professional geologist to look at the cliffs and specifically contest the results of a study Massey had contracted to a mine engineering company. University of Pennsylvania folklorist Mary Hufford testified regarding the cultural importance of the landscape that would be destroyed by the Edwight mine. Hufford had conducted ethnographic research on the Hazy Creek watershed in the heart of the mine site for ten years. She documented not only the importance of the forest, but also illustrated the contradictions in the permit sections that deal with cultural and historical resources. For example, permits (including Edwight) routinely indicated that no part of the mine site had been historically used as cropland. Hufford quoted the National Historical Record definition of cropland and used her own research on Hazy Creek to illustrate that some plots did, in fact, qualify.

Compared to other appeals I observed, I thought CRMW presented a greater quantity of professional, expert testimony that attacked specific portions of the permit—what the Surface Mine Board always said they must do. This time, however, there was a marked difference in the board's attitude toward the appeal.

Chairman Michael challenged Hufford to identify where the permit violated regulations on cultural and historical resources. Hufford explained one such case, but Michael, in a condescending tone that lacked any professional courtesy, pointed out that the regulation applied only to resources registered on the National Register of Historic Places. Hufford's argument, while thorough and accurate, was moot. Michael began what would become a recurrent theme throughout the day: the SMB was not the appropriate forum for Hufford's testimony or CRMW's appeals.

As the hearing dragged on, the board's attitude went from confrontational to rude. According those present, the board at first didn't want to allow Bonds to deliver a closing argument, suggesting that the appellants had not presented any evidence. Michael, in delivering the board's findings, said in no uncertain terms that the SMB's mandate was to uphold the laws that permit mountaintop removal mining. He said the SMB did not have the authority to stop mountaintop removal and that the appellants should take their cause elsewhere.

* * *

The SMB's reception of the Laxare and Edwight appeals could not have been more different. Outright hostility replaced cordial respect as the board's dominant attitude. It was plain to see that the board did not want to hear any more appeals like those CRMW had presented.

In the winding course from the newspaper advertisements to the informal conferences and SMB hearings, there is no place in "the chase" for people to say, "Mountaintop removal is wrong and should not be allowed." A strong rebuttal can be made to Chairman Michael's assertion that the SMB is not the appropriate venue for the kind of evidence CRMW provided. Arguably, specific technical points like the existence of abandoned mines or historical features are cause for review under the federal Surface Mine Control and Reclamation Act, which the SMB and DEP are charged with upholding. Even when people can point to details like these, however, the pertinent laws and regulations set such a low threshold that the companies and the DEP are not required to provide effective safeguards. The bureaucratic maze also gives credence to Congressman Ken Hechler's warning to President Carter that SMCRA would not work because enforcement agencies were too susceptible to industry influence.

If the DEP and SMB throw up their hands and say they don't have the authority to restrict mountaintop removal or other mining practices, the sometimes spoken, sometimes unspoken message to citizens is that they need to go to the legislature.

Overloaded Democracy

Between 2000 and 2002, a rash of deaths caused by collisions involving coal trucks led to a public outcry for new regulation. During a twenty-month period, twelve people were killed in collisions with coal trucks. While the truck drivers were not always at fault, citizens argued that the trucks were too big, too heavy, and not effectively policed for use on winding coalfield roads. Coal truck weight regulations and lack of enforcement had been a dirty secret swept under the rug, for the most part, for decades. Existing laws limited all vehicles on West Virginia roads to gross weights of 65,000, 73,500, or 80,000 pounds, depending on the type of road.[21] Most roads used by coal trucks were small roads maintained by the state and limited to loads of 65,000 pounds. Bridges on these roads had their own weight limits, sometimes as low as 24,000 pounds.

In response to the public outcry, Mike Caputo, a member of the West Virginia House of Delegates and of the United Mine Workers, introduced a bill in 2002 to increase enforcement of existing weight limits. The coal industry introduced a competing bill to raise weight limits to 120,000 pounds with a 5 percent variance on enforcement, effectively making the new limit 126,000 pounds.[22] Governor Bob Wise offered a compromise bill to raise weight limits and increase enforcement. Debate climaxed in a special session of the legislature during the summer of 2002. Caputo offered an amendment to the governor's bill eliminating the weight increase. The amendment passed in the House of Delegates by one vote, effectively killing the bill. Opponents of the weight increase celebrated Coal's first public defeat in recent memory. While it was no small victory, celebrating an outcome that, in effect, preserved the status quo indicated Coal's institutional power in West Virginia.

Coal found several new friends in the legislature after the 2002 election cycle and returned to Charleston seeking a weight increase in 2003. The United Mine Workers, Coal River Mountain Watch, Ohio Valley Environmental Coalition, and West Virginia Citizen Action Group again joined forces to fight the industry bill.

The activist community followed the industry's bill as it breezed through the state Senate. In the Senate's Energy, Industry and Mining Committee, the committee's general counsel explained the particulars of the bill. When a senator asked a question that counsel could not answer, counsel stepped to the front row of the gallery to consult with Bill Raney, president of the West Virginia Coal Association. After the meeting, Janice Nease and other CRMW members asked, in a joking-but-not-really-joking tone, whether Raney had written the bill. Raney replied in a similar tone that he had not.

The only serious threat to the new weight limits would come in the House of Delegates Judiciary Committee. As he had in the previous year, Delegate Caputo offered an amendment to the bill to remove the weight increase, while keeping increases in fines and electronic reporting measures insisted upon by the governor.

At a public hearing before the Judiciary Committee meeting, a bridge inspector from the state Division of Highways spoke out against the weight increase. He detailed specific reasons why raising weight limits for bridges on the proposed road system was not safe from an engineering perspective. Engineers, however, did not design the proposed coal transportation system. Roads were selected for the system based on the amount of coal hauled on them in the previous year, not the construction standards of the roads, nor their ability to safely carry heavy loads.

The committee's hearing room was obviously built before citizens were welcome to attend meetings. A large conference table took up most of the room. When we arrived, people already lined the walls of the room two and three deep. By the time the meeting started, over seventy spectators were packed into the room, with more in the corridor outside. Coal truck supporters held a rally on the capitol steps outside the meeting room. There were television, radio, and newspaper reporters. Supporters of the weight increase outnumbered opponents about 2:1 at the capitol. Supporters included coal association representatives, coal executives, and a few actual truck drivers. Stickers and buttons easily identified Coal's supporters: Friends of Coal, I ♥ Coal, and others referring to specific companies. About thirty minutes into the meeting, Judy Bonds scrawled a sign that read, "Thou shalt not follow others into wrongdoing."

As committee members filed into the room, Delegate Jim Morgan joked with Delegate Caputo, "You're not offering any amendments to this [bill], are you?" Debate on the bill lasted all day, with many tense exchanges between delegates. The primary points of discussion were amendments offered by delegates Mike Caputo and Steven Kominar. Like his 2002 amendment, Caputo's would keep the increased enforcement provisions, but reduce the weight limit to 80,000 pounds. Kominar (who had family connections to a coal trucking firm in Mingo County, West Virginia) offered an amendment to preserve the coal association's intent to raise weight limits and clarify some of the constitutional questions that had arisen during previous debates.

Cost was one of the many pertinent issues in the debate. A 1980 federal study estimated the cost of upgrading the West Virginia's roads for hauling coal. Adjusted for inflation, the price tag came to $2.8 billion. At the time of the committee hearing in 2003, the state had taken no action to upgrade these roads. During a Senate committee hearing, the coal association introduced a new amendment to the bill that would impose a one-cent per ton surcharge on coal hauled by truck to raise money for road maintenance. At the end of the meeting, Chuck Wyrostock, a lobbyist for the West Virginia E-Council (part of the coalition opposing the bill), approached coal association president Bill Raney and ceremoniously handed him a penny.

The following excerpts of the Judiciary Committee discussion of the coal truck bill and amendments are taken from my own notes and recollection. Unless indicated by quotation marks, all of the text should be treated as paraphrased comments.

* * *

Delegate Caputo asked a string of questions of counsel. He emphasized that the enforcement provisions would not apply to roads outside the coal haul system even though the provisions would raise the weight limits on those roads.

Counsel estimated that revenue from the one-cent surcharge would generate $400,000 and that license fees in the plan would generate between $2.5 and $3.5 million—all ballpark figures based on coal hauling statistics from previous years.

At one point, several CRMW members laughed audibly. I later learned that a delegate sitting across from them whom I couldn't see had fallen asleep—her head fell and hit the table. Committee chair Jon Amores repeated an announcement he had made at the beginning of the meeting, that House rules forbade expressions of approval or disapproval, and said that laughter fell under those regulations.

Delegate Barbara Fleischauer asked a series of interesting questions. She established, by questioning counsel, that no public hearings would be held on raising weight limits statewide to 88,000 pounds. She asked about the constitutionality of this provision. "Are we selecting one industry for special treatment?"

Counsel responded that language in the Kominar amendment would deal with this question, adding that "I think it is problematic, the way it is written," and that the constitutional questions would depend on case law.

FLEISCHAUER: Could this lead to challenges to the law forbidding local bills?
COUNSEL: I'm comfortable with the language in the Kominar amendment.

FLEISCHAUER: Would this be inappropriate statewide?

COUNSEL DID NOT RESPOND.

FLEISCHAUER: Would other resource haulers be unfairly discriminated against?

COUNSEL: Coal is a unique part of the economy and it would be a valid public policy to provide economic stability to that industry.

Following this exchange, counsel wanted to abstract Kominar's amendment because it addressed many of the questions being raised. Caputo and others objected to this request because his (Caputo's) amendment was supposed to be considered first. Chairman Amores explained that Caputo's amendment would be considered for adoption first, but allowed Kominar's amendment to be abstracted to address the questions.

The Kominar amendment offered the following changes to the coal truck bill:

1. It would leave the weight enforcement division within the Division of Highways rather than moving it to the Public Service Commission.
2. It would remove a provision that exempted trucks from any weight restrictions for hauls of five miles or less (a provision that would have directly benefited Massey Energy's mines in Coal River).
3. It would restructure penalty provisions so that they applied to shippers and haulers.
4. It would increase the one-cent surcharge to five cents per ton.
5. It would require the Division of Highways (DOH) commissioner to report the new weight ratings of all roads upon completion of his assessment.
6. It would require all shippers shipping loads over 80,000 pounds to report weights electronically.

Delegate Bonnie Brown asked counsel about the lack of a fiscal note for the bill. Counsel conceded that the bill would add a financial burden to the Public Service Commission, and that all revenue generated by the fees and fines would go to the highway fund. When pressed for financial information, counsel said that the bill was designed to be revenue neutral, but a financial note could be requested.

DOH commissioner Fred Van Kirk was called to respond to technical questions relating to the bill.

DELEGATE CAPUTO: How adequate are the funds in the bill to repair and upgrade roads and bridges?

VAN KIRK: The "money is not all that great."

CAPUTO: What is the cost of a new bridge?

VAN KIRK: A thirty-to-forty-foot bridge could cost $200,000.

Caputo read from a letter Van Kirk wrote stating that weight limits on bridges in McDowell County ranged from 48,000 pounds to 120,000 pounds and that only one bridge could carry 120,000 pounds. Van Kirk responded that the letter referred only to U.S. Highway 52 (the primary artery) in McDowell County.

CAPUTO: Can the DOH justify rating a road at 120,000 pounds with a bridge that is rated at 32,000 pounds?
VAN KIRK: No sir.
CAPUTO: Have we built bridges for 120,000 pounds?

Van Kirk hedged, but said no.

CAPUTO: The bridge design criteria are not for 120,000 pounds; some will hold 120,000, but are not designed for them?
VAN KIRK: The design vehicle used is a five-axle truck weighing 90,000 pounds and considers other variables like speed and wind.
CAPUTO: Would heavier trucks wear out a bridge faster?
VAN KIRK: Yes.
CAPUTO: What is the lifespan of a bridge?
VAN KIRK: Forty to fifty years.
DELEGATE JOHN OVERINGTON: Would you divert funds from other parts of the state to service coal haul roads?
VAN KIRK: No, that would not be our policy. We would ask the entity requesting an upgrade to contribute to that upgrade.
OVERINGTON: Would more damage be done by one 120,000-pound truck or two 80,000-pound trucks?
VAN KIRK: Axle loads are the determining factor, I don't know.

Delegate Corey Palumbo went back to the same question.

VAN KIRK: It would depend on the configuration of the trucks. A heavier load in the same truck would cause more damage. I don't know if it's possible to determine one truck versus two trucks.
VAN KIRK: Most all roads would need bridge work to be rated for 120,000 pounds. There are some sections that could handle 120,000.
DELEGATE BROWN: What is the upgrade cost estimate?
VAN KIRK: DOH's wish list for upgrades statewide is $10–$12 billion.
BROWN: We don't have that. What is the procedure for investigating complaints of overweight traffic on bridges?
VAN KIRK: We send out weight crews to investigate whether the violation is repeated.
BROWN: McCorkle Avenue and Corridor G [main roads in and around Charleston] would be designated as coal haul roads under this bill.

VAN KIRK: The designation of roads is based on a history or anticipation of coal hauling. Primary consideration is the structural integrity of roads and bridges.

BROWN: Population density is not considered?

VAN KIRK: Not per se.

BROWN: What about traffic history or pedestrian traffic?

VAN KIRK: No. Safety would be considered.

DELEGATE RUSTY WEBB: [Based on a rumor] is it the intention of the DOH to reduce loads to their current level after implementation of this bill with the exception of some steel haul roads?

VAN KIRK: That would be my intention, to hold current limits and upgrade to 80,000 pounds.

DELEGATE FLEISCHAUER: Current limits are set "scientifically?"

VAN KIRK: Yes

FLEISCHAUER: How will you prioritize your review? Have you considered expense?

VAN KIRK: No.

FLEISCHAUER: How many roads are currently rated at 65,000 pounds?

VAN KIRK: The vast majority.

FLEISCHAUER: How many bridges are in the state?

VAN KIRK: Between 6,500 and 6,700.

FLEISCHAUER: And how many of those are on roads rated for 65,000 or 73,500 pounds?

VAN KIRK: That would be in conformity with the distribution of roads at those ratings.

FLEISCHAUER (asks for data related to the previous question): What are penalties for hauling overweight on 65,000 or 73,500 pound roads?

VAN KIRK: Graduated scales from 1 cent per pound up to $1,600.

FLEISCHAUER: Where does the money go?

VAN KIRK: To the board of education in the county where the violation was.

FLEISCHAUER: Comment on the $2.8 billion figure for improving damaged roads.

VAN KIRK: That's based on a 1980 federal study of upgrading roads for coal hauling. Based on those [today's] federal standards it would be even higher. The state generated the $2.8 billion number for bare minimum safety standards. The $2.8 billion is a current estimate based on inflation.

* * *

After a lunch break, debate continued for several hours. About thirty people had gathered outside the packed committee hearing room as debate resumed. A truck driver standing beside me spoke to another trucker. "That over there is the one that's always on TV," he said, pointing out Judy Bonds on the other side of the room. "I'd like to know what her daddy did. I bet if you went back far enough, there is coal in there somewhere. I don't understand why they don't understand that coal is all we got. They got to give us this 120. They got to!"

Debate culminated in a series of votes. Tension hung heavy across the room as Caputo finished his final statement and asked for a roll call vote. The delegate who had joked with Caputo in the morning mouthed the words "I'm sorry" to Caputo as he voted against Caputo's amendment. A delegate from Logan County, visibly distraught, with her face in her hands and voice trembling, voted against the amendment. The amendment failed fifteen votes to ten. Caputo and Delegate Fleischauer offered several more amendments, but the outcome was clear—the coal industry won. The remainder of the meeting was torturous for members of the activist community—watching their hard work go down one vote at a time. The only concession the committee agreed to was a provision for one representative from the United Mine Workers to sit on the board that would monitor the coal transportation system. After losing several votes and seeing that this provision was approved on a 13–12 vote, Caputo quietly exclaimed, "Oh, sweet Jesus."

* * *

The fallout from the committee meeting was heavy. Despite all their hard work, the words of support from so many people, and the apparent rectitude of their position, many in the activist community felt physically defeated. The mood was somber and wounded for a couple of days as activists contemplated reasons for their failure.

To most people familiar with state politics, one large reason for the legislative outcome was clear and marked with a dollar sign. The People's Election Reform Committee (PERC-WV), a cooperative effort led by the Ohio Valley Environmental Coalition and West Virginia Citizen Action Group, confirmed the place of money in the coal truck debate. PERC compiled information on Coal's campaign contributions in the 2000 and 2002 election cycles and drew a direct connection between contributions and the different outcome of the two votes. The data were taken from official reports filed by candidates with the secretary of state's office.

The PERC study established that legislators who received campaign contributions from Coal were more likely to support the coal truck weight increase. While that seems obvious, the study provides important documentation on giving to specific candidates. Coal gave nearly $90,000 to returning House members who had supported the weight increase during the 2002 special session. Coal concentrated more than one-third of its contributions to members of the House Judiciary Committee, increasing donations within that committee by more than 100 percent. Contributions to Judiciary Committee chairman Jon Amores increased nearly tenfold. A March 2002 fundraiser for Governor Bob Wise's reelection campaign raised $73,500—mostly from coal companies. Wise received $62,250 from coal companies in March 2003, the month the coal truck bill passed. In the 2000 election, Wise received $115,600 from Coal, and another $120,340 for his inaugural celebration. After the House of Delegates approved the weight increase, PERC analyzed Coal's campaign contributions to those who voted for and against the bill. Delegates who voted for the bill received a total of $104,660, while those who voted against it received a total of $23,545.

* * *

Reflecting on the coal truck effort several months after the climactic 2003 committee meeting, delegate Mike Caputo felt like the coalition of labor and activists had succeeded in many ways.[23] Within communities like Coal River were several reactions to the new 120,000-pound weight limits. Some coal truck drivers commented that they were making more money now than they had before the coal truck issue came up. The drivers credited wage increases to the attention activists brought to the issue. Others blamed the activists for reducing their weight limits. Despite the fact that drivers carried signs through the capitol declaring that 120,000 pounds was the only savior of the coal trucking industry, many later complained that the new weight limit was actually a reduction compared to the weights they had been hauling illegally. Either way, Caputo identified some successes from the effort he spearheaded, one of which was making the coal industry admit that it breaks the law.

Caputo surmised that everything in the new coal truck law was an improvement on the previous law except for the weight increase. Along with the 120,000-pound limit, the bill imposed electronic real-time reporting of vehicle weights; reporting requirements for coal shippers, haulers, and receivers; as well as new enforcement provisions and fines. Still, he concluded that the 120,000-pound limit was too high a price to pay for these improvements.

When asked how the coal truck debate might have developed had the UMWA and activist groups not worked together, Caputo suggested they would not have had a prayer. Recognizing that the respective organizations would have differences over issues, most notably mountaintop removal, Caputo credited the pact between the union, community groups, and environmental organizations for getting any coal truck legislation passed at all.

* * *

The tightly controlled regulatory process illustrated by the informal conference and the Surface Mine Board hearings, combined with the legislative debate over coal trucks, illustrate Coal's power within the state of West Virginia. Shut out of the regulatory apparatus and defeated in the state government, coalfield residents' and activists' anger over the lack of effective regulation is doubled by their frustration with their inability to participate in an honest democratic forum. Delegate Caputo suggested that a public referendum would have found 80 percent or 90 percent of the state opposed to raising coal truck weight limits. Those numbers may be exaggerated, but his characterization of public opinion related to the industry was accurate. A 2004 poll commissioned by the Appalachian Center for the Economy and Environment showed likely West Virginia voters opposed mountaintop removal mining by a margin of two to one. The poll reinforced the notion that popular sentiment was not reflected in state policies regarding the coal industry. These examples illustrated the protection the state provides Coal. That this regime was regularly defended in the name of economic opportunity and development added insult to activists' injuries, especially those who lived in coalfield towns that had been economically depressed for decades. A closer analysis of the state's economic development policies and practices begs the question, "Whose development is it?"

6. Whose Development Is It?

Perhaps the most striking characteristic of West Virginia's economic development is that there seems to be no focus on the quality of jobs created. There has been no long-term plan to develop any particular kind of workforce, other than the poorly paid service sector. Nor has there been a focus on reducing poverty and inequality as part of economic development efforts.[1] Among the projects supported by the state in 2003 and 2004 in the name of economic development were a Victorian-themed outlet mall in Wheeling, a Cabela's outdoor outfitters warehouse and retail store near Wheeling, a new minor league baseball stadium in Charleston, and two NASCAR racetracks (one of which was to be built on a strip mine site in Logan County). Beginning in 2000, West Virginia dramatically expanded its gaming industry by legalizing so-called gray video poker machines and allowing casino table games in certain venues. All of these industries employ people and all of the projects supported by the state will bring construction and other related jobs to West Virginia. As a policy, however, the state's economic development efforts do not form a coherent and effective plan to create jobs and long-term economic growth in West Virginia. Projects like the Hatfield-McCoy ATV trails, shopping malls, racetracks, and baseball stadiums create geographically isolated, relatively low-paying service jobs that typically offer no benefits. Nearly all baseball stadium employees will be employed only five or six months per year; racetrack workers possibly less than that.

Implicitly, if not explicitly, the state's various development policies protect Coal's status as the dominant economic engine in southern West Virginia. In 2001, the legislature passed Senate Bill 603 to allow county and regional economic development agencies within West Virginia to develop their own land use master plans. The explicit goal of the bill is to allow local economic development authorities to work with mining companies to create alternate land uses for post-mining reclamation to those provided under mining regulations. This approach gives gave official credence to Coal's assertion that mountaintop removal promotes development by creating flat land. (It also contributes to a geographic imbalance and general incoherence of economic development within the state.)

SB 603 gave rise to efforts like the Boone County Land Use Master Plan commissioned by the Boone County Community and Economic Development Corporation, whose draft plan included the following section.

METHODOLOGY

The Boone County Land Use Master Plan is a county-wide plan developed to provide opportunities to help diversify the local economy and provide recreational opportunities to enhance the quality of life for the citizens of Boone County, West Virginia, by identifying land made available through current and future transportation systems and coal mining activities in correlation with current proposed water and sewage systems and current and proposed community development activities.

Senate Bill #603 allows for alternate land use categories for previous or current surface mine sites. The earlier requirements for reclamation were limited to returning to area back to the Approximate Original Contour (AOC). Reclamation options now include Industrial, Commercial/Retail, Residential, Agricultural, Recreational, or Commercial Forestland sites.[2]

The methodology allows coal companies to negotiate mountaintop removal reclamation plans with local authorities. In addition, the master plan describes various demographic information and existing utilities that serve Boone County. Notable among the demographic statistics were increases in the county's unemployment rate and school children classified as "low income." From 1996 to 2001, West Virginia produced more coal than in any other period in state history. During that time, Boone County was at or near the top of coal production among West Virginia counties. Yet, during that same period, Boone County's unemployment rate nearly doubled, increasing from 5.6 percent to 10.4 percent. The percentage of students in Boone County schools classified as low income increased by 7.6 percent, to a total of 57.0 percent.

The draft plan's executive summary listed all active surface mines in Boone County along with information on their size, location, and proximity to four-lane highways and available utilities. Permits in the summary covered approximately 10,626 acres, of which 6,665 were deemed "post-mining usable."[3] Of the fifteen mine sites listed, none had existing water or sewer service, five had electricity, and ten had gas.[4] The plan zoned the sites for development based on proximity to the county's main roads: US Route 119 (the only four-lane highway in the county), and WV Routes 3 and 85. Only three of the existing surface mines listed in the summary were within five miles of US 119, and only six within five miles of US 119, WV 3, or WV 85.

SUMMARY

As a result of the passing of Senate Bill #603 in the 2001 Legislative Session, Land Use Master Plans are being developed to assist the counties in West Virginia. The Boone County Land Use Master Plan will provide Boone County Community & Economic Development Coroporation [*sic*] with the ability to sieze [*sic*] development opportunities for alternate land uses of transportation systems and surface mine sites. The plan, adopted by the Boone County Commission, will set the standards for development on such properties, having a positive impact on the economic status and enhancing the quality of life for the citizens of Boone County.[5]

Policies like the land use master plan lend political and bureaucratic support to Coal's insistence that flat land from mountaintop removal is necessary for economic development. Such policies also justify removing reclamation regulatory power from the state Department of Environmental Protection and give discretion to local development boards.

Activists, on the other hand, love to ask when and how existing mountaintop removal sites will be developed. In a presentation at the activists' 2002 Coal Summit, hydrogeologist and activist Rick Eades mapped 95,000 acres of mountaintop removal sites that existed in the Coal River basin at that time. Eades suggested there were already enough flattened acres to build five 5,000-acre recreational parks, ten 1,000-acre prison sites, fifty 500-acre shopping mall sites, one hundred 100-acre trailer parks, four hundred 50-acre school sites, and have thousands of acres left over.

Meanwhile, prisons became a favorite job creation program in Appalachia. The cost of one prison built on a mountaintop removal site in Kentucky soared to over $40 million as the land settled beneath the structure. The facility project became the most expensive federal penitentiary in the country, nicknamed "Sink Sink." Structural problems have surfaced at a high school built on an MTR site in McDowell County, West Virginia. McDowell County is also home to trailer parks populated by victims displaced by record flooding in 2001 and 2002. Activists used data like these to argue that Coal had already stripped more land than could possibly be developed, even if development efforts were genuine.

* * *

None of the projects put forth in the name of economic development—like the Hatfield-McCoy ATV trails, highways, and the racetrack on reclaimed strip mines—will bring systematic, sustained growth to the southern counties. Projects such as these create a charade of development on these sites, but they comprise a paltry fraction of stripped land across the region.

Despite the fact that Coal has failed generation after generation of citizens who have lived through its boom-and-bust cycles, it remains the centerpiece of state-supported economic development policies. Within the state, Coal's supremacy is apparently not questioned. Beyond the coal industry itself, West Virginia applies the economic model of the extractive industry to other sectors of the economy. In all of the examples offered, the state caters to corporations focused on large-scale development that will, in theory, bring jobs. In each case, this approach to development impedes or restricts the ability of people to access local resources and apply local knowledge and culture to generate income.

The development model applied by West Virginia, based on the idea of "comparative advantage," was a favorite around the world in the late twentieth century, reflected in neoliberal governments and international development institutions like the World Bank and the International Monetary Fund. If a locale can produce a commodity better (i.e., cheaper) than anyone else, the theory goes, that commodity should be the focus of the locale's entire economy.[6] West Virginia has a comparative advantage in producing coal because coal is plentiful and West Virginia is close to the major energy markets and shipping ports on the East Coast.[7] Wyoming coal is cheaper to produce, but shipping costs and higher quality made Appalachian coal the preferred fuel for the East. As the boom-and-bust cycles of the coal industry have shown over and over again, people suffer when an entire economy is tied to the whim of the market for the one commodity. Even more frightening, towns like Whitesville and others across the Appalachian coalfields have languished through the last years of the twentieth and into the twenty-first centuries—a period of booming coal production.

West Virginia itself, however, serves as a wonderful example of the ongoing failure of the economics of comparative advantage to create a healthy economy. Despite its comparative advantage in coal production, after roughly 150 years of industrial coal extraction, West Virginia ranked at or near the bottom of every economic category in 2000, including median household income (fiftieth),[8] percentage of adults with access to the Internet (forty-sixth),[9] and persons over age twenty-five with at least a bachelor's degree (fiftieth).[10] West Virginia ranked at or near the top of inglorious categories like prevalence of obesity (third), prevalence of smoking (second), cancer deaths (third), cardiovascular deaths (third),[11] smokeless tobacco use (first),[12] ATV deaths per capita (first),[13] and total persons below the poverty line (fifth).[14]

In the coal industry, as in the banana industry mentioned at the beginning of part II, comparative advantage combined with locally fixed production and integration with global markets creates an inflexible economy tied to the fate of one industry that is dependent on unpredictable distant consumers. A diverse economy protects citizens against boom-and-bust cycles and generates a thicker web of social interactions. West Virginia economic development officials claim to promote diversity by supporting the tourism and gaming industries. This creates an image of diversity, but a growing, vibrant economy has not emerged from these efforts.

How development is defined and measured accounts for part of the flaw in economic development policy. With its continuing inability to break out of economic stagnation and poverty, despite repeated efforts, West Virginia has much in common with developing nations around the world. Like many international development efforts, West Virginia's economic development plans have, for at least two decades, been based on neoliberal ideology that includes a focus on overall economic growth measured by statistics like gross domestic product (GDP). Measures like GDP fail to recognize that poverty and inequality are not necessarily reduced by general increases in economic production. Many economists (and even the World Bank) have come to see alleviating poverty and reducing inequality as basic components of any economic development program, even to the extent of judging many of the bank's own projects to be failures.[15] The bank's 2006 world development report asserts that leveling economic and political fields is crucial for reducing economic inefficiency and generating success for an economic development program. The report recommends an "equity lens" that brings new perspectives to development programs. Among recommendations for this lens, the report suggests that "the best policies for poverty reduction could involve redistributions of influence, advantage, or subsidies away from dominant groups. . . . The dichotomy between policies for growth and policies specifically aimed at equity is false. The distribution of opportunities and the growth process are jointly determined."[16]

That is, economic growth programs must emphasize reducing poverty and inequality. The report also asserts that the success of a comprehensive economic development program must involve direct democratic participation among social equals. West Virginia's economic development policies have consistently focused on large-scale projects that appeal to the already powerful within the state—most notably, the coal industry—or out-of-state interests. State efforts do not include its own citizens as equal participants in a democratic process. If anything, the public input apparatus in the coal permitting process works in a de facto, if not explicit, way to channel public input into ineffective ways away from decision making.

Economist Amartya Sen argues that development can, in fact, create economic growth that benefits everyone by increasing what he calls "freedom."[17] However, Sen devotes no critical attention to what *development* actually means. Development in and of itself does not necessarily create greater freedoms for everyone in an economic system. A valuable contribution to economic analysis, however, is the idea of *capability,* which Sen uses to account for things like religious and cultural beliefs that are not typically included in economistic analyses. Examples such as ignoring the value of multimillion dollar ginseng resources lost to mountaintop removal or restricting farmers' ability to plow near streams demonstrate how West Virginia's extraction-based economic development model restricts the capability of its citizens to engage in cultural and economic practices that do not fit the model. An empirical analysis of decades of economic development schemes shows the state has not created new high-quality jobs nor have they created a vibrant or diverse economy.

State economic development schemes have enclosed commons resources like forests and streams and given millions of dollars to corporations that have exacerbated the poor economic condition of the state by reducing health care benefits and providing poorly paid service sector jobs—a trend solidified when Walmart displaced Weirton Steel as the state's largest employer in 1998.[18] In December 2004, Charleston's *Sunday Gazette-Mail* reported that Walmart was the largest employer of people whose children were enrolled in the state-sponsored health program for uninsured children. Walmart accounted for three times as many uninsured children as the second-highest employer listed on application forms.[19]

* * *

At the public comment hearing for the environmental impact statement on mountaintop removal held in Charleston in July 2003, a preacher spoke in favor of the coal industry. He said, "We do have an environmental problem in West Virginia; that problem is poverty." The preacher reflected the same attitude found in the people who accuse activists of being on welfare and collecting a government check. The attitude also reflects a common accusation made against activists everywhere: that they are against economic development altogether.

A professional consulting group surveyed West Virginians' feelings toward state economic development efforts in the late 1990s. In comments made to a *Charleston Daily Mail* business editor in 2000, one consultant commented: "One of the strongest assets that the state has going for it is its sense of place that people genuinely feel. The way the state is embraced and revered is striking. The problems in the state seem to be almost personally felt. . . . [Interviewees have] been through this before. They felt that they had openly given their opinions and shared ideas for success for West Virginia many times in the past—and that these efforts were neither acknowledged nor implemented."[20]

I asked many activists what ideas they had for economic opportunities in their communities. Patty Sebok proposed a recreational campground for Indian Creek, a popular recreation area for local residents now used by Massey for a strip mine and haul road. Judy Bonds imagined developing retirement communities in the region with specialized services for the elderly. The state had already given special status to several locations including the cities of Bluefield and Morgantown as "retirement zones." Vivian Stockman pointed to a report by the New Apollo Project that suggested thousands of jobs could be created in the alternative energy industry.[21]

Whose Development?

Despite Coal's insistence that West Virginia needs flat land to develop, Rick Eades's analysis of mountaintop removal development efforts indicates that thousands of acres of land have already been flattened by mountaintop removal. The rhetoric of development used by Coal and by the state goes hand in hand in maintaining an economic regime that holds the southern coalfields in a state of suspended development. Recalling descriptions of the park at Montcoal and the various manufacturing businesses that once operated in Coal River, a correlation can be seen between the expansion of mountaintop removal with its accompanying boom in coal production and the decline of noncoal businesses and broader community resources in the coalfields.

Helping ensure that the system stays in place are laws like West Virginia's coal severance tax that requires companies to pay for each ton they mine. Though it sounds like a plan that would give money back to the communities where coal is mined, the severance tax, which is centrally administered and redistributed by the state, actually pits towns and counties across the state against one another. The tax is distributed to all municipalities in West Virginia according to population, regardless of whether they are in the coalfields. In a 2003 public appearance, CEO Don Blankenship stated that in 2002,

Massey Energy mined 15 million tons of coal at its Coal River mines along Route 3. All of those 15 million tons passed through the town of Sylvester. For its trouble, Sylvester received $404.05 from the coal severance tax in 2003. For 15 million tons, that would be 0.000027 cents per ton. The same year, the town of Martinsburg, in Berkeley County, which has no coal reserves, received $31,023.43 from the coal severance tax. Why would legislators from Berkeley, or any other county, want to change a system that gives such benefits with no direct costs? When reform efforts in the coalfields look for allies in the legislature, as they did in the debate over coal truck weight limits, policies like the severance tax often influence officials who might lend their support, but must consider the economic impact on their own districts.

The pattern that emerges from these disparate examples of economic development in West Virginia is that there is no systemic pattern to West Virginia's economic development. The inconsistent approach is reminiscent of David Whisnant's characterization of the Appalachian Regional Commission's efforts as "development by dipsy doodling."[22] The only links between projects like mountaintop removal, race tracks, baseball stadiums, shopping malls, and the gaming industry are that developers and corporations want to undertake the projects and they don't interfere with Coal.

The explicit focus of economic development in southern West Virginia is coal mining—an industry that will cost the state millions of dollars in environmental, health, property taxes, and other externalities. Pursuit of jobs at all costs makes the state susceptible to bad decisions that hurt the state and its people in the long run. Whether it is tourism, gaming, or road construction, the state's approach to development seems to be based on the corporate extraction model: large-scale projects that exploit a particular resource. Viewed in isolation, the projects may create jobs, but they don't fit together to form a coherent strategy for developing a workforce or vibrant economy. A profound consequence of this approach to development is that it restricts access to resources that local people could use to develop economic opportunities on smaller scales and following other models.

PART III

Symbolic Capital, the Commons, and Community Activism

> Now I wander around, touching each blessed thing,
> The chimney, the table, the trees.
> And my memories swirl round me like birds on the wing.
> When I leave here, oh, who will I be?
> —Kate Long, "Who Will Watch the Homeplace?"[1]

In this section, I present two broad sets of features that distinguish the community activism of Coal River Mountain Watch and the Friends of the Mountains from other forms of social activism. Chapter 7 explores the significance of prominent women's leadership in the movement to stop mountaintop removal. The role of women is related to the decline of the union and the shifting cites of organizing within the community. Though women have always been active in social issues in the coalfields, the union's historically dominant role in organizing activism limited women's ability to rise to leadership positions. Organizing outside of the union affords women greater flexibility to link together social issues that a labor perspective may not have addressed directly. As such, women are able to forge a more comprehensive approach to social justice built upon different symbolic capital foundations.

This approach to justice both draws from and contributes to a broad conceptualization of the commons. In chapter 8, I examine how a commons approach to environment and community sets the mountaintop removal movement apart from other environmental and activist positions. The commons approach includes humans as active participants in the environment. In contrast, the narratives that have greatly influenced modern discourses of environment—industrial progress and wilderness protection—both exclude humans from the environment. A commons perspective allows activists to create a more comprehensive discourse in which environment and economy are not opposed, but are necessary and complimentary components of any community.

The discussion of the commons in this section is heavily indebted to Mary Hufford, who has written extensively on the commons, social and physical, based on years of very public ethnography in the Coal River region.[2] In the course of her research she engaged many residents in conversation and discussion of local knowledge of and about resources, watersheds, places, practices, and many other topics. Conversations I had with Hufford revealed not just overlaps in geographic area and ethnographic consultants, but also that many concepts she had discussed with local residents showed up in my subsequent interviews. It would be impossible individually attribute the circulation of these ideas through the community. Rather, I acknowledge the direct and indirect debts this discussion of the commons owes to Hufford's work.

7. Gender, Solidarity, and Symbolic Capital

The prominence of women in leadership positions is a signature characteristic of Appalachian community activism, including in the Coal River Mountain Watch (CRMW) and the larger Friends of the Mountains (FOM) networks. Women's leadership in Appalachian activism is nothing new. Mother Jones was not a native Appalachian, though she is certainly a standard bearer for strong women in the region. Elizabeth Engelhardt (2003) traces the "tangled roots" of feminism and environmentalism in the region's literature. From Widow Combs (who lay down in front of a bulldozer in 1977) to Florence Reece to Coal River Mountain Watch, women have long played important roles in pushing for social change in the coalfields.

But why? What leads women in Appalachia to take on leadership roles so often? And why did this tendency resurface in community-oriented activism specifically in the late twentieth century? Several factors are associated with this complex social phenomenon. First, neoliberal restructuring in industry shifted the locus of organizing in the coalfields and society more broadly away from trade unionism and toward community-based organizing. Second, men and women derive symbolic capital—resources that contribute to status and identity—from different social environments in Appalachia (and elsewhere).[1] Third, women, for historical reasons, actually go about organizing in different ways than men do.

Several historical contingencies have changed the primary sites of organizing (the first of these factors). The shifting locus of conflict with industry and capital away from trade unionism and toward community organizing is an effect of neoliberal trends in economy and politics.[2] A brief list of factors associated with this shift includes the decline in trade unionism in general, the decline in the United Mine Workers of America (UMWA) specifically, the restructuring of capital, the restructuring of the mining industry, and the changing role of the state in relation to capital. This shift is apparent around the world, but Appalachia's coalfields provide a particularly clear example.

Second, women derive symbolic capital from different sources than do men. This has two dimensions. The locus of women's identities in Appalachia's coalfields has historically been closer to the homeplace, which doubled as the workplace for many women. This offered women more freedom to transcend traditional constraints on labor and link together broader community issues into a single activist cause. Also, men's symbolic capital has historically been related to their capacity as breadwinner and derived from the commercial workplace and, perhaps of greater importance in Coal River, its interlocutor, the union.[3] The union's declining membership numbers and its loss of prestige and power in recent decades compromised a primary source of men's symbolic capital. Women are able to take advantage of the historical fact that they were always involved in union activism—usually in informal but meaningful ways. In the union climate that developed after 1980, it became easier for women to create a social space outside the hierarchy and patriarchy of the United Mine Workers. From this space, centered in the more traditionally female-gendered spaces of home, family, and community rather than in the traditionally masculine spaces of the coal mine or the union hall, women can address a broader range of organizing themes that transcend a conventional labor perspective.

Drawing on this community-based space, women tend to emphasize different qualities in organizing than those typically associated with labor organizing. One male community activist summarized locally recognized differences in leadership styles. Women, he argued, fostered a more collaborative and cooperative approach to activism. Based on his own experience, he described an archetype of male leadership that he calls the "charismatic asshole."

Working with these broad themes of gendered activism, I highlight characteristics of CRMW and their collaborators on matters of leadership, style, and activism.

* * *

CRMW's ascendance in the coalfields and in the state activist community owed much to the changing status of the union and the socioeconomic shifts in capital and politics. The union's fading created the need for a new structure to represent local people against the power of the coal industry and the state. Even with the union in a weakened state, CRMW and the FOM coalition had nowhere near the power of the UMWA, particularly in formal power centers like state government. But the activist community filled an important social role locally and in the state by providing a social space in which citizens could air grievances against the industry and state, as well as create and organize new practices, identities, and forms of activism to reflect their changing interests and values. Much like the way that access to the mountains as a physical commons is necessary for the practice of culturally valuable activities like digging ginseng, the social space created by the activist community functions like a kind of civic commons.[4]

The CRMW and FOM communities are indelibly marked by the fact that many of their leaders are women. At the same time, CRMW owed much to the union's legacy in Coal River. From its inception through 2003, virtually every prominent figure associated with CRMW had some personal connection with the UMWA.[5] After 1935, the UMWA provided a crucial social space in which concerns could be brought against the coal companies or the state. In addition to their incorporation of certain organizing and protest strategies historically used by the union, people in Coal River were accustomed to having such a social organization to represent people against power. That they created a group like CRMW testifies to the historical influence of the union in the community. CRMW draws both on the institutional legacy of the union and the rank-and-file tradition. The two are distinct in Coal River, evidenced by the implicit challenge continuous wildcat strikes posed between the rank and file and union leadership. Organizing outside the union structure gives the activist community the freedom to make more bold critiques of both the union and the industry.

Opponents of both CRMW and the UMWA have noted their similarity and often conflated the two, particularly after they collaborated to fight the weight increase for coal trucks. An anonymous caller to the Charleston *Gazette*'s "Readers' Voice" column said, "I am glad Judy Bonds got money for her mountaintop mining stance and enriched her own pockets by it [referring to the Goldman Environmental Prize]. She is a puppet for the United Mine Workers against Massey Coal."

Historically, women's symbolic capital in the coalfields was most closely associated with the homeplace. It would be emphatically incorrect to see this as a devaluation of women's work. In the early days of mining, women's work consisted of child rearing, cooking, canning, gardening, gathering, and producing necessities like soap and butter. Much of this work was done collectively in social settings with other women. Before the New Deal, these responsibilities were absolutely necessary for subsistence in an economy where work was uncertain and social welfare programs nonexistent.

Women's spaces and roles in the home and in the community contributed to their prominence in organizing in these spaces. Men's roles as citizens were formed in the mine and in the union—institutions that have been both rigidly hierarchical and constrained by labor laws. Because their roles in activism were outside mine and union, women had greater freedom to address a broader range of issues using a broader range of tactics than men did.[6]

Deriving significant portions of their social standing from the workplace—usually the coal mine—reinforced men's role as breadwinner. The union remade the workplace for the coal miner by giving him powerful backing to confront bosses who had operated with relative impunity before mines were organized. Miners' comments about the wildcat strikes of the 1970s bear this out most clearly. A man's identity was significantly tied not just to being a coal miner, but to being a *union* coal miner.[7]

Men's social and political roles forged through the union influenced other common male communal interactions like those at church, hunting, or town councils. Men took on leadership roles in local politics and churches, but these activities were not political in the same sense as the union, and certainly were not seen as venues through which to challenge the union. The union still has greater power in labor and politics than community organizations do, but its structure inhibits its members' ability to oppose the union's position or to work on issues outside the union. As Paul Nelson commented, when one man poured out his water during the wildcat strikes in the 1970s, everyone walked out. In practice, the union concept of solidarity gave miners a great deal of power, but it and internal union politics effectively prevented expressions of dissent and debate *within* the union over workplace issues.

The UMWA has, at times, functioned as a form of overbearing power during periods marked by corruption and fierce internal politics.[8] In addition to unpopular positions such as the selective strike policy, the union actively supported positions on health and safety legislation in the 1960s, and black lung policy in both the 1970s and 1980s that significant portions of the rank and file opposed. While actions on the health and safety bill represented the corrupt union leadership under president Tony Boyle, the latter cases on black lung policy came after the Miners for Democracy movement achieved substantial reforms in the union. The push for a federal health and safety bill peaked after an explosion at the No. 9 mine in Farmington, West Virginia, in 1968. After an initial outcry, the UMWA backed a less-stringent bill offered by industry-friendly congressmen against a bill sponsored by, among others, West Virginia Representative Ken Hechler.[9] Hechler bused widows of the Farmington disaster to Washington D.C. to lobby for the safety bill, which eventually passed. A similar lobbying effort helped overcome union opposition to a stringent black lung disability bill. Comparable wrangling accompanied several years of debate that resulted in the 1977 Surface Mine

Control and Reclamation Act. Many coalfield residents, including many union miners, supported abolition of strip mining. Hechler led the abolition effort in Congress.[10] The union supported control and regulation of strip mining embodied in a bill sponsored by congressman Morris Udall.[11] In each of these cases, the union leadership bargained with industry and backed bills that lacked support from large portions of the rank and file. In each case, women stood alongside many rank-and-file miners working against the union leadership's official position.

At the turn of the twenty-first century, mountaintop removal served as another prominent symbol for this trend. The UMWA tried to create middle ground on the issue of mountaintop removal, articulated in an op-ed column by president Cecil Roberts emphasizing both regulation and "responsible" mining.[12] When a 1997 lawsuit threatened three hundred union jobs at a union mountaintop removal site in Logan County, Roberts and the UMWA rallied to protect those jobs by supporting mountaintop removal.[13] Caught in the crossfire were many union miners who were outspoken critics of mountaintop removal and the union's defense of the practice.

While the union played a historically important role in differentiating men's and women's social spaces, the decline of the union has also compromised an important source of men's symbolic capital. All older miners— nearly all older residents—in Coal River expressed pride in the union. In Coal River at the dawn of the twenty-first century, workers at nonunion mines outnumbered union workers by a large margin. Union sympathy remained high, but was overshadowed by Massey Energy's dominating presence.

Nonunion workers refigured their masculine identities in response to the nonunion workplace. Some identified vigorously with Massey Energy and against the union and activists. When Massey first began operating in Coal River, it brought in many nonunion workers from other mines outside the area. The company attracted and appeased local workers by offering expensive perks like vacations, fishing boats, shotguns, and other gifts. Such benefits dried up in the late 1990s. As Massey's stock value dropped and the company struggled to make profits, the company repeatedly cut workers' pay and benefits. A 2003 article in *Forbes* magazine documented how Massey's reluctance to raise wages during the short-lived 2002 boom in the coal market caused an exodus of experienced miners. *Forbes* reported that, in 2003, over 50 percent of Massey's workforce were under the age of twenty-five.[14]

Symbols of masculinity connected this trend to masculine symbolic capital. Rather than the power and cache of being a union miner, especially at the height of the wildcat era in the 1970s, consumer goods that symbolize power, independence, and defiance became prominent markers of masculinity. Expensive pickup trucks, boats, four-wheelers, motorcycles, and the like became common among young miners. Often, trucks driven by Massey workers (especially the younger workers) stood out because of decals and stickers flaunting their opposition to the union, environmentalists, and the community's distaste for Massey Energy. Bumper stickers with the Massey logo said things like, "I mine coal . . . you're welcome," and "Earth First! We'll mine the other planets later." One full-size pickup truck, jacked up with custom suspension and mud tires, featured a large decal with the familiar Calvin character pissing on the words "Tree Huggers."

Other miners, particularly former union members, were more likely to go quietly about the business of providing for their families. Danny Howell, the union miner who delivered newspapers rather than work at a nonunion mine, met one of his former co-workers at a gas station not long before our interview. The man, who had gone to work for Massey, told Howell about the long hours he worked. As the conversation ended, he said, "I guess that's what I get for being a scab."

Such casual use of the word "scab" testifies to the drastic shift from union to nonunion mining in Coal River. As recently as the early 1990s, that same gas station, like many businesses in Whitesville, would likely have had a sign pledging support for the UMWA. The meaning of scab has itself completely changed when it can be casually thrown around over a gas pump by someone who would himself be labeled a scab.

Strong Women and Charismatic Assholes

The characteristics that mark Appalachian community organizing do not derive simply from the shift in the locus of organizing from the union to community groups. The leading women in the mountaintop removal (MTR) coalition go about the business of organizing in different ways than men. Strong female leadership was one of the first things that impressed John Taylor about the MTR movement. Taylor, a former lawyer for the UMWA (who has a long history of experience with male and female leadership from his own family as well as with union activism in Detroit auto factories and later in the Black Lung Movement), professed an admiration for female leadership, noting that women at the front of many Appalachian movements have a different style of leadership than men. He characterized the archetypal male leader in such movements as a "charismatic asshole"—a white male, bright, articulate, talented, and at least somewhat ambitious. The key for Taylor is that this male archetype is charismatic, but not collaborative. He fights to attain and maintain a grip on power and decision making. The key characteristics of female leadership Taylor listed include emphasizing collaboration and consensus.[15]

While the word "asshole" is less applicable, CRMW does reflect the general differences between men's and women's activism that Taylor described. Aside from cofounder Randy Jarrold (who left the area in 2000), most men in operational roles in the organization had experience in professional work settings and union organizing. They tended to emphasize the need to focus the group's energy and resources and to plan specific strategies for activism. While prominent women activists were guided by the general ideas of stopping Coal's destructive practices, they were more likely to focus on whatever problem was at hand, which often did not fit neatly within a defined strategy. Men were more likely to focus on tangible outcomes, including taking credit for accomplishments. Women tended to privilege their working relationships with other groups—especially other women—over taking individual credit for CRMW.

More generally, the women involved in CRMW and other groups, most notably the Ohio Valley Environmental Coalition (OVEC), tended to bear out Taylor's idea that female leadership is characteristically collaborative. Advantages of female leadership that Taylor described include a broad, inclusive, and nonhierarchical approach to organizing that works toward consensus. Disadvantages include sometimes inefficient use of time and meager resources. And the collaborative approach to work sometimes obscures accountability for specific projects. Of course, this analysis is itself a male approach in that it assumes the importance of efficiency and accountability—hallmarks of a male-dominated corporate culture.

If Union Is What Union Should Be . . .

"It's something kind of spiritual," said Elaine Purkey of organizing. Purkey was never active in union or community organizing until the Pittston strike of 1989.[16] Along with her husband, a union miner, Purkey worked hard during that sixteen-month standoff. She began writing and performing songs during the strike. After her initial involvement with the UMWA, Purkey became a community organizer with the West Virginia Organizing Project and performed at events hosted by community and labor groups. She described as well as anyone can the similarities and differences between union and community organizing. "I once described community organizing to a cousin of mine and he thought I was talking about a church organization. And he said, 'Is it a church that you're talking about that you work with?' I said 'No, but it's close.' There's a camaraderie there that you share with other people. It's a brotherhood and a sisterhood. And if union is what union should be, you go into one of those organizations, you're gonna see that, you're gonna feel that."

Purkey's own transition from union organizing to community organizing gave her a particularly good perspective on the key differences between the two. She highlighted themes of trust and involvement as important distinctions between the empowerment that community groups try to foster and the solidarity built by the union.

> I think we lost more than we gained in Pittston. And I've always differed with Cecil [Roberts] and some of the other guys on this—but I think we lost more than we gained simply because they operated on a need-to-know basis. . . . I was down here talking to all the women and the men who weren't UMWA members, and the people that were working really, really hard in that strike and giving up their lives to work in that strike, to see to it that it was won—listening to them and the mistrust that it was creating: "Well, what has he [Roberts] got to hide?" "Why won't he let us know what's going on?" "Why doesn't he trust us?" "If he doesn't trust us, why should we trust him?" And it was really hard to keep that thing going where they would just go out and do what needed to be done, no questions asked. I mean, that's one thing—you can order your members to do that. And they're obligated to do that because they've taken an oath when they become members of the UMWA.[17]

Purkey highlighted a central difference between the union concept of solidarity, expressed most directly by honoring picket lines, and the kind of togetherness that community organizers try to foster. The concept of solidarity flows through MTR activism, and particularly through CRMW because of its strong union influences. The importance of solidarity historically and the contested nature of solidarity in the present begs analysis.

One of the problems, Freda Williams suggested, was that many workers came to ask how the union would benefit them personally.[18] It is exactly this sentiment that Massey and many other companies exploited to break unions in coal and other industries. Massey's gifts, vacations, and perks benefited each miner and his family individually. The expensive consumer items that became symbols of masculine power benefited individuals. As miner Clyde McKnight said most succinctly, young miners tended not to "look at the health care, pensions, retirement that you need to look at down the road."[19]

Ideally, organizing in the nonprofit activist organizations is geared toward empowerment and cultivating a kind of solidarity that is distinct from that of organized labor. In the short term, activist organizing is oriented as much toward process as results. The characteristics associated with female leadership coincide with community organizing in emphasizing participation and empowerment—increasing involvement and investment in the activist process—as ends in themselves. Stopping mountaintop removal and other specific tangible results always guide activities, but increasing involvement and number of participants is a short-term product.

"We wanted to look at the long term and the importance [of] education and training, not actually getting the job done right now the fastest way possible, or getting actual results," said Elaine Purkey of the West Virginia Organizing Project, a community organizing effort that operated from 1991 to 2002. "We wanted results, but we wanted to train and to teach so they would stay active and do other things. And union is not that way. Union has a set of rules that you go by—you do this; you can't do this because of the laws that govern what you can and can't do. . . . Other than one union person teaching another union person about [worker's] rights . . . there's not a whole lot of training that goes on in union."[70]

The seeming lack of success frustrates several different kinds of people in the movement. Those who have already been through conversion and empowerment often thirst for victory, and their patience is tested by having to cultivate more brothers and sisters in the struggle. Others who have professional organizing experience, particularly with unions, are frustrated by the slow pace of individual empowerment and what sometimes seems like a lack of strategic direction.

When successful, however, empowering new people to write their first letter to the editor, give their first television interview, or take part in direct action events creates a solidarity that is "thicker" than honoring a picket line. This active involvement and sense of investment in and connection to a movement is a more active and participatory relationship than that created by the union, even during its wildcat heydays.

Wildcat strikes were effective in the short term in some cases and not in others. After the Miners for Democracy movement toppled the corrupt Boyle administration and won democratic reforms, the United Mine Workers has prided itself on its internal democracy. Rank-and-file miners elect their representatives, and internal union politics are notoriously fierce. The conflict between leadership and rank and file stems, at least in part, from the laws to which Purkey alluded. Labor laws put tangible restrictions on union activities, and the leadership is responsible for seeing that those laws are obeyed. The grassroots power of the rank and file, illustrated in the wildcat strikes of the 1970s, showed that their allegiance to union solidarity gave miners more power than labor laws allowed or more power than union leadership was willing to grasp. This led to conflict between the rank and file and union leadership on the one hand, and between the rank and file and the industry on the other.

Freda Williams's comments about the individual and collective benefits of union membership remind us that unions and community organizations create a kind of civic commons—a space for pursuing a common good, which can be undermined by those seeking individual benefit or recognition. CRMW and the FOM provided many coalfield residents a forum to air their grievances and protest Coal's treatment of citizens. The shape of coalfield activism reflects the influence of the UMWA because union is the best historical example of a political and social structure to represent people's interests against power. By emphasizing individual involvement and empowerment, activist organizations have the opportunity to create a stronger sense of connection for members than the union did. Involvement may also help guard against feelings of alienation caused by some of the corrupt dealings of the UMWA.

Though a great deal of similarity among community organizing groups distinguishes them from trade unions, there is also much variation in these groups' appearance. Within the Friends of the Mountains coalition, no two groups look or act alike as organizations, though they work together in a spirit of collaboration. Despite certain similarities—like strong female leadership and emphasis on collaboration—each of these groups has different forms of expertise and style to contribute to the coalition.

The frenetic tone and pace of CRMW's office often carries over to their public hearings, organizational meetings, and protests. When I mentioned that CRMW's style reminded me of John Taylor's description of Boone County miners of the 1970s as "just more militant" than others, Judy Bonds quickly corrected me.

"We're not militant," she said, emphasizing that the group's point of view is rooted in the region's culture.[21] Her insistence on the distinction between "militant" and "confrontational" reflects CRMW's effort to appeal to their constituency. Militancy reminds people of the turbulent wildcat period. CRMW works to root their activism in a commonsense understanding of coalfield life and culture.[22]

Wildcat strikes that pitted the rank and file against the union leadership in many cases, along with labor laws that have tightened over the years, prevented the strikes of the 1970s from changing the status quo of the mining industry. Miners exercised their collective power through wildcat strikes, but the wildcats also created financial hardship for the miners, the union, and the industry. Those hardships, at least in part, precipitated the industry's reorganization in the late 1970s and early 1980s.

Coal's institutionalized place in West Virginia's politics and economy makes the prospect of abolishing mountaintop removal even more difficult. Stopping mountaintop removal demands a dramatic change to the status quo of Appalachian mining and politics. Even though strongly influenced by the union's wildcat legacy, CRMW and its collaborators do not imitate it. Judy Bonds said of the union's stance on mountaintop removal, "They need to realize the closest they ever came to stopping strip mining was in the 1960s when underground [union] coal miners worked together with citizens."[23]

While the frenetic pace and confrontational style may not look as consensual as OVEC's leadership, CRMW's activism reflects the experiences and personalities of its staff and its membership. Many people in Coal River are deeply, if not always vociferously, against mountaintop removal. A 2004 poll of likely voters in West Virginia found that MTR opponents outnumber its supporters two to one.[24] There are no local polls to gauge public opinion, but my experience in the community led me to believe well over half of the residents opposed mountaintop removal and resented the general attitude with which the coal industry treats coalfield residents. CRMW's more confrontational brand of activism is rooted in its members' anger generated by personal, visceral feelings of violation by the coal industry.

Personal testimonies characterize the relationship between CRMW and its constituency. Nanette Nelson described feeling a sense of relief and support when she met Julia Bonds and Patty Sebok for the first time. People who are angry and frustrated with Coal and the community often don't know where to go or what to do until they meet someone from CRMW. Boone County resident Tommy Jarrold described Bonds as "Little Mother Jones." Jarrold gave fiery speeches at public hearings near his home in Peytona, but didn't come to rallies or protests. CRMW's confrontational style appeals to its coalfield constituency, many of whom do not speak publicly or travel to rallies.

* * *

The shifting locus of organizing away from the union and toward the communities highlights more than just gendered patterns of organizing. From the platform afforded them by the social, political, and economic circumstances of the coalfields, leading women espouse a set of values that challenge the dominant interpretations of coalfield history and culture. Though it sometimes looks like a reactionary defense of place and identity, conversations with activists reveal ideas for alternative forms of economy and politics, rooted in the region's history and aimed at preserving certain values into the future.

During a 2003 debate between Massey Energy CEO Don Blankenship and citizen activist Cindy Rank, Blankenship said that the meaning of the coalfields derived from the hard-working people who go out every day to create "value." Rank argued that the value of the coalfields lay in the attachment people feel to place, community, and the landscape of the mountains.

Blankenship's use of the word "value" provides an opportune point from which to differentiate forms of value. The value that Blankenship indicated was a monetary one, something to be created by extracting, processing, and shipping goods. Rank's value—the value espoused by many activists—is an intangible concept that is generated between people and through interaction with the landscape.

Rank's value is reflected in the values professed by many community activists. Those associated with Coal River Mountain Watch are especially likely to evoke themes of the homeplace to argue for the nonphysical values of the mountains. Home, in this sense, is a shifting concept, not necessarily a specific place.[25] In most cases, the "home" many people grew up in and around no longer exists. Home may have been Marfork Hollow, White Oak Hollow, Cherry Pond Mountain, Indian Creek Hollow, or any of the too-many-to-count places that Coal has destroyed socially and/or physically. The rivalry between Clear Fork and Marsh Fork high schools, for example, was once so intense as to start fights and discourage interschool dating. The rivalry no longer matters because both schools were closed—Clear Fork in 1992, Marsh Fork in 2004. Students from both districts are now bused to the same school an hour away.

The concept of home invoked by Coal River Mountain Watch and other activists is more appropriately read as a set of values describing the experience of people who grew up in the mountains before the so-called coal crisis set in the 1980s. "The mountains" as commons—a place of shared story, action, and experience—stands against the corporate-state view of mountains as "useless" and "overburden."[26] Coal's industrial landscape, including slag heaps, valley fills, and slurry impoundments, reflects Blankenship's notion of value and the theme of industrial progress. The activist community's idea of home situates their approach to mountain culture in a social space where women have more symbolic capital. In this space, activists can differentiate their perspective and protect it from industry apologists who seek to protect jobs.

Within the activist community, CRMW represents a specific coalfield constituency with its confrontational style and sometimes-abrasive rhetoric. It may not look or sound like other activist groups, but the leading women at CRMW share with others in the Friends of Mountains network the collaborative features that Taylor attributed to women's leadership.

Battle of Blair Mountain: Reprise

At the old ball field in the bend of Coal River in Racine, near the mouth of Indian Creek, Mother Jones addressed marching miners on their way to organize the mines of Logan County in 1921. Usually a fiery speaker who spared no obscenity in challenging workers to confront their employers, Mother Jones urged caution this time, sensing that danger loomed on the march. Not that miners weren't prepared: a group of men broke into the company store in Edwight to steal guns and ammunition for the trip. Men from Coal River, including Freda Williams's father, met miners from Kanawha and other counties as they crossed Lens Creek Mountain and continued on to Logan.

The encounter at Blair Mountain is the stuff of history and legend. A mob of Logan miners, National Guardsmen, and hired thugs, all led by the Logan County sheriff, ambushed the marching miners on Blair Mountain. What amounted to a small war raged for several days until the miners retreated, but not before the U.S. Army was called in to put down the march.

A group of miners from the march, including union president John L. Lewis, was charged with treason and tried in Jefferson County, West Virginia. In the late 1990s Jefferson County wanted to demolish the original jail that held the miners to make way for a parking lot. Fortunately, a group of preservation organizations and the union worked to save and restore the building.

The Battle of Blair Mountain is one of the greatest pieces of American labor history and a touchstone of coalfield mythology. Most coalfield residents think of Blair Mountain as the foundational moment in the creation of the United Mine Workers. While it is one of the most important moments in UMWA history, it did not establish the union in southern West Virginia. In fact, many mines in Logan, Mingo, and McDowell counties weren't organized until passage of New Deal legislation in 1935.

Nevertheless, Blair Mountain symbolizes the spirit of the union in the imagination of union sympathizers to this day, making the new battle over Blair Mountain all the more painful.[27] A subsidiary of Arch Coal, Inc., planned to do mountaintop removal on more than three hundred acres of Blair Mountain, including the 1921 battle site. Surely the United Mine Workers would rally around their most sacred ground. Surely the union would stand up to any company that would so disrespect the memory of that tragic encounter. Surely the union would come to the emotional aid of those whose souls already weep over the destruction of their homeplace.

No one doubted that the union would come to the rescue, except for the fact that this was to be a union mine. Union miners were actually going to methodically and efficiently remove their own history—the field where their own fathers and union brothers fought for their union.

The proposed mountaintop removal incited a grassroots effort to save Blair Mountain by getting it listed on the National Register of Historic Places. Residents, amateur historians, activists, and scholars picked over the mountain looking for artifacts, picked through archives looking for documents, and picked through bureaucracy looking for the necessary processes for registration.

The telling characteristic of their effort was that the union was not involved. Eventually, though, union leadership negotiated with Arch Coal, Inc., to preserve a small section of Blair Mountain as a historic site commemorating the battle.

Vigilance

In her award-winning song, "Who Will Watch the Home Place," Kate Long asks, "Who'll watch the home place / . . . When I am gone from here?"[28] The name Coal River Mountain Watch seems to respond to the theme of vigilance over the coalfields. CRMW and other groups that embody female-driven community activism not only watch the homeplace, they define it. Community activism characterized by women's leadership defines value in a way that challenges Coal's institutional dominance of the region. Through their definition of the homeplace, groups like CRMW and the FOM illuminate the social and historical meaning of the landscapes that are being destroyed by mountaintop removal.

Though their activism garners mixed results when measured by actual reforms in the coal industry, CRMW fills an important structural role within the region. The decline of the United Mine Workers in both membership and political power—particularly in Coal River—created a need for a new interlocutor to mediate relationships with industry. CRMW doesn't enjoy the power that the union once held, but it does work to empower local people and provides a social forum for residents to air grievances against the industry.

MTR is rarely visible from the road in West Virginia, and few people have access to good vantage points from which to see the expansive projects. Many people who live surrounded by MTR operations don't realize the extent of the destruction until they see aerial photographs of what is around them. Coal River Mountain Watch has often provided this service. With partners from several different organizations, they have arranged free airplane tours of the coalfields for residents, activists, and journalists. By circulating pictures in print and on the Internet, they have alerted many to the extent and intensity of mountaintop removal. Seeing mountaintop removal in an aerial photograph or in person creates a kind of empirical knowledge. Within the social framework created by CRMW, the moral violation that mountaintop removal represents is self-evident to most coalfield residents. Watching mountaintop removal in progress from a hill overlooking a new operation on Kayford Mountain was a surreal experience for me and several others in November 2004. The wind against the bare trees drowned out what little noise we might otherwise have heard from the machinery. With our eyes fixed on the steady motions from the mine—end loaders and dump trucks—we watched in a silence that I could only describe as mourning. The experience was so profound that one of our guests on Kayford Mountain that November day pulled out his checkbook and made a donation to CRMW on the spot.

CRMW also provides the newly aware with opportunities to do something about mountaintop removal. The group nurtures new members and activists by walking them through their first activities—sometimes literally. Judy Bonds has coached many people through their first on-camera interviews. Standing beside the reporter, Judy says, "Pretend the camera isn't there, just talk to the reporter."

The acts of seeing and watching—of confronting the industry—are a valuable service in the community. CRMW struggles to overcome the various obstacles to organizing. Though their activism is well received by many within the coalfields, their base of active, empowered members is rather small. Even so, CRMW makes sure Coal's activities are noticed and counted. CRMW has been extremely successful at organizing media attention to their fight, particularly after the Goldman Prize in 2003.[29] With the help of the entire coalition, CRMW has been making people around the United States see mountaintop removal too. In 2003, activists began traveling throughout the country presenting a road show to civic and student groups in conjunction with a bipartisan bill in Congress that would abolish mountaintop removal. The emotionally gripping slide show includes narration from several coalfield residents that introduces viewers to the difficulties and injustices of living in the coalfields. The presenters then ask their hosts to write letters asking their congressional representatives to support the Clean Water Protection Act.[30]

There are two telling characteristics of efforts like the road show and the preservation of Blair Mountain. First, community organizations are leading the way and epitomize a new structure for representing community interests. The second notable trait of these efforts is the prevalence of women in leadership roles, especially when compared to the union. The shifting locus of organizing is most evident in the United Mine Workers' absence in the Blair Mountain preservation campaign. Many coalfield residents—some but not all of whom were already part of the activist community—felt compelled to save Blair Mountain from the dishonor and violation of mountaintop removal even without the union's support. The people who joined the fight were those who would have been on the picket lines if the union had called for them at Blair Mountain, and were in large part the people who were on the picket lines in the 1970s. To the extent that people who were (and would still be) grassroots union members have begun working outside the union, their effort resembles, at least structurally, the wildcat tradition of the 1970s.

8. Commons Environmentalism and Community Activism

During the 2004 session of the West Virginia legislature, a prominent Senate committee chairman sought advice on how he could legally bar "environmentalists" from committee meetings. In response to the idea, Patty Sebok of Coal River Mountain Watch said, "That's okay. I'm not an environmentalist; I'm an activist."[1]

The distinction is not superficial. Challenging conventional and stereotypical ideas about environmentalism found in the public imaginary, in common political discourse, and to some extent, in the literature on the environmental movement, is a defining characteristic of CRMW and the Friends of the Mountains network of activists. In this chapter, comments from activists, their opponents, and selected arguments from literature on environmentalism illustrate activists' treatment of the environment as a kind of commons that emphasizes myriad social and cultural relationships. This view includes how activists understand environment, community, and activism, and how all three are intertwined with a perspective on social justice. Employing this form of commons environmentalism, activists construct themes of community and identity as distinctive features of their various forms of activism.

From this perspective, I argue that CRMW transcends four common problems in environmental and social activism. First, by framing their activism in terms of community and identity rather than under the rubric of organized labor, they evade labor regulations and neoliberal authority over labor, and also challenge claims to prosperity based on neoliberal models. Second, the approach to commons environmentalism within the Friends of the Mountains network, with its emphasis on lived experience in the environment, challenges the common mythologies of industrial progress and wilderness preservation, both of which exclude humans from much of modern western environmental thought. Third, by including lived community experience, their activism breaks free of portrayals of environment and economy as an either-or, zero-sum game. Fourth, the network approach to activism transcends the exclusivity of the local by building solidarities between localities and regions and by laying bare the trans-local lines of power and capital that link them together.

* * *

Speaking at the United Mine Workers Labor Day Celebration during the 2000 gubernatorial campaign, Republican incumbent Cecil Underwood, a former coal executive, charged that growing calls to end mountaintop removal were the work of "extreme environmentalists." Several outspoken critics of mountaintop removal were in the crowd that day, but none fit any readily available definition of an extreme environmentalist that the governor seemed to employ. Activists at Coal River Mountain Watch were the daughters, wives, and sisters of coal miners. Some were coal miners themselves. All had grown up in a region with strong environmental and labor sensibilities—but those sensibilities are very different from discourses about environmentalism and labor found in mainstream American politics. In short, they are not "tree huggers," despite efforts by the coal industry, state, and sometimes the union, to paint them as such.

Mountaintop removal is certainly an environmental issue, no matter if you speak to a coal miner or a member of Greenpeace. Local sentiments, reflected in CRMW's activism, do not root environmentalism in abstract concepts or ideologies. Rather, their environmentalism is rooted in the lived experiences and contingencies of everyday life in the coalfields. Environmental and class issues are especially salient in communities struggling to overcome chronic economic woes. As the controversy over mountaintop removal grew in the 1990s, economic circumstances operating on multiple scales effectively cleaved local sentiment into three camps: those who supported the industry because of the jobs it created; those who opposed Coal's practices, but did not act out of a perceived lack of alternatives or inability to challenge the powerful industry; and those whose outrage moved them to action, including forming groups like CRMW.

But are these people environmentalists? I asked Patty Sebok to describe what she meant when she described herself as an activist and not an environmentalist. "Well, you know, most people when they think of environmentalists, they say, oh, they protect lizards and frogs and salamanders and that's all they're worried about. And they eat vegan, or vegetarian, and they recycle, and I mean, you know they're different than us—you know they are. And a community activist is just an ordinary, everyday person that has to go out in the community and do something because your damn government is doing you wrong."[2]

Freda Williams made the distinction by saying that an activist works on broader issues in the community. "I care about the environment, of course . . . clean water, clean air . . . But as an activist, when you know someone has got a problem, you go talk to that person. If it's something you can help them with, then you get busy and do what you can to be of help to them. So, to me . . . that's an activist. An activist doesn't always solve the problem . . . but you may be able to find an inroad somewhere that helps to find a solution."[3]

Continuing her distinction between environmentalism and activism, Williams's description of environmentalism blurred into social justice. "An environmentalist is someone who really cares . . . [for] the entire planet, but especially around the areas where they live. Such as the damage that's going on here with the coal min[ing] that's destroying plant and animal life and doing so much destruction to the people. This destruction is just forced on the people, and there's no reason for it. If the coal industry would mine legally and responsibly, we wouldn't be in the struggle we're in today. The two could live side by side. But not when this type of mining is coming right down into communities."

A third CRMW activist, Julia Bonds, described how the group's focus developed to include environmental and social issues. "In our mind, we wasn't an environmental organization because . . . our mission was . . . to establish justice in the coalfields. But the more we tried to establish justice in the coalfields, the more we found out that social issues and injustice runs hand-in-hand with the environment. And in that respect, I think you would call it an awakening to the fact that you can't separate social and environmental injustice; they run hand in hand."

I asked Judy, "What does being an environmentalist mean to you?"

She responded: "Preserving and protecting the land and air and water for future generations—stewardship."

I asked, "Is CRMW an environmental organization?"

Judy sighed and said, "I reckon."[4]

* * *

At first glance, it seems difficult to call these women tree huggers. The distinction they embody between extreme environmentalism and the industrial apocalypse of mountaintop removal runs deep into the very fabric of the community. Coal River Mountain Watch activists are not the environmental extremists described by the former governor, but describing what they are is more difficult.

In their own comments, it is clear that CRMW activists have a strong environmental sensibility based on interaction with the mountain environment as a critical part of the community they value. Any community must have common spaces—both physical and social—in which the common activities of community are performed. In the commons of the mountains, people hunt, fish, garden, and gather an assortment of wild forest products.[5] CRMW's activism draws on both members' individual and collective identities forged in the locally meaningful social spaces of the mountain landscape and their union activism. Out of their past and present comes a particular understanding of what their community is and a cooperative approach to protecting and reviving it by asserting its value against the claims of value employed by nonlocal entities like the industry and state.[6]

Who Are the Activists?

Since she joined the group, Julia Bonds has been the most prominent public face of CRMW. A combination of intelligence, determination, and an incredibly strong personality made Judy a leader not just within Coal River, but in the West Virginia activist community. The Goldman Foundation recognized Judy's work in 2003. The Goldman award, given annually to one activist from each continent, is generally considered the most prestigious award for environmental activism in the world.

Goldman brought attention to Bonds and to CRMW. Judy's story of how she became an activist was publicized in media outlets around the world. Judy was living with her daughter and grandson near the mouth of Marfork Hollow where she had lived most of her life. Marfork Coal, a Massey subsidiary, started operations in the hollow in the early 1990s. The company bought out residents of the hollow, until eventually only Judy and a couple of neighbors remained. One day, Judy's grandson Andrew yelled to her from the creek where he was playing, "Hey, maw maw, what's the matter with these fish?" When Judy looked, the creek was running black with mine waste and Andrew held two hands full of dead fish. Judy traces the roots of her activism to that moment of horror.

If few of the activists that now make up the so-called environmental movement in the coalfields ever thought of themselves as environmentalists (including Bonds), how did they come to describe themselves as such? Judy once quipped that she first thought of herself as an environmentalist "when they started calling us that." But the journey from feeding—literally—off the proceeds of coal to actively opposing the coal industry is not something to be taken lightly in southern West Virginia. For each activist, something had to happen in their lives for them to take action.

While Judy's story has been told far and wide, other figures in the movement have equally compelling personal testimonies. These stories illustrate the process of becoming an activist. Contexts and motivations vary, but common themes emerge. People often describe an awareness of the harm being done by the coal industry, but a reluctance to acknowledge it. Most activists describe a moment of transformation—an awakening, a conversion experience—in which they decide they must act. These stories offer a sample of the ideas motivating these activists. From these stories emerge discourses of justice, democracy, and community that are born on the narratives of environment and economy.

Freda Williams

Freda Williams has perhaps the longest personal history of activism in the coalfields. Her father was a UMWA organizer who moved around from camp to camp. One of Freda Williams's prize possessions is a framed black-and-white photograph on an end table in her home near the old Leevale Colliery mines. The photo shows the group of men who were tried for treason for their participation in the infamous 1921 Battle of Blair Mountain. Williams points to her father, just over the right shoulder of UMWA icon John L. Lewis. "During the mine war my older brothers were toddlers and my oldest sister was an infant.... The coal company forced them out of the coal company house and they went to live in a tent. So mom was left with the two toddlers and the infant while dad went to ... the march to Blair. ... Mom couldn't get diapers for my sister ... so she used the red bandana handkerchiefs that the men used to identify with the union.... It had to be a really rough way to live."

When I asked Freda if she ever thought she would spend her retirement years doing the kind of work she became known for in the activist community, she brushed it aside:

> Never did give it much thought because, in growing up, I was always aware of the injustice in the coalfields. And simply because dad was a union organizer, I think it was more obvious to the entire family.... To give you an example, my two younger brothers would play with the black boys in the community. We didn't live in the same camp, but the camps are close.... Because they did, because these boys played with the black boys, we were considered white trash.

> And, so growing up and learning the lessons from dad and from my mother, we knew that these types of things were not fair, and it just wasn't right. . . . It made it harder on the families that wanted to integrate. But, we did it anyway.[7]

Williams has carried her formative coal camp experiences with her throughout her professional life. Working for the telephone company in Charleston as a young woman, she helped organize a chapter of the Communications Workers of America. Upon returning to Coal River, Williams and her late husband developed and ran the first cable television service in the area, including offering free cable to schools and other public services. She wrote her first letter to the editor in 1968 in response to the first strip mine she became aware of in the area. Through the 1990s, Williams became increasingly alarmed at mining activity on Kayford Mountain and the Brushy Fork slurry impoundment and was part of the group of citizens who formed Coal River Mountain Watch in 1997.

John Taylor

John Taylor had never been in any environmental group. Based on his childhood in West Virginia that fostered what he described as a personal connection to nature, he considered himself an environmentalist—but he had never been an activist. As an attorney for the UMWA and later representing miners seeking black lung disability benefits, he considered himself a "black lung guy." From his grandfather's legacy as a UMWA organizer near Morgantown to his own activism with the United Auto Workers, Taylor's personal history is perhaps the most radical of anyone affiliated with the activist community. Through his own experience working in automotive factories to his connections with the black lung movement in the 1980s, he developed a historical perspective on social activism in West Virginia. Taylor was already familiar with and appalled by mountaintop removal from Penny Loeb's 1997 article in *U.S. News and World Report* when he first encountered CRMW through the Ohio Valley Environmental Coalition.

"This movement is the place for me," he recalled thinking about CRMW. "The environmental movement . . . are the only people, forces that are actively taking on the coal industry. I mean, who else? Is the union taking on the coal industry? No. Is the government? No. Is Communist Party USA? No. Nobody is. It's hard for me to express the depth of my feeling against them. Because they hurt my people—my family. My granddad died of black lung disease. I take that personally."[8]

Robert and Dottie Washington[9]

> ROBERT: Neither one of us had been what you would call activist. Most of that
> was because the jobs that we had held . . . my job in particular was a coal
> industry job. And I guess when our home got flooded and we realized how
> bad it was going to get, it was time to make some hard choices about the
> way we had been living. And, so we made the choice. We said we don't want
> to be a part of the problem here, let's be a part of the solution. So, we gave
> up working in industrial-type jobs or corporate-type jobs and said let's . . .
> what talent we do have, let's give it to [CRMW].

Though Robert and Dottie Washington had been aware of and alarmed by
the effects of the coal industry on the community, the Dorothy flood of 2001
that literally reached their doorstep finally drove them to activism. After the
flood, both Washingtons became active members of CRMW and the Sierra
Club. When asked if he had ever considered himself an environmentalist
before, Robert responded,

> I had been reading about environmental problems and I realized that air pollu-
> tion was a problem, water pollution was a problem—I realized that there were
> some environmental problems dealing with coal mining. I saw that there had
> been an increase in flooding because of mountaintop removal mining. It was
> sort of like things were coming to this head for the last year. I was not happy
> working where I was working . . . I got laid off, so it just like all came together
> to push us to make some choices about how we had been making our living.

Robert had first heard of CRMW while working for a company that ser-
viced mine equipment. He describes his first impressions and the thoughts he
wrestled with during the period before he and Dottie joined the movement,
a moment he describes as a "coming out":

> When I was working for the coal company and [CRMW] were in their old
> offices, they had these pictures up on the windows. And we'd go by and look
> at the pictures . . . of the slurry impoundment up on, uh, Brushy Fork. . . . I
> had been on that slurry impoundment, because of the job I had. So, I was up
> there and was frankly amazed at the size of it and worried about the size of it.
> So that was the issue that we first thought CRMW was involved with. Then
> we knew that they were involved in an anti-mountaintop removal mining. . . .
>
> You know, people rationalize things. And I rationalized, well, you know, the
> company I work for . . . none of our clients are mountaintop removal mines. . . .
> Our clients do have mountaintop removal mines, but [my company doesn't]
> service the mountaintop removal part of it. So I was rationalizing all of this
> stuff. . . .

Then we were approached . . . by someone who needed a speech written and Dottie had agreed to write the speech. But, we said we'll ghostwrite it . . . we're not going to be acknowledged as having written it. And so, in preparation for that, they started giving me information about mountaintop removal. This was about six months before we came out, so to speak. I started reading the facts and figures and was like, Oh my God! And so we wrote the speech, gave it to the person who needed it, and just sort of . . . that seed just sort of set there and started germinating in my mind and, [I thought], you know we can't continue this.

The Washingtons came into the movement during the heat of the coal truck battle in 2001. Robert framed the matter in terms of business ethics and public policy, based on his previous work experiences:

I had looked at the [coal truck] issue and thought, you know, this is just not right. You can't reward people for breaking the law. . . . Whatever you do, whatever business you are in, you have to do it within the confines of the law. When I was in banking, we had regulatory agencies that came in. We couldn't say, "Well, we want to [do] this our way, no matter what the regulations say, because if you don't let us do it this way, we're going to go out of business." . . . You fit the business . . . within the parameters of the regulations. The coal industry is one of the few industries that I see that just totally disregards that. . . . Every job that I've had, the business had to meet the regulations . . . that was just something you planned [for].

Paul and Nanette Nelson

"I had always wanted to be [an activist]," said Nanette Nelson, a retired public school employee. Both Nanette and her husband, Paul, a disabled coal miner, lived in the community of Peytona all their lives. They came to CRMW during the coal truck campaign in 2001. In their fifties, both Nelsons were very outspoken about abuses of the coal industry that had employed and fed them their entire lives.

Nanette continued, "I would get so mad and furious with everything going on and I thought, well, what do you do about it, you know? I ran into Patty [Sebok] and Judy [Bonds] over at Madison. I hate mountaintop removal. I hate strip mining with everything in me. I hate this clear cutting. I hated all that, coal trucks . . . and didn't know what to do about it, and then we met up with them."

Nanette first heard of mountaintop removal when she sat on a jury for a 1998 court case in Boone County Court.

NANETTE: I had heard of it [MTR] but I had never seen one because there was none around our area. Well, they took us up on the mine site . . . in these vans and [the judge] and the lawyers was on the van. . . . I raised my hand and said, "Can I ask some questions." The judge turned around and said, "Depends on what it is." And I asked him, I said, "When are they going to reclaim this?" And they said, "It's been reclaimed." They pile up rocks and sprayed green stuff on it like it was going to grow there. They even had a excavator, a huge—I mean huge—big excavator there just sitting and rusting, they sprayed that stuff on it like that grass was going to grow on that thing. It had been reclaimed. And I just . . . it made me sick at my stomach. . . . I told Paul when I got out of there, I said, "I'm joining every environmental group . . . I just wanted to get into some environmental groups."

PAUL: And we did. [We've joined] everthing coming and going.

NANETTE: Greenpeace and Sierra Club was the ones I had heard of. Coal River [Mountain Watch]—I feel connected with because it's here.[10]

The Nelsons are an example of how CRMW spread out from its base of operations in Whitesville. Their involvement enabled the organization to address issues on the lower end of Coal River. The area around the communities of Racine and Peytona became, in many respects, the most active and contentious area in Coal River. All the attention brought to coal trucks in Whitesville and Sylvester caused a shift in truck traffic in surrounding towns, especially after a court ruling limited the number of coal trucks passing through Sylvester to seven thousand per year (down from more than twenty thousand). After the ruling, trucks bypassed the towns by traveling through the mountains on private coal company roads that come out near Peytona. (Truck traffic increased dramatically in that area from 2001 to 2003.) In addition, the Nelsons helped coordinate opposition in the area to a proposed Massey Energy mining and processing complex near Peytona on Drawdy Creek. The new complex would rival the Elk Run plant at Sylvester as the largest such complex in the region. Paul and Nanette learned from activists like Mary Miller and Pauline Canterberry, the duo that spearheaded efforts in the town of Sylvester.

Mary Miller and Pauline Canterberry

"Well, in the beginning," said Pauline, "we said if we was going to be able to fight this, we had to laugh our way through it. If we didn't, we would probably end up crying ourselves to death, watching our homes being destroyed."

No one has as much fun with their activism as Mary Miller and Pauline Canterberry, the so-called Sylvester Dust Busters. Their struggle began in the late 1990s when neighboring Elk Run Coal Company planned two additions to their coal preparation facility. First, the company removed a natural bluff that had shielded the town of Sylvester from the plant since its opening in 1981. On the new site, Elk Run installed a stoker plant that crushes coal to a fine powder and stockpiles it. Prevailing winds in the valley carried dust from the plant, covering the town in a dusty black fallout.

After the uproar over dust was already underway, the company applied for a permit with DTE Edison, a large electric utility based in Detroit, to build a synfuel plant at the Elk Run site. To make synfuel (which a plant foreman for a different company called "s-i-n fuel"), diesel fuel, pine resin, or other chemical combinations are sprayed onto raw coal that is then baked.[11] Several Sylvester citizens began researching synfuel. Combined with the effects of the coal dust, they feared they would be further exposed to chemicals carried into town by the wind.

After several residents who lived at the foot of the plant sold their property to Elk Run and moved, Pauline became the leader of the opposition movement.

> After [CRMW member and former Sylvester resident] Sharon sold out—it got so rough, she finally sold out . . . it come down the line and my name was on top of the list. I looked up and I said, "What do I do?" I had left city council. I chose not to run anymore cause I wanted to fight the coal dust battle. . . . I didn't want to do anything where anybody else would be held responsible for what I done. Only me . . . I said, "Oh, Lord, what do I do know?" I was seventy years old, seventy-one at that time.
>
> I said "What do I do," and that's when [Mary] came on board and we got in touch with [Coal River] Mountain Watch. Sharon had already been talking [to them]. They give Sharon clues about, you know, where to go, and then they started helping us. And through them, through them and their organization, and also OVEC and WVOP[12] . . . we went to legislature. We tried to get a law passed on dust. We were told that they already had one, that nobody uses it, that nobody goes by it. That got us into rallies and things where we could, you know, bring out the fact of what they were doing in the town of Sylvester. And the first thing I said, I said, "We're gonna put Sylvester on the map. We're gonna let the world know what they're doing to us here." 'Cause Sylvester is 65 percent elderly people. And, you know, coal mining people don't get rich, by any means. And what you make, you put in your home and things. And so that's what they've got here. And you gonna do this, and it's destroying us? . . . I know it's destroying me. I could go to my daughter's or something, but I don't want to do that. I want my own life."

I asked Pauline if she had ever joined an environmental group before. She replied, "I was the last person in the world I would have thought would have been an activist."

When I asked why, she said, "'Cause I've spent my life teaching Sunday School and singing in the church choir." She didn't associate those things with people she considered activists, adding, "But I believe in standing up for my rights."

I asked Mary and Pauline if they had ever sued anyone before they took Elk Run to court over the coal dust.

MARY: No.

PAULINE: Never even thought about suing anybody.

MARY: I'm not the kind of person to sue to get money.

PAULINE: Never thought I'd be in a courthouse. The last time I was in that courthouse over there, up in that judge's chambers, was when I adopted my son in 1963.

PAULINE: [Shutting down Elk Run] wasn't our goal. But I feel just like this about it now: if we can't stop it any other way, shut 'em down. Why should we have any compassion for them? When I have to listen to an employee sit in a courtroom and say, "Well, if I use the technology that they're developing now to stop the coal dust then I'm not going to get my bonus"—that's a little hard to take.[13]

* * *

Running through these testimonies are themes of personal transformation, rights, commons, and community. There are strong senses of history, propriety, and integrity. All of these activists have a sense that wrong is being done and they have decided to do something to confront that wrong. Together, they are learning that to confront power, they must do more than simply demonstrate that wrong is being done. They must develop a principled way of addressing their needs for environmental, economic, social, and political justice. But how do these themes fit into a definition of environmentalism and how does this style of environmentalism relate to others?

Fields of Environmentalism

Environmental economist Joan Martinez-Alier identifies three broad trends in global environmentalism: wilderness protection, eco-efficiency, and what he calls the environmentalism of the poor.[14] He associates wilderness protection with Sierra Club founder John Muir and identifies the sacredness of nature and affiliations with deep ecology as the movement's defining characteristics. Martinez-Alier links eco-efficiency with concepts like ecological modernization, wise use, and scientific management of resources, and with the other major American environmental father figure, Gifford Pinchot.

Martinez-Alier's focus falls on his third grouping: the environmentalism of the poor. Like its close cousins livelihood ecology and liberation ecology, the environmentalism of the poor focuses on a material interest in the environment as a source and a requirement for livelihood rather than the sacredness of nature. The environmentalism of the poor is "not so much a concern with the rights of other species and of future generations of humans as [it is] a concern for today's poor humans."[15]

Bourgeois Environmentalism

While I generally agree with Martinez-Alier's characterization of the three trends, a few modifications must be made to apply them more appropriately to the West Virginian, and more broadly, American context. To tailor the environmentalism of the poor to Coal River, I employ a social practice theory approach to individual and collective identities. That is, how do people construct their identities as individuals and groups through shared and meaningful practices? Examples like Coal River demand attention to the pragmatics of site-specific social contexts. Identities are built on understandings of local history, culture, economics, and politics that are collectively negotiated and contested.[16]

State and regional groups who represent a wilderness protection perspective tend to be dominated by more affluent middle- and upper-class groups whose activities I characterize as bourgeois environmentalism. In addition to wilderness protection, they tend to focus on recreational areas and issues like logging in national forests and protecting view sheds in scenic places. These activities often conceptualize the environment and landscape as a consumer good primarily for recreational use.[17]

In West Virginia, a prime example of such activism is reflected in the debate over wind power projects. Two groups of energy producers announced plans to construct so-called wind farms on the Allegheny Ridge in the Monongahela National Forest. Together, the wind farms would include 366 state-of-the-art wind turbines reaching up to four hundred feet above the ground. Running along the northeastern side of the state, the ridge is the highest geologic formation in West Virginia and contains the state's highest altitude point, Spruce Knob.

The proposed wind farm sparked a debate that divided the state's environmental community largely along class lines, most notably within groups like the West Virginia E-Council and the West Virginia Highlands Conservancy. These groups have stronger presence in the northern part of the state and have programs specifically to protect the Monongahela National Forest. The constituencies of these groups also tend to be more affluent than those of Coal River Mountain Watch.

Julian Martin, a retired high school teacher and Boone County native, was a member of the Highlands Conservancy board of directors and a regular participant in the Friends of the Mountains coalition and various anti-MTR activities. Martin also strongly opposed the wind farms in the Allegheny Ridge. In 2003 he outlined his reasons and summed up the wind debate in a colorful description of the Highland Conservancy's internal conflict over the issue.

> The Highlands Conservancy, I think, was organized to . . . save the highlands. You know, where the real gorgeous places are. . . . I grew up right next to a slate dump, so I had no idea West Virginia was beautiful for years. I said, "Are you kidding me? What the hell are you talking about?"
>
> The wind thing . . . is local because there are people living there who don't want these windmills right above their house. I'd like for them to put them all in Kanawha County, right behind my house, anywhere they want to, but leave those beautiful places alone. Put 'em on strip mines, put 'em on mountaintop removal, but . . . for God sakes, I don't want to go up there on the highest mountain in West Virginia, Spruce Knob, and look out there at windmills.
>
> [The Highlands Conservancy has] all these people, each one going a different direction on different things. And man, it's a zoo. And it covers the whole state, so you got people way up in the Eastern Panhandle, and I'm down there trying to say, "Wait a minute, wait a minute, they're destroying southern West Virginia." [Wind supporters say,] "Yeah, but windmills are going to save the mountains." And I said, "Bullshit. Windmills are not going to save one mountain. They'll destroy all the mountains and put the windmills up in the beautiful places too, so it won't matter. It ain't gonna stop mountaintop removal."[18]

Martin's comments about the conflict among environmentalists over the wind farms reveals a passionate connection to West Virginia's "beautiful places." People all over West Virginia describe a personal relationship to particular places, be it Spruce Knob or a lesser known, but personally mean-ingful, feature of the landscape. Arguments like Martin's for protecting places like Spruce Knob and Dolly Sods (a national wilderness area) reflect genuine passion for the crown jewels of West Virginia's mountain beauty, but they also reflect class divisions within the state and its environmental community. Dolly Sods, Spruce Knob, and the entire Monongahela National Forest are attractions—places that visitors consume by gazing upon their beauty. Be they tourists from urban areas like New York City or Washington, D.C., or tourists from Charleston, West Virginia, the people who are most likely to visit these scenic places have a very different orientation to them as part of the environment than does someone who lives beneath a mountaintop removal site in southern West Virginia.

Environmental historian William Cronon and others highlight this distinction. Cronon criticizes the wilderness focus because it excludes humans from the landscape. Richard White, in his essay, "Are You An Environmentalist or Do You Work for a Living?" further argues that wilderness advocates do not consider people's need to interact with the landscape in their work.[19] This apparently clear distinction between landscapes of production (where people work) and landscapes of consumption (where people live and recreate) reflects class differences that enable consumers of places like Spruce Knob to work in one place and travel to another for recreation. People who live in beautiful places, be they coastal waterways or the mountains of West Virginia, need to make a living from the landscapes that tourists frequent. Cronon and White argue that the obsession with wilderness protection is an ineffective environmental strategy because it cedes moral ground to wise-use advocates.[20] Though their rhetoric ranges from clumsy to absurd, the coal industry takes advantage of this gap in class status in environmental strategy by arguing that coal provides jobs and alleviates poverty.

Corporate Environmentalism

Crudely speaking, the coal industry's rhetoric justifying mountaintop removal is a wise-use argument. Mountaintop removal is good for West Virginia, the argument goes, because the mountain landscape is "useless." Mountaintop removal allows them to efficiently extract coal to provide the nation with much-needed "affordable" energy. Flattening the land constitutes an "improvement" because the flat land can be used for future development.

The cold rationality of those terms is frightening for those familiar with the Appalachian landscape. The pinpoint focus on coal systematically overlooks and denies any value to other features of the landscape and creates what Mary Hufford calls "non-intersecting public spheres." Hufford has compiled cyclical interactions between people and the landscape in Coal River to create what she calls the Seasonal Round.[21] A small sample of activities includes clearing cemeteries and planting gardens in spring, gathering berries in summer, canning vegetables when they ripen, digging ginseng in early fall, hunting squirrel when nuts fall from trees, and hunting deer in the winter. Much like Terre Satterfield's "talking past," hearing coal executives and local activists describe these nonintersecting public spheres seem as though the two sides are describing two different planets.[22]

Like wilderness protection, Coal's rhetoric also systematically excludes humans from the landscape. The activities detailed by Hufford represent cultural practices that have accumulated over many generations of mountain living. These activities were essential to mountain subsistence in an era when mining work was irregular and poorly paid. Today, few if any people depend exclusively on such activities for subsistence, but they still play an indispensable role in social cohesion and maintaining community.

In addition to excluding humans, the myopic focus on coal as West Virginia's only marketable resource excludes other resources that could support economies of varying scales. Southern West Virginia is continuously told not just by the coal industry, but also by its government and by many of its citizens, that coal is all there is. No persuasive evidence shows that a genuine effort has ever been made to diversify the region's economy. After taking office in 2000, Governor Bob Wise created a special commission to promote economic development in the southern counties, but he appointed Art Kirkendoll as director. Kirkendoll, a Logan County businessman with strong ties to the coal industry, was associated with a mob that attacked marchers (including then Secretary of State Ken Hechler) while they reenacted the 1921 march to Blair Mountain.[23]

The coal industry's rhetoric justifying mountaintop removal resembles window dressing around a program of political, social, and economic domination of West Virginia. Through all eras since industrial coal extraction began, consistent patterns link the coal industry and state politics. Economic development has always privileged coal in explicit forms (like the broad form deed and Governor Arch Moore's secret tax breaks) and implicit forms (like maintaining development regimes that effectively prevent noncoal development in the coal-producing counties). Empirical analysis of economic trends of the past fifty years shows that, rather than diversifying, the economy of southern West Virginia has in fact grown even more dependent on coal. The systematic exploitation of coal resources at the expense of other economic opportunities and at the expense of communities and humans warrants a designation with a much stronger connotation than wise use or scientific management.

Radical Environmentalism

Martinez-Alier does not designate any particular brand of environmentalism as radical, but the radical label is very important in the United States. While terms like radical and extreme are discursive labels that have no concrete definition, it can be useful to discuss where and how such terms are applied. In the United States and abroad, environmental activists employ a spectrum of tactics. Some people see themselves as activists if they make a donation to a group like the Sierra Club. Examples of "radical" activism in the American imaginary include Greenpeace activists attacking whaling ships and the Earth

Liberation Front (ELF) setting fire to housing developments under construction in environmentally sensitive places.

Radicalness can only be measured in comparison to other tactics and beliefs. I think it safe to say that most Americans would label ELF-style arson a radical action. But the radical label is applied to many activists in cases that are not so clear. In addition to Governor Cecil Underwood's comments accusing "extreme environmentalists" of trying to stop coal mining, West Virginia Coal Association spokesman and legendary West Virginia University football coach Don Nehlen claimed that Coal's opponents were only a dozen "wackos" whom he characterized as "flies" to be swatted.

As described at the beginning of this section, the label environmentalist itself is used as a derogatory term in many West Virginia circles. Challenging the status quo often draws the radical label. Because of Coal's status in Appalachian history, politics, and economics, and coal's status as a target of global environmental concerns like the Kyoto Protocol and other efforts to combat global warming, many in West Virginia see environmentalism of any sort as a radical enterprise. While there is no hard and fast definition of a radical, the following sections evaluate Coal River Mountain Watch and the activist movement within the context of broader environmental movements and in the historical, political, economic, and social contexts of southern West Virginia. That is to say, are CRMW activists radical? Are they extremists? Are they wackos?

Environmental Justice and the Commons

As appealing as it may be, Martinez-Alier's "environmentalism of the poor" does not translate seamlessly to movements in the United States. While he associates his term loosely with the American environmental justice movement, his tendency to focus on indigenous and peasant groups in the Third World seems to overlook a case like CRMW. Martinez-Alier is "concerned with the majority of humankind, those who occupy relatively little environmental space, who have managed sustainable agroforestal and agricultural systems, who make prudent use of carbon sinks and reservoirs, whose livelihoods are threatened by mines, oil wells, dams, deforestation and tree plantations to feed the increasing throughput of energy and materials of the economy within or outside their own countries."[24]

Livelihoods in Coal River, West Virginia, are at once threatened and sustained by mines and extractive industries. CRMW does, in many ways, cultivate an indigenous image by drawing attention to cultural heritage, historical events, and pastimes that mark theirs as a distinctive American culture. Many activists claim genealogical traces of American Indian heritage and draw on themes of Indian respect for nature. They emphasize cultural interactions with the landscape like digging ginseng and ramps, fishing, and hunting. In 2003, CRMW sponsored an essay contest in local schools with the prompt, "What my mountain heritage means to me." Aided by the visual impact of mountaintop removal, these and other narratives of heritage and culture form the basis for an argument that MTR threatens a distinctive culture.

But the indigenous shoe does not completely fit either. One neighbor of mine told me that she and her husband were moving because her husband, a miner, had gotten a job in a Nevada gold mine. The area where they were moving, she said, wasn't a big city but, "it's not like here, they have stuff. You don't have to drive an hour to Walmart." Coal River residents, including CRMW activists, are on the periphery of American politics and economics, but they are very much integrated into the American market patterns of consumption, including its energy dependency and large ecological footprint. The fact that the nearest Walmart (or most any other store) is an hour away doesn't stop people from driving to it on a regular basis.

Given Martinez-Alier's environmental triad, CRMW does seem to fit best within the rubric of environmentalism of the poor versus both wilderness protection and eco-efficiency. Yet, even this category, which Martinez-Alier associates with indigenous agroforesters, does not adequately describe CRMW's strategic focus on reforming rather than dismantling their local economy by pursuing sustainable economic development.

The environmental justice (EJ) movement is a better fit for CRMW within existing theoretical perspectives on environmental activism. Perhaps CRMW's greatest contribution to EJ is helping transcend its historical associations with race. Initially phrased as environmental racism, EJ was long equated with racial discrimination in the United States.[25] But CRMW represents a movement driven primarily by socioeconomic class issues.[26]

CRMW and the Friends of the Mountains network are indicative of a move toward broader, more comprehensive community activism that extends beyond single issues to situate momentary concerns within larger cultural frameworks. Geographer David Harvey's theoretical approach to environmental justice focuses on the need to create a workable concept of justice in practice—in people's everyday social interactions.[27] The fight against mountaintop removal, environmental justice, and the environmentalism of the poor are ultimately moral rather than environmental concepts. Fundamentally, their arguments are about human interactions and social relationships, and the inequalities that govern them. The environmental component of environmental justice comes from a focus on a shared environment or landscape as a common basis for conversation about social change. The goal of the conversation, Harvey asserts, is to create "a principled way in which to talk about the need to regulate human relationships and our collective endeavours so as to achieve a particular set of goals under a given set of ecological, historical, and geographical conditions."[28]

Here, a perspective that joins together concerns about the environment with everyday human relations reinforces a commons approach to environmentalism. Anthropologist Donald Nonini defines the commons as "those assemblages and ensembles of resources which human beings hold in common or in trust to use on behalf of themselves, other living human beings and past and future generations of human beings, and which are essential to their biological, cultural, and social reproduction."[29] Among other things, any community must possess as part of its constitution a shared understanding of its relationship with the physical environment, economic arrangements, and a workable concept of justice. This depends on creating spaces in which differing public spheres must intersect and speak to one another.[30] Mary Hufford's public ethnography stitches together the biological and physical commons of the Coal River landscape with the social concept of the commons in the public sphere. Drawing on an inclusive commons perspective that sees environment and economic opportunity not as opposing forces, but necessary and complimentary components of a lived community that is at once local and trans-local, the Friends of the Mountains movement attempts to forge a public space between the two equally unsatisfactory myths of industrial progress and wilderness protection.

Harvey ultimately criticizes the environmental justice movement, however, for being fixated on local issues that obstruct the creation of a broader discussion of justice. He describes what he sees as a fervent attachment to the local and reluctance to work across issues as "militant particularism." Herbert Reid points out that a similar criticism is applicable in an Appalachian context to thinking based on colonial trauma or regional identity, which he likened to "traps."[31] The locally situated, yet thoroughly networked forms of activism embodied by CRMW and the Friends of the Mountains more accurately represent a form of "place-based globalism."[32]

Coal River Mountain Watch is a decidedly local organization that is focused explicitly on stopping mountaintop removal locally and across Appalachia. The group transcends this local focus by connecting mountaintop removal to larger social, political, and economic forces that drive the coal industry. Members of CRMW and FOM have traveled nationally and internationally to speak, meet, and work with other local and regional organizations. They work with larger environmental groups (the "Big Greens") to extend their expertise and financial resources. Some have participated in larger meetings including at the World Social Forum. Within these broader coalitions, CRMW often plays the role of the frontline activists who live with the effects of coal on a daily basis, a feeling Judy Bonds often described as living "in the belly of the beast."

Rather than inhibiting work between localities, CRMW's attachment to place gives them entrée into activist networks that work toward exactly the broader discussions of justice that Harvey invokes. By following the coal ripped from their mountains, for example, to the far-flung power plants where it is burned, to air pollution issues, to the buildup of methyl mercury in the food chain, to water pollution issues stemming from the dumping of power plant ash, and finally to a household power switch, CRMW inserts itself into everyday lives of people around the country and into networks of activists around the world that confront a diffuse, systemic problem in local contexts.

Approaching mountaintop removal and its affiliated ills using an approach to commons environmentalism aids CRMW and FOM in transcending problems commonly associated with place-based or single-issue social movements. Relying on the importance of lived experience in the commons, they are able to carve out conceptual space in the apparent dualisms between industrial progress and wilderness preservation and between economy and environment. Their approach affords a strategic position outside the confines of organized labor and facilitates a social movement that does not depend on the United Mine Workers—itself a noteworthy accomplishment in the coalfields. Finally, the use of commons environmentalism by Coal River Mountain Watch and the Friends of the Mountains should serve as a model of how a distinctive attachment to place can aid rather than inhibit formation of partnerships across place and across issues. Their activism grows from a physical and civic commons that is necessarily local, but also necessarily in conversation with much broader discussions of justice that transcend place and call into question multiple, nonintersecting interpretations of the same "local."

Conclusion: John Henry, Efficiency, and Community

John Henry was a steel-driving man, but why did John Henry drive steel? Like most children, I assume, I learned the words to the song without knowing or even thinking about what he was doing in the first place. I knew it was about a man competing with a machine. I knew that John Henry won; I knew he died, and I knew that was supposed to mean something.

The origin of the John Henry legend has traditionally been attributed to West Virginia around the time railroads expanded into the new frontier seeking the region's rich raw materials. John Henry would have been one of many newly freed black workers brought to the region after the Civil War. Henry, his co-workers, and the evil steam hammer were laying tracks through Big Bend Mountain that would make up the Chesapeake and Ohio Railroad.[1] The Chessie, as it was known, would bring industry, development, and progress to the mountains. Though there are many interpretations of the legend, John Henry still serves as a parable for the shift to modern industrial society and its ramifications. The social struggles represented by the conflict over mountaintop removal belong not to John Henry's era, but to a subsequent social shift that West Virginians and Americans in general struggled with at the turn of the twenty-first century. Nevertheless, the relationships between corporate efficiency and community bonds are similar enough to warrant revisiting the parable.

I once interviewed a retired mine foreman who had worked with my grandfather. Together, they reflected on the changes in work and life that had occurred during their lives.

We've gone in my lifetime from when everybody had to farm these hillsides in order to help pay the bills. [The hillsides] are all grown up now. That was an agricultural society. We went to a mechanized society and we've gone now to another level where everybody is trying to make a million dollars in the stock market. . . . We've brought up a society and taught them it's a shame to have to work with your hands. That it's not right to have to get out there in that coal mine and work like that, or work on a farm. There's been a tremendous change in the way a man makes a living in my lifetime.[2]

As a child, I thought John Henry's death made his triumph over machine a hollow one. Folklorist Archie Green provides another perspective on John Henry framed within the context of American labor lore. "Did John Henry die only because he was black, or because all workers are doomed who defy modernity? How do losers function in a society caught up by worship of competitive sports and entrepreneurial spirit? Ideally, the C&O contractor or capitalist who brought the steam drill to Big Bend should have been honored by song. . . . Are we perverse in having elevated a defeated driller to Olympus?"[3]

As a child, I could not understand John Henry's status as a mythic symbol for labor pride. As Green indicates, John Henry's status as an American folk hero defies our society's manic drive to worship champions. Under the logic that elevates sports heroes and CEOs as role models, all people who labor for a living should be seen as losers. But that is a perverse understanding of our society in which people have to work to make a living.

The lessons taught by Appalachia's mountaintop removal fight extend far beyond the coalfields. The struggle shows how we as a society are still struggling with the profound lessons that John Henry attempted to teach, though in new forms created by neoliberal globalization. Mountaintop removal is a graphic case that shows how, instead of serving our needs as a community, modernity in the form of mythical industrial progress (discussed in chapter 8) can work against our needs as a community.

In 2004, the Discovery Channel aired a series called *Mega Excavators* that provided a who's who of mammoth strip mining machinery. The program glorified machines like Big Muskie, the biggest dragline ever built, as if they were heroes competing against the Earth like John Henry competed against the steam hammer. A dragline operator interviewed for the program talked about the fast pace and stress of loading three hundred hauling trucks in a twelve-hour shift. Each moment that the dragline is not loading is a moment the $100 million equipment is not paying for itself.

Industry certainly rode in on the Chessie, and untold tons of timber and coal have rolled out. Certain kinds of development and progress followed.

The way *Mega Excavators* presented surface mining, it is the best mining method ever devised. "A mechanical digger has been the goal of man since he first made tools," the narrator declared.

Draglines certainly represent progress in efficient extraction, but what of John Henry? He died, remember? Just because he *could* beat the steam hammer, docs that mean he *should* have? Maybe we need to think about what John Henry accomplished. In beating the steam hammer, he became a hero for black and working class people who find pride and dignity in their work. Coal miners, like those I met in the South section with the roof cracking and popping over their heads, took pride in the fact that they worked well in dangerous conditions. What, then, do machines like the steam drill and dragline accomplish? Just because we *can* move one hundred tons of earth with one pass of a dragline, does that mean we *should?* Pride in the case of efficient machines would appear to be reserved for engineers, manufacturers, and mine operators—not the miners themselves. It's hard to understand how a miner could take pride in the destruction of a place he or his loved ones once valued. Maybe better questions to ask of mechanized industry are, "Is this progress?" and "Do we even have a choice?" As we struggle to integrate principles of social justice and reconcile the economic imperatives of neoliberalism with the needs of communities, we would do well to ask, What is the purpose of efficiency?

John Henry, obviously, gave up his life in confronting the machine. Those who capitulated to mechanization gave up a lifestyle. Not a life of hard work, driving steel or digging coal, but a life that is not mediated by ever more efficient machines. As machines get bigger and better (portrayed on programs like *Mega Excavators* as a seemingly natural, inevitable, and apolitical progression), people have to get out of their way. The arrival of draglines changed the Appalachian landscape forever, in ways less obvious than decapitating mountains and filling valleys. Mountaintop removal has reshaped the social landscape. The steam hammer displaced John Henry's co-workers. Draglines displace workers, residents, mountains, streams—entire ecosystems and familiar social formations.

* * *

Theologian and ecologist Thomas Berry takes a deep historical perspective to describe what he sees as flaws in Western thinking about the environment.[4] He faults the term "environment" for being anthropocentric and argues that humans must see themselves as integrated within larger ecological and cosmological systems that govern the Earth and the universe. Not wanting to sound like a Luddite, Berry acknowledged that science and technology have provided great benefits to society. Berry's argument, however, is that science has "stolen the planet Earth" from us by asserting itself as a cosmology. Science, he argues, must operate within an acceptable cosmology that does not assert itself as being above and removed from the processes that govern the universe. Looking historically, he suggests a fundamental shift in the purposes of knowledge. Prior to the Enlightenment, he said, the goal of knowledge was not efficiency, but fulfillment—two very different objectives.

Hearing coal operators and state officials pronounce that "mountaintop removal is the best way of mining coal ever," and that "topsoil substitute is better than native topsoil," lends credence to Berry's suggestion that efficiency has usurped human concerns in our society. At some point, efficiency transforms from a servant to a master—from a means to an end in itself. Coal was for decades the only reason many towns existed in the mountains. Now, across Appalachia's coalfields, Coal is bearing down on those same communities. Already, the mountains are littered with places that used to be, but are no more.

As a society dealing with the growing pains caused by a global neoliberal system, we are faced with difficult choices about our social, political, and economic systems. Anthropologist Eric Wolf described abstracting economic and political activity as fundamental characteristics of the modern system.[5] He argues that all economics and all politics occur within a social and political context (political in a broad sense referring to power relations between people, not simply partisanship). In contrast, our assumption that economy is a thing unto itself allows our society to worship the market to the extent that we allow it to determine social and political contexts. Similar to Wolf, anthropologist Steve Gudeman views economy as an extension of culture, reflecting the cultural characteristics and values of the society from which it emerges.[6] When we indiscriminately yield to the demands of corporate efficiency, following his view, we grant economy and corporations control over our material, cultural, social, and spiritual needs.

In the contentious local spheres where people struggle over issues like mountaintop removal, abstractions like economy and landscape meet real people in particular contexts of space and time.[7] It is where the macroeconomic machinery of neoliberal globalization appears in the form of mine closings, consolidations, and job losses. It is where the abstract vagaries of landscape become the familiar homeplace. In these contentious spheres, the impetus of corporate efficiency meets valued lifestyles and meaningful relationships. In Coal River, theory becomes situated in conflict between coal industry initiatives like mountaintop removal and people's desire to protect the mountains that have been their home for generations. At the same time, those residents who seek to preserve livelihoods that depend on the coal industry emphasize the importance of the industry for the economic health of the region. Out of conflicting points of view emerge conflicting interpretations of history giving rise to contentious practices in the present.

In the spaces of specific communities, the local, the historical, the economic, the environmental, and the social converge in the realm of experience. At this intersection, participants form, accumulate, and embody knowledge, understandings, and experiences that influence how they live their lives and perceive their world.[8] I have used "community" throughout this book in a very broad sense as a shared interest, belief, or position that creates a relationship between people.[9] Though the common bonds at the root of any particular community are arbitrary, all communities turn their arbitrary bonds into an assumed and unspoken fact that is seemingly "natural" and outside the realm of opinion or negotiation.[10] In times of conflict, the natural sense of identity shared by a community is disrupted and the shared interest breaks down into different points of view. Resolution of conflict involves identifying disagreements and negotiating a shared understanding of how to overcome them.

One of the simple yet profound lessons taught by the mountaintop removal conflict is that nature, or the landscape of the mountains, has a social history. Just as society works to make its bonds seem natural, it also gives nature social and historical elements.[11] One of CRMW's basic accomplishments has been its insistence that there are different interpretations of the history of the mountains and the communities of Coal River. An older man told me about a confrontation he had with armed guards patrolling mine property. When I asked him when this had happened, he didn't reply with a month or even the year. He said simply, "It was turkey season." People in Coal River often narrate space and time with stories of hunting with their fathers or children, playing in the mountains as children, or working in their garden. Testifying to the social history of nature draws attention to the fact that landscape is socially constructed: mountains are not just mountains. They are places known, used, and understood through personal experience.[12]

The work of recreating the mountains as a social space began with John Flynn and Mary Hufford and has continued through the acts of many volunteers from within Coal River and without. The seemingly simple act of making explicit something that everyone knows but never discusses is necessary to create a movement to change the political and social forces giving rise to and undergirding the regime of mountaintop removal.[13] The significance of the movement is not just that it raises alternative interpretations of the mountains, but that it also opens social spaces in which those interpretations can circulate and challenge the dominant narratives offered by the industry and government. This commons social space is reminiscent of several theorists, but also distinctly rooted in local meanings and expressions.

Just as nature is inseparable from social forces, economy is also socially and culturally constructed.[14] The particular economic structures and practices that sustain any community are taken for granted, as if they were a part of nature. People like the activists in Coal River Mountain Watch demonstrate that life in the coalfields has always meant more than just mining coal. Although mining has been the primary economic activity in southern West Virginia since the late 1800s, it has not always been so, nor has mining ever been the only source of jobs. Opening the social history of that economic arrangement to investigation is necessary to recognize and question the source of its authority and to propose alternative economic activities.

Failing to engage in social introspection and yielding our social values to the natural forces of economic markets has profound implications for the meaning of democracy. Twentieth-century social and political theorists like Antonio Gramsci, Hannah Arendt, Jurgen Habermas, and others forged analytical categories in their efforts to understand the emergence of movements including fascism and totalitarianism.[15] As recipients of this tradition we are grateful, but categories like the state, corporations, the mob, and labor unions are not entirely applicable to the circumstances that face us at the beginning of the twenty-first century. What good are "the state" and "the corporation" as analytical categories if you can't tell where the state ends and the coal company begins?

West Virginia has had a litany of public officials who came directly from and returned directly to the coal industry. Chief among recent examples are former governor Cecil Underwood and former DEP secretary Michael Castle. At the national level, in the George W. Bush administration, interior secretary Gale Norton made a career as an attorney representing mining interests in Colorado. Her chief deputy, J. Stephen Griles, was a coal industry lobbyist prior to taking his post in the Bush administration. David Laurisky, who served as head of federal Mine Safety and Health Administration, was a lobbyist for a mining company in Utah. Laurisky's boss, labor secretary Elaine Chao, is married to Kentucky Senator Mitch McConnell, a longtime friend of the mining industry.

* * *

Appalachia's mountaintop removal nightmare illustrates a pattern of relations among corporations, government, labor, communities, and environment that appears across the United States and around the world. The industrial exploitation of the mountains, in the past and in the present, resembles an updated version of the banana republic stereotype. So-called economic development projects in West Virginia (more appropriately described as job creation programs) create very few good jobs and no coherent plan for sustained development. The rhetoric of economic development is used to put a fresh coat of whitewash on a very old economic regime in the mountains. It creates a few jobs under some trendy terms, but all the while guards the preeminence of the extractive industry.

In the past, the United Mine Workers represented workers and their communities in dealings with companies and the state. The relationship wasn't always rosy. The union went through periods of serious corruption and internal political squabbles. But on the whole, the union provided representation that most coalfield residents were grateful to have. Speaking at a fundraiser for the West Virginia Citizen Action Group in 2003, UMWA president Cecil Roberts claimed that the union was the first environmental group in West Virginia. The audience, largely made up of community and environmental activists from the southern part of the state, gasped. As poorly tailored as the statement was for that particular audience, Roberts was right. The union led the first fights against "straight piping": running sewage lines straight from the house to the creek.

In fact, it is easy for some people to imagine that the United Mine Workers, in its heyday, would have stood up against the ill effects that mountaintop removal visits upon coalfield towns. But the reprise of the Battle of Blair Mountain illustrates just how impossible the union's position is in the twenty-first century. The union's desire to maintain its membership makes John L. Lewis's concession on mechanization during the 1949 contract negotiation look like a deal with the devil. Unable to organize significant numbers of new miners and desperate to hold onto the active members they have left, the UMWA cannot take a stand against mountaintop removal, even though most MTR jobs are nonunion and large numbers of the union's rank and file oppose the practice.

The success of community organizing efforts like Coal River Mountain Watch and Friends of the Mountains, admittedly modest in scale when compared to the United Mine Workers, illustrates just how important community issues are to labor organizations. The neoliberal trends that began in the 1960s severed ties between corporations and communities and set the tone for the assault on organized labor that accelerated into the twenty-first century. As it pertains to the coal industry, this is reflected in the fact that coal companies no longer have local offices that are accessible to the public. While Coal has always been tied to transnational capital, the local face of Coal today has been enclosed in fortified compounds that are virtually impenetrable to the public. This arrangement is a far cry from the post–World War II days when a miner could get fired from one job and find another without missing a shift, or when unemployed miners would walk from one mine office to the next looking for work. Union members and sympathizers have historically looked to the union for representation on community issues, but now that the relationship of the corporation to the community has become especially abusive, the rank and file and the citizenry demand exactly the kind of representation that the union cannot—and the state will not—offer.

Media trends within West Virginia provide yet another example of traditional institutions failing to represent the concerns of working class people. Attorney Joe Lovett noted the importance of the Charleston *Gazette*'s coverage of coal issues in supporting the coal reform efforts that emerged in the late 1990s. Changes in management, the media business, and the political climate, however, have made the *Gazette* less willing to challenge the state's business establishment. The *Gazette* has been locally owned for its entire history, and former owner Ned Chilton was an icon in West Virginia's progressive community. Several specific people contributed to the *Gazette*'s bold stance on coal issues. Award-winning environment reporter Ken Ward wrote an extensive series of articles on mountaintop removal mining. Longtime investigative reporter Paul Nyden contributed investigative pieces about the finances and corporate practices of Massey Energy. Editorials from Dan Radmacher brazenly challenged the coal industry and state politicians. During 2003 debate over increasing coal truck weight limits, Radmacher criticized Democratic Governor Bob Wise for betraying the progressive community that helped get him elected and labeled him a "coal whore."

Needless to say, the business community resented much of the *Gazette*'s coverage, which it called "anti-business." Coal executives listed the *Gazette* along with West Virginia's workers' compensation laws and tax structures as impediments to doing business in the state.

In the days after the 2004 election, comments circulated through the progressive community about the *Gazette* becoming more reluctant to print editorials and columns critical of the coal industry and other business interests. The newfound sensitivity to the "anti-business" label was an ominous sign for the activist community, which relied on the *Gazette* to counteract Coal's propaganda machine.

Traditional political and social institutions like the United Mine Workers and, increasingly, the media, have failed in various ways to represent the needs and interests of coalfield residents who want real alternatives to the coal industry and mountaintop removal coal mining. So far, community organizing like that of Coal River Mountain Watch and the Friends of Mountains coalition offers a venue in which to discuss and advocate alternatives. While these efforts have achieved modest results, they have succeeded in sustaining a counterpoint to industry and government propaganda, and have led to other efforts like the People's Election Reform Coalition (PERC). Closely related to the activist community, PERC has sponsored legislation for publicly financed political campaigns.

Law—the institutional avenue that MTR opponents have used most successfully—has also been closed off to them. Four lawsuits successfully established that mountaintop removal mining violates the Clean Water Act. Several northeastern states have sued coal burning power plants in the Midwest and Mid-Atlantic on the assertion that their emissions violate the Clean Air Act. Many environmental conflicts, most notably the dispute over old-growth timber in Oregon, have turned on arguments over endangered species habitat.

As demonstrated in chapter 5, there is no place in the regulatory process for people to stand up and say, "Mountaintop removal is wrong and should not be allowed." Laws like the Clean Water Act and the Endangered Species Act endow streams and endangered species with rights that *people* do not have. Activists in southern West Virginia cannot argue that mountaintop removal is wrong because it affects people and the landscape, but they can say that mountaintop removal destroys critical habitat for the endangered Indiana bat.

Reactionary arguments that such applications are outside the original intent of the law have been used to change the regulations. After a federal judge decided that mountaintop removal violated the Clean Water Act's definition of "fill," and the so-called buffer zone rule under the Surface Mine Control and Reclamation Act, the Bush administration changed those rules specifically to accommodate mountaintop removal. Other proposals would have changed the Clean Air Act, Endangered Species Act, and mine permitting procedures.[16] Changing laws because they have been used toward ends that are contrary to the goals of industry and the state makes explicit the complicity between the two, undermines the rule of law, and renders the practice of democracy virtually impossible.

* * *

While the processes and circumstances affecting the business climate, the media, labor, communities, and the environment are so profoundly apparent in Appalachia's mining regions, they are by no means exclusive to that or any other geographic area. The restructuring of capital that affected the mining industry has also reshaped all of the institutions of society on a global scale. The dynamics that play out with grotesque clarity in Coal River are also at

work across the United States and around the globe. A few well-known examples include the spread of Walmart and similar retail stores across rural
and suburban landscapes, the offshore flight of manufacturing jobs, and the
pervasive factory farms of the agribusiness industry.

Capital restructuring is by no means synonymous with the economics of
comparative advantage, but comparative advantage has been a popular model
for developing postcolonial economies, especially when they are under the
direction of a monetary institution like the World Bank. West Virginia's economic development efforts provide a clear example of the continued failure
of the comparative advantage model to establish a healthy economy that provides for citizens' needs. West Virginia has enjoyed a comparative advantage
in coal production for 150 years, yet its citizens have always been exposed to
the fickle coal market. Even at the dawn of the twenty-first century when coal
production was at an all-time high, West Virginia struggled to provide basic
services to many citizens in the coalfields. In fact, it is because of Coal's success that coalfield communities face even more dire economic circumstances
than they have faced during previous bust cycles. There are fewer noncoal
job opportunities now than in years past. Meanwhile, the state continues its
perpetual efforts to catch up with the national and international economies.
The sometimes-silly projects that come under the name "development" like
the baseball stadium and racetracks create a façade of a healthy economy. At
the same time, hard-working people in the coalfields struggle to maintain
basic services (like municipal water systems that sometimes leak over 90
percent of the water they pump),[17] as well as free themselves from dangers
like coal waste impoundments, flooding, and blasting.

It is only because of southern West Virginia's homogenous economy, engineered by the coal industry and the state, that mountaintop removal is
possible. With so few jobs and such a pitiful economy, enough people are
willing to accept mountaintop removal—even though some mountaintop
removal miners themselves describe their own paychecks as "blood money."

People in southern West Virginia and in communities everywhere have
practical ideas for making a living for themselves and their communities
outside of the coal industry or state economic development plans. The problem is that even if CRMW and their friends are right, it doesn't matter. The
activists are almost always accurate in their portrayals of state and industry
power and its effects on their own lives. They are almost always accurate in
describing conflicts of interest and inconsistencies in the law and its application. Even if their logic is sometimes not thorough or complete, the moral
thrust of their arguments generally hits its mark. But none of that matters if
the armor of power cannot be pierced by argument.

Restrictive economic conditions along with the foxes guarding the pro-
verbial henhouse make democratic governance impossible to achieve. How
are people supposed to live lives guided by democratic principles when they
have no choice in the economic activities that provide for themselves, their
families, and their communities? After all, democracy is also an analytical
category like the state and the corporation. Of what use is democracy when
it is upheld and proclaimed by members of the West Virginia legislature
where coal truck owners make laws regulating coal trucks based on industry
needs rather than engineering specifications? Democracy as a concept is of
no critical value when we fail to discriminate the practice of democracy from
the mere name of democracy.[18]

* * *

Like the steam drill that killed John Henry, the machinery of the modern
economy creates efficiency and soothes the sore muscles of hard times. Flip
a light switch. You know what's going to happen. We take for granted that
our electricity is going to work, so much so that we have totally forgotten
the incredibly complex architecture of our electric grid. Among the lessons
learned from the 2003 blackout in New York state and parts of the Midwest
is that the delivery of electricity is an incredibly complicated endeavor. Regardless of its complexity, anyone who wants to see it can follow a straight
and continuous line linking your light switch directly to flooded homes in
the community of Dorothy, the black slurry in the Coal River, and the coal
dust blanketing Sylvester. Under the soothing hum of fluorescent lights, we
as a society tend to overlook that our conveniences might be killing people
in Coal River and across Appalachia.

Thomas Berry's idea that the goal of knowledge should be fulfillment
rather than efficiency gives us a historical perspective on the problems of
the modern economy. I take Berry's sentiment to mean that maintaining our
social and environmental fabric requires attention to human and communal
values that may be inefficient, nonrational, or otherwise at odds with the
mechanical efficiency of the global neoliberal economy.

A colleague once asked if I thought of globalization as an "unmitigated
evil." It certainly is not. Globalization makes it possible to distribute goods,
services, and information on unprecedented scales. But when the costs include the occlusion of democracy and the disembodiment of our communities, we must at least ask how much is too much. When society allows
capitalism to proceed without a workable concept of justice that is applied
through everyday practice, we sacrifice things like community, environment, and basic ethics to the invisible hand of the market. In her study of

the farm crisis of the Midwestern United States, Kathryn Dudley uses the term "moral economy" to describe how many farming families came to attribute moral agency to the market by saying that a neighbor whose farm was foreclosed somehow "deserved it."[19] But by treating market effects as if they were politically neutral or natural, we fail to recognize how powerful political interests are shaping our communities. We fail to treat economy as a means to sustaining and reproducing ourselves physically and socially and bow to economy as an end unto itself.

William Greider uses "moral economy" to describe something completely different.[20] Recognizing the same tendencies that Dudley described, Greider advocates reforming capitalism to make it function within a socially acceptable moral framework.

Though the day-to-day experience and process of local organizing is slow and continually frustrating, the very existence of Coal River Mountain Watch and Friends of the Mountains is cause for hope. The activists represent a fundamentally different approach to community, history, economy, and environment that is at odds with traditional political and economic dogma of neoliberalism. Coalfield history, along with the political and economic circumstances surrounding mountaintop removal, clearly illustrates two basic points. First, for an economic regime to serve as a means to healthy social formations—communities—rather than as an end unto itself, it must be built around a workable concept of justice in practice. Second, in fundamental opposition to neoliberal theory, a social structure is needed to effectively organize the collective interests of communities in opposition to powerful industrial and political interests.

CRMW and the Friends of the Mountains illustrate what such a structure might look like, outside the models of trade unions and corporations. Through their innovative configuration and practices, activists at CRMW and FOM advocate and emulate a workable concept of justice. Reinterpreting the meaning of the mountains, the community, and the commons in a way that proclaims the existence of meaning outside the callous cash value of a ton of coal flies in the face of economistic analysis, the foundation of neoliberal political economy. A sense of justice that critically examines the relationship of economy and the people who both create it and depend on it challenges the tendency to let abstract forces like "the market" make moral decisions about the worth of things like labor, environment, and community.

To the extent that democracy can still be meaningfully practiced by people under circumstances like those found in the coalfields, it is in the form of participatory activism like that of CRMW and FOM. Theirs are the faces of an expressive democracy in practice, not just in name. Coal River Mountain

Watch and its allies have not stopped mountaintop removal. But given the union's declining power, that a group of people is mobilizing on their own behalf—that they are accepting the challenge posed by the machinery of neoliberalism—is in itself a valuable contribution to social movements in Appalachia.

* * *

"That nine pound hammer killed John Henry," sang Tennessee Ernie Ford, "it ain't a gonna kill me." Actually, John Henry probably swung a fourteen-pound hammer, but who's counting? Who needs a hammer at all when you have a $100 million dragline? Defeating the dragline might kill us. But, looking around southern West Virginia, we can see that our communities are going to die if we don't. John Henry put up a good fight. Despite the odds stacked against them, activists at Coal River Mountain Watch and the Friends of the Mountains have accepted the challenge and decided to fight the dragline and its mechanical efficiency. Standing up to the industry that has shaped their lives for generations is the first step toward reclaiming the pride and dignity of their community.

Epilogue

My formal field research period ended in late 2003 and early 2004. Since then I have made many visits to the Coal River region, though never for as long as I would have liked. I have attended several events related to MTR, coal, and energy policy issues. I have incorporated the issues into my various teaching roles, and I have included coalfield activists in my classrooms and communities at every opportunity. Strong continuities endure between the movement against mountaintop removal as it existed in 2003 and the various forms that have emerged through 2010. Coal issues in 2010 were no less contentious in the coalfield regions of Appalachia. Strong grassroots opposition persisted, as did entrenched industry and political forces supporting mining. Several important developments warrant specific mention.

Efforts challenging the coal industry and regulatory agencies continued to succeed in federal district courts. Working with grassroots organizations and national environmental law organizations like Earth Justice, Joe Lovett and others have successfully challenged several specific pieces of mine regulation and enforcement, including the so-called Nationwide-21 permit procedure (authorization from the U.S. Army Corps of Engineers to put fill material in U.S. waters). As with previous legal victories, the Fourth Circuit Court of Appeals has overturned all of these challenges.

Barack Obama's election gave activists cautious optimism that new leadership at Environmental Protection Agency (EPA) might be more friendly to their cause than had the EPA leaders under George W. Bush. The Obama EPA drew attention to the issue by ordering new reviews of pending MTR permits and by rescinding some noteworthy permits. Two years into the administration, however, the activist community was frustrated at the EPA's piecemeal approach and President Obama's unwillingness to reinstate language defining MTR overburden as "waste" rather than "fill"—reversing the change made early in the Bush administration to accommodate mining.

The environmental nonprofit organization Appalachian Voices led legislative efforts against MTR by advancing the Clean Water Protection Act. The bill, first introduced in the U.S. House of Representatives in 2002 and in each subsequent Congressional session, would reinstate language changed by the Bush administration and would outlaw most valley fills. A companion bill was first introduced in the Senate in 2009. The House bill, originally sponsored by Republican Christopher Shays of Connecticut and Democrat Frank Pallone of New Jersey, had bipartisan support from the beginning. The Senate bill, however, brought with it the most noteworthy Republican name to date—Lamar Alexander of Tennessee. Alexander's status as cosponsor was impressive not only because of his stature within the Republican Party, but also because he represents a coal-producing state. Appalachian Voices opened a permanent office in Washington, D.C., and continues to bring coalfield residents to lobby on behalf of the Clean Water Protection Act on a regular basis.

Shortly after my formal research concluded, the specter of mountaintop removal permits on Zeb Mountain in east Tennessee brought a new group of young MTR activists into the movement. Members of the Friends of the Mountain coalition, including Coal River Mountain Watch, began collaborating with an Earth First! group from Tennessee that, along with many other key participants, gave rise in 2005 to Mountain Justice Summer (an organization seeking abolition of MTR, steep slope strip mining, and all other forms of surface mining for coal). Clearly drawing on civil rights models, the effort brought a cadre of young activists to Coal River for a series of educational and activist efforts. The goal of CRMW, as many early activists emphasized, was not confrontation, but building community solidarity and offering local residents spaces and resources with which to express their frustration with coal industry practices. The incorporation of Earth First! and the subsequent organizational models of Mountain Justice were decidedly more confrontational, with elements of anticapitalist and anarchist countercultural themes.[1] This constituted a clear break with much of the CRMW tradition that created both enthusiastic hope for new directions in the movement and serious misgivings among many community members and longtime activists.

These conflicted feelings culminated in a intramovement meeting in Charleston that included the organizers of the Mountain Justice movement and other leading MTR movement figures with reservations about the new trends. I attended the meeting, which was mediated by a Charleston minister respected by activists for his longtime participation in social justice issues. Foundational members of the MTR movement explained their efforts to build credibility within local communities and with the state regulatory agency and the local public through nonconfrontational tactics. Many felt that the abrupt shift (as they perceived it) toward tactics associated with Earth First!—including civil disobedience—could undermine years of community organizing. Mountain Justice organizers responded with respect for activists' concerns, but asserted their own sense of urgency that called for new ideas and tactics in the effort to combat mountaintop removal and associated industry practices.

Mountain Justice Summer 2005 brought many young activists to Coal River. They participated in a "listening project" in which participants visited with local residents to learn about their experiences and concerns. The summer culminated in an activist demonstration at the West Virginia Capitol. This event had a decidedly different air than the somber Funeral for the Mountains in 2000. Counterculture cheerleaders performed anti-MTR routines and young activists on stilts shouted anticapitalist slogans.

Mountain Justice Summer succeeded in bringing new ideas, tactics, and participants into the movement. It also alienated some activists and offended some Coal River residents. As they had before, opponents slugged out their differences in letters to the editors of local newspapers, among other venues. Organizers and sympathizers lauded young people for being invested in the cause and caring enough to come to Coal River. Opponents accused participants of skinny-dipping, drug use, and offering drugs to local children.

The meeting in Charleston became a model of sorts for the different forms grassroots activism took between 2005 and 2010. The more community-oriented, nonconfrontational organizing persisted in many forms, while civil disobedience and the countercultural flare increased. Mountain Justice continued through the end of the decade, playing a strong role alongside more traditional organizing as a key component of MTR opposition.

Savvy organizers within the movement found productive ways to use the tactics together. In several key events, seasoned coalfield residents provided powerful firsthand testimony that yielded credibility to the movement. Meanwhile, youthful enthusiasm and civil disobedience often drew public attention and new interest to the cause, particularly among young people and college students.

Organizers employed this model on the largest scale yet at the September 2010 Appalachia Rising event in Washington, D.C. The event included both coalfield residents, youthful activists, and college students in a long weekend of teach-ins to educate newcomers about various issues associated with coal and mountaintop removal. Since I was teaching at a university in Washington at the time, I invited two coalfield residents to speak to my class on Monday afternoon. Lorelei Scarbro of Coal River, who had become an outspoken opponent of MTR beginning in 2005, accepted my invitation. (The other was too excited to be arrested for the first time to accept my invitation.) The weekend would culminate with a rally in Freedom Square on Pennsylvania Avenue followed by a march around the EPA building, ending in front of the White House.

The event advertised the opportunity for civil disobedience for those who were willing to risk arrest, but no other details were made public. People familiar with Washington were curious about the civil disobedience action. Knowing that the U.S. Park Police do not like to arrest people in front of the White House, we wondered what the civil disobedience action might be.

I attended the rally and march. On the steps of the EPA building, Scarbro delivered an impassioned speech to the crowd of several hundred marchers. In her measured, deliberate style, Scarbro accused the EPA of not properly enforcing existing mining laws and putting families like hers at risk. As the march continued toward the White House, Scarbro and I left and traveled to campus for class.

As she was speaking to my class and responding to students' questions, we learned of the organizers' civil disobedience strategy via a Twitter feed on Scarbro's cell phone. The target was not the White House. Rather, as the march turned west onto Pennsylvania Avenue, those risking arrest occupied the lobby of a PNC Bank branch just northeast of the White House. PNC Bank was one of many financial bodies holding major investments in coal companies that practiced MTR. As Scarbro described to my students the challenges of living in Coal River, including the difficult social and family divisions like hers—her nephew and son-in-law both worked for Massey— she also gave us updates on who was getting arrested at PNC. In total, several dozen protesters were arrested.

The Appalachia Rising event illustrates how organizers within the movement opposing MTR created a tenuous balance between the credibility and gravitas of coalfield residents like Scarbro and many others with the visibility of civil disobedience. Sadly, one of the activists who most passionately embodied both strains of activism could not attend the Appalachia Rising event in Washington. Judy Bonds was diagnosed with an aggressive cancer in summer 2010 and died in January 2011. Judy's passing points to one of the future battles over MTR—the exposure of coalfield residents to health risks resulting from mining activity. In 2008, the West Virginia University Department of Community Medicine released the first of several studies indicating that coalfield residents face greater risk of heart, lung, and kidney diseases, as well as overall mortality, than do residents of noncoal producing counties. In response to the study, then Governor Joe Manchin III told the Charleston *Sunday Gazette-Mail* that any substantial response to health risks should be the federal government's responsibility.[2] Subsequent studies are underway, including studies comparing cancer rates in the coalfields to noncoal producing areas.

Appendix: Cumulative Local Impact of Surface Mining

Permits issued for surface mines on Williams Mountain and Kayford Mountain in Coal River illustrate the explosion of mountaintop removal mining that began in the late 1980s. Of twenty-eight permits issued for the two mountains between 1976 and 2003 totaling 15,577 acres, only five permits totaling 2,147 acres (about 14 percent of the total acreage) were issued before 1987.

Table 1. Williams Mountain Quadrant[1]

Operator	Parent	Permit #[2]	Facility Name	Acres[3]
Elk Run	Massey	505792	East Stollings	1,238
Elk Run	Massey	507586		411
Elk Run	Massey	600687		60
Elk Run	Massey	601189		236
Elk Run	Massey	601487		246
Elk Run	Massey	602688		344
Independence	Massey	501400	Ramo Surface	80
Jack's Branch	Massey	007984		131
Omar Mining	Massey	007076		316
Omar Mining	Massey	502387		268
Omar Mining	Massey	503190		97
Independence	Massey	501200	Laxare East	1,534
Independence	Massey	502401	Lexerd	837
Elk Run	Massey	502898	West Stollings	1,087
Total Massey Acres:				6,885
Asset Mining	Peabody	503095	Frozen Hollow	388
Pine Ridge	Peabody	502995	Williams Mtn.	194
Total Peabody Acres:				582
Total Williams Mountain Acres:				7,467
Percentage of Quad:				20.18%

1. Based on USGS 7.5 minute topographic map quadrants.
2. The last two digits of the permit number indicate the year the application was submitted.
3. All data except for parent company taken from DEP records.

Table 2. Kayford Mountain

Operator	Parent	Permit #	Facility Name	Acres
Catenary	Arch	300800	Kayford South	712
Catenary	Arch	301795	Samples Ext.	83
Catenary	Arch	302390	(White Oak Hollow)	499
Catenary	Arch	302490	Cabin Creek	2282
Catenary	Arch	303593	Stanley Heritage	1098
Catenary	Arch	601287	Samples	203
Total Arch Acres:				4,877
Princess Beverly	Horizon[1]	300599	Kayford Mtn. 5	459
Princess Beverly	Horizon	301492	Kayford Mtn.	224
Princess Beverly	Horizon	302791	Kayford Mtn. 2	377
Princess Beverly	Horizon	600989		209
Princess Beverly	Horizon	603586	Kayford Mtn.	289
Princess Beverly	Horizon	z002781	Notomine Surface	1000
Total Horizon Acres:				2,558
Cumulative Acres:				7,435
Percentage of Quadrant:				20.09%[2]
Total Permitted Acres on Williams & Kayford Mountains:				14,902
Percentage of Two Quadrants:				20.01%

1. The Princess Beverly mine shut down in 2003. Later that year, Horizon sold its reserves on Kayford Mountain to Massey Energy.
2. Catenary and Princess Beverly straddle three topographic quadrants. They are all close enough in proximity that they could fit within the spatial area of any one of the quadrants. This percentage estimate is based on the spatial area of a quadrant at 38°00'00"N.

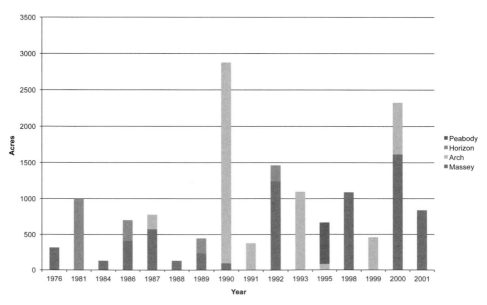

Mountaintop Removal Timeline: Kayford and Williams Mountains.

Notes

Introduction

1. Throughout this text, I use "Coal" to refer to the coal industry, particularly its corporate bodies; "coal" refers to the black mineral found inside the mountains.

2. See McNeil (2005).

3. From the mountainous literature on neoliberalism and globalization, I draw from Harvey (1989a, 1989b, 1996, 2005, 2006) Neil Smith (2005), Dicken (1998), Castells (1996, 1997) Comaroff and Comaroff (2001), and Stiglitz (2002).

4. Holland and Lave (2001: 4–5).

5. Gregory (1998: 3).

6. Eller (1982: 3–38).

7. Corbin (1981: xvii–xviii).

8. Montrie (2003).

9. Burns (2007).

10. Watts (1998).

11. Hinson (2000: 327–34).

12. See Montrie (2003) on the history of activism against strip mining in Appalachia.

13. Nonini (2007).

14. Ward, "Bush Hauling in Coal Contributions"; "Coal Operator Makes Case over Buffet"; Frankel, "Coal Operators Get Chance to Talk with Candidate."

15. Several transnational companies have become owners of Appalachian mines. Some mines in Coal River are owned by RAG International, a subsidiary of RAG Aktiengesellschaft based in Essen, Germany.

16. Harvey (2005: 19).

17. Harvey (2005: 23).

18. For entry into the rich literature on community organizations in Appalachia, see Fisher (1993), Couto and Guthrie (1999), and Montrie (2003).

19. Satterfield (2002: 8).

20. U. S. Census Bureau. *Statistical Abstract of the United States.*

21. I borrow the term "civic professionalism" from Herb Reid and Betsy Taylor (Reid and Taylor 2002; Reid 2006). "Pragmatic solidarity" comes from Paul Farmer (2003: 26).

Part I. The Worst Goddamn Thing I've Ever Seen

1. Julia Bonds was known to her friends as "Judy." I use both names interchangeably throughout this text. See description of hybrid pseudonym use in the introduction.

2. Subsidence refers to surface cracks and fissures caused as the ground settles into abandoned underground mines.

3. In the eastern United States, mountaintop removal and surface mining for coal has also been done in Virginia, Kentucky, Tennessee, Pennsylvania, and Ohio. I focus on West Virginia, but for information on other states, see Montrie (2003).

Chapter 1. Welcome to Coal River

1. Personal communication with anonymous Sylvester resident, July 2000.

2. Other forms of strip mining were practiced in Coal River since the late 1940s.

3. Consolidation and mazelike subsidiary structures within the coal industry make names very confusing to trace. Eastern and Addington Brothers were among the largest producers in the early 1980s. Eastern Associated and Eastern Associates are often used interchangeably in local speech. Both refer to Eastern Associated Coal Corporation. While it owned and operated mines in Appalachia as an independent corporation, Eastern has since become part of Peabody Energy and Addington, after several name changes and bankruptcies, became Horizon Resources.

4. All comments attributed to Jack Spadaro in this section are taken from an interview conducted December 10, 2003.

5. All comments attributed to Randy Jarrold [pseud.] are taken from an interview conducted July 16, 2000.

6. The company I refer to as Massey Energy or just Massey was known for most of its existence as A.T. Massey Coal Company. Through several corporate mergers and spin-offs, it has become known as Massey Energy. Massey is the largest coal producer in West Virginia and fifth largest in the nation. It is well known for its nonunion, or "union free" mines and its long-standing antagonistic relationship with the United Mine Workers. www.masseyenergyco.com.

7. Gross (1995: 227–41) describes the continuation of these trends in the NLRB under President Ronald Reagan who appointed conservative ideologues to the board early in his first term.

8. In May 1981, approximately two thousand UMWA members marched from a nearby rally onto the Elk Run property, damaging several company buildings and vehicles. This is described in detail in chapter 4.

9. Only one preparation plant has retained its union contract since Massey took over the mines from Peabody. The plant employs around two dozen workers.

10. New York City's Central Park offers a good size comparison. That park that people get lost in every day is "only" 848 acres.

11. Interview with Ken Hechler, June 27, 2003.

12. End-dumping refers to simply backing a dump truck up to the edge of the mine site and dumping spoil over into the valley without compaction or other design or engineering criteria.

13. A coal waste impoundment collapsed, washing away communities in Buffalo Creek, West Virginia, and killing 125. See Erikson (1976).

14. SMCRA permits states to run their own regulatory programs if they are at least as stringent as the federal guidelines enforced by the Office of Surface Mining.

15. Address delivered at the Hobet 21 coal mine, August 3, 1996, quoted in Purdy (1998: 130).

16. See appendix.

17. Moore was later convicted on federal corruption charges.

18. Nyden, "Super Tax Credits."

19. Interview with anonymous Dorothy resident, May 15, 2003.

20. Interview with Bernie Stanley [pseud.], July 5, 2003.

21. See appendix.

22. Interview with Pauline Canterberry and Mary Miller, April 8, 2003.

23. Interview with Freda Williams, July 11, 2000.

24. Interview with Ernie Harless [pseud.], October 15, 2003.

25. Interview with Pauline Canterberry and Mary Miller, April 8, 2003.

26. Interview with Elizabeth Casto, August 29, 2003.

27. Memo to Whitesville Businesses, June 2003.

28. Tipples were the forerunners of processing or preparation plants. Though modern plants are much more sophisticated operations, coalfield residents often use the three terms interchangeably.

29. Interview with Freda Williams, April 30, 2003.

Chapter 2. Fighting Back . . . Again

1. Fisher (1993; 2004).

2. Hufford (2001, 2002a, 2002b).

3. The Lucy Braun Association formed in the mid-1990s to bring together scientists and laypersons for a project monitoring sections of the mixed metaphysic forest in Appalachia. The association has not met since 1997. See Wills, et al., "Patterns of Forest Health."

4. Comments attributed to Randy Jarrold [pseud.] throughout this section come from an interview conducted July 16, 2000.

5. Interview with Joe Lovett, June 6, 2003.

6. Michael Castle was an appointed official of the West Virginia state government. While I have used pseudonyms to refer to many private citizens (including the president of Elk Run Coal Company), I have not altered names of elected or appointed public officials.

7. Personal communication with James Simon [pseud.], June 2000.

8. People often conflate the state Department of Environmental Protection (DEP) and the federal Environmental Protection Agency under the term "environmental protection."

9. The issue of wastewater impoundments is of particular importance since a large impoundment collapsed in Kentucky in October 2000 spilling an estimated 300,000

gallons of polluted sludge into the Big Sandy and Ohio Rivers. Of local concern in Coal River, one very large impoundment holds wastewater just above an elementary school, and another impoundment in the area will eventually have a dam over nine hundred feet high.

Chapter 3. What Are We Fighting For?

1. See Eller (1982: 7–22), Weise (2001).

2. See Tilley on phenomenology of landscape (1994).

3. See Beverly Brown (1996).

4. Hufford (2002b) and "Ramp Suppers, Biodiversity, and the Integrity of 'The Mountains.'"

5. See Eller (1982: 38).

6. I use dialogic and dialectical to refer to a model of action common to anthropology and social sciences. Rather than a linear model of cause and effect, a *dialectical* model is a mutually constituting, multilinear relationship. *Dialogic* is a more recent term that emphasizes the duration and dynamism of such relationships, as in an ongoing dialogue that is always informed by past statements and anticipation of future statements. I use the term *moral* outside of any particular religious tradition to refer to a systematic way of determining right from wrong that is found in all cultures.

7. Sixty-nine percent of surface acres and 74 percent of mineral acres in West Virginia counties sampled by the Appalachian Land Ownership Task Force (1983).

8. Nonini (2007).

9. Acronyms used in this section to denote different organizations include CCC (Citizens Coal Council, a national coalition), MWA (Mountain Watershed Association, PA), KFTC (Kentuckians for the Commonwealth, KY), CRMW (Coal River Mountain Watch, WV), and OVEC (Ohio Valley Environmental Coalition, WV).

10. Comments from Teri Blanton, Beverly Braverman, Julia Bonds, and Vivian Stockman come from a community meeting held on January 17, 2004.

11. Longwall mining is an underground method that cuts away very large blocks of coal, usually around one thousand feet across and tens of thousands of feet long. Longwall mining causes rapid and profound changes to the surface above as it subsides.

12. Here Stockman referred to the Apollo Alliance, a multifaceted effort to stimulate jobs and promote clean energy options within the United States. See http://apolloalliance .org.

13. Hypothetical name suggested by speaker.

14. Interview with anonymous resident, June 4, 2003.

15. Personal communication with an anonymous worker, August 2003.

16. Personal communication with an anonymous worker, June 2000.

17. Discussed in detail in chapter 6.

Part II. Banana Republic, Neoliberal Style

1. Personal communication, August 2003.

2. Nesbitt and Weiner (2001).

3. Montrie (2003).

4. Slocum (2006: 43–45).

Chapter 4. Strained Solidarities

1. Gorn (2001: 170). This is not to say that racial harmony existed in the coalfields. Racial divides remained, but a class consciousness emerged in many communities that enabled the union to organize. See Freda Williams's comments in chapter 8.

2. Alinsky ([1949] 1970).

3. BCOA is the industry bargaining association. The fund was actually administered by a three-person panel that included Lewis, a representative of the industry, and a "neutral" third party (initially Senator Styles Bridges of New Hampshire). Effectively, Lewis was able to control the panel and thus the fund (Alinsky [1949] 1970: 325–45).

4. Woodrum (1999: 115–17).

5. Comments attributed to John Taylor come from interviews conducted on July 2, 2003, and August 19, 2003.

6. Interview with Paul Nelson and Nanette Nelson, June 4, 2003. Union policy held that if one shift at a mine walked out, no other shift could work until the striking shift returned. If the midnight shift walked out, the mine would shut down at least until the beginning of the following midnight shift.

7. Amherst Coal Company v. United Mine Workers of Am., Civil Action No. 75-0510-CH, 5–6 (S.D. W. Va. 1975).

8. *Amherst Coal Company*, Civil Action No. 75-0510-CH at 10.

9. DuPont and Union Carbide were to of the largest plants in the sprawling chemical industry in the Kanawha Valley surrounding Charleston.

10. Interview with George Snodgrass and Mary Snodgrass [pseud.], June 2003.

11. Interview with Jimmy Jackson [pseud.], June 5, 2003.

12. Clark (1981: 114–37).

13. Ragsdale, "Coal Firm Damaged in UMW Rampage."

14. Gallagher, Andrew. "'Sheer Acts of Terrorism' Cited by President of Elk Run Coal Co."

15. Interview with Ronnie White [pseud.], July 2000.

16. Personal communication, anonymous former resident of Sylvester, July 4, 2003.

17. Interview with anonymous Sylvester resident, April 2003.

18. The Elk Run conflict was in May 1981. The UMWA fought another bitter and often violent strike against Massey at its Rawl mine in Mingo County in 1984.

19. Interview with anonymous union member, October 15, 2003.

20. See Clark (1996).

21. For broad description of macroeconomic restructuring along with social and political implications, see Dicken (1998) and Harvey (1989), among others; Morgan, "Oil Firm Holdings in State Extensive."

22. Interview with Paul Nelson and Nanette Nelson, June 4, 2003.

23. Interview with David Jarrell and Kathy Jarrell [pseud.] April, 2003.

24. Interview with anonymous miner, October, 2003.

25. Here McKnight is referring to Massey's injunction against the UMWA after the Elk Run confrontation in 1981.

26. Clyde McKnight's comments are taken from an interview conducted June 19, 2003.

27. Interview with Danny Howell and Kay Howell, April 9, 2003.

28. Boyle rigged the 1968 union election and later had his challenger, Jock Yablonski, murdered along with his wife and daughter (Hume 1971).

29. The Stanley Heirs land is an heirship of nearly fifty acres on Kayford Mountain. The land is owned by heirs of the Stanley family but one of the heirs, Larry Gibson, has become prominent in the movement against MTR and as a primary caretaker of the land.

30. Roberts, "Responsible Mining: UMWA Wants Communities, Environment Protected."

Chapter 5. The Chase

1. The importance of the railroad in the transformation of the region is widely documented. See especially Waller (1988), Ronald L. Lewis (1998), and Weise (2001).

2. Weise (2001).

3. Appalachian Land Ownership Task Force (1983: 21). The Appalachian Land Ownership Study was begun in 1979. While certain pieces of information were published earlier, like the newspaper articles cited later in this chapter, the study was published in its entirety in 1983. The study sampled fifteen West Virginia counties including leading coal producers Kanawha, Raleigh, Logan, Mingo, and McDowell. Absentee interests here combine ownership located outside the state and outside the county but inside the state. The percentage of surface acres is based on a sample of 35 percent of the state total. The percentage of mineral acres is based on a sample of 54 percent of the state total.

4. Helen Lewis, Johnson, and Askins (1974); Caudill (1963).

5. Billings and Blee (2000: 12–15) argue that the colonial model must extend beyond its exclusive focus on coal to include agriculture.

6. Eller (1982) also directly addresses this theme of integration.

7. Morgan, "Oil Firm Holdings in State Extensive."

8. Described in chapter 1.

9. Companies can also appeal DEP decisions, such as violation citations, to the Surface Mine Board.

10. Cases in which appellants represent themselves without an attorney.

11. Described in the section on Indian Creek in chapter 1.

12. Joe Bowden, along with several other names used in this section, are pseudonyms.

13. See chap. 2, note 9, above.

14. One woman accidentally pointed out just how absurd the formal recording and reply procedure was when she asked a simple, factual question about the location of a proposed mine in relation to her property. Under the DEP's own rules, the facilitator of the conference was not supposed to answer, even though he knew where the mine would be and could have easily provided the information using the map at the meeting.

15. Valley fills, as described in chapter 1, are the large deposits of debris from MTR sites constructed in adjoining valleys. In Kentucky they are often referred to as hollow fills.

16. Interview with an anonymous Dorothy resident, May 15, 2003.

17. West Virginia Department of Environmental Protection. Surface Mine Board Members. http://www.dep.wv.gov/smb/Pages/boardmembers.aspx; accessed March 5, 2011. The

description of board members reflects board membership in 2003 and 2004. The URL has changed since then. This URL reflects a current link to the current board members.

18. Described in chapter 3.

19. Peters, Dillon et al. v. DEP, 265.

20. Interview with Janice Nease, September 18, 2003.

21. The maximum federal weight limit for commercial vehicles on interstate highways was established at 80,000 pounds in 1994.

22. During the debate, people used the numbers 120,000 pounds and 126,000 pounds interchangeably.

23. Caputo's comments in this section are paraphrased from a personal interview, December 9, 2003.

Chapter 6. Whose Development Is It?

1. Inequality in development refers not only to income, but also social and cultural resources like political access and education. See Gillespie (2001) and Sen (1999).

2. Executive Summary, *Boone County Land Use Master Plan*, 3.

3. When adding up the acreages, I rounded down any fractions of acres. The summary designates as "post mining usable" 65 percent of the permitted area.

4. The summary lists eighteen permits. Because four of them (Twilight I, II, and III, and Upper Big Branch) are contiguous, I considered them one mine site.

5. Executive Summary of the Boone County Land Use Master Plan (Draft), p. 26.

6. This sketch is dramatically oversimplified and is meant only to illustrate the most cursory ideas behind comparative advantage. For a more thorough explanation of comparative advantage and development theories, see Rist (1997), Peet and Hartwick (1999), Sen (1992, 1999), and Stiglitz (2002).

7. Forty-seven percent of West Virginia coal is exported out of the United States. www.wvcoal.com.

8. U.S. Census Bureau, *Statistical Abstract of the United States*, Table 687. "Household Income—Distribution by Income Level and State: 2004" 454.

9. Progressive Policy Institute. Technology Project. www.neweconomyindex.org/states/2002/westvirginia.html. Data cited comes from a URL that is no longer in service. Similar data from the 2007 State of the New Economy Index indicate their accuracy. West Virginia ranked forty-eighth overall in 2002 and fiftieth overall in 2007 in a broader index of economic indicators including technology criteria.

10. U.S. Census Bureau. *Statistical Abstract of the United States*, "Educational Attainment by State: 1990 to 2005," 145.

11. Deaths and mortality are per 100,000 residents. United Health Foundation. "America's Health: State Health Rankings: West Virginia 2010."

12. Center for Advancing Health. "Young Users of Smokeless Tobacco Lack Awareness of its Dangers."

13. "W.VA Had Record 27 ATV Deaths in 2002."

14. U.S. Census Bureau. "Individuals and Families Below Poverty Level—Number and Rate by State 2000 and 2004." *Statistical Abstract of the United States*, 457.

15. Gillespie 2001 (8–13).

16. World Bank (2005: Overview, 9–10).

17. Sen (1999). Sen's concept of freedom refers to things like freedom from hunger, persecution, or religious discrimination. Freedom in this sense is a way of measuring economic performance on a sliding scale that varies according to cultural values rather than fixed and culturally ignorant categories like gross domestic product.

18. In 2003, Bethlehem Steel reneged on its health care obligations to pensioners, leaving thousands of retired miners without health insurance. Horizon Resources did the same through a 2004 bankruptcy court decision. See also Frankel, "Workplace Changing at Dizzying Pace."

19. Heys and Wison, "Wal-Mart Tops State CHIP List."

20. Hohmann, "Residents Want Input on Economy."

21. Apollo Alliance. "The New Apollo Project." www.apolloalliance.org.

22. Whisnant (1994).

Part III. Symbolic Capital, the Commons, and Community Activism

1. Kate Long, Feeny Feemster Music (BMI).

2. Hufford (2001, 2002a, 2002b)

Chapter 7. Gender, Solidarity, and Symbolic Capital

1. My use of symbolic capital is based primarily on the work of Bordieu (1977, 1983, 1984, 1990).

2. Described in introduction.

3. Commercial workplace refers to places of paid employment, which, in Coal River, are most often coal mines. This is not meant to diminish the economic importance of the home and work traditionally performed by women in Appalachia.

4. See Hufford (2002a) and Reid and Taylor (2002) on civic commons in Appalachia. Holland and Lave (2001) refer to what CRMW and FOM have created as a "community of practice." The social space I describe is also very similar to what Couto and Guthrie (1999) call a "mediating structure" and, more loosely, Habermas's "public sphere" (Habermas 1991; Calhoun 1992; Fraser 1992) and Harvey's "social solidarities" (2005).

5. The year 2003 marks the end of my extended field research, but also indicates a watershed within CRMW as an influx of new activists entered the group, reflecting a new activist strategy in 2004 (McNeil 2005b).

6. Good discussions of gendered spaces and organizing can be found in Appleby (1999) and Maggard (1999). Also see Anglin (1993) and Fisher (1993) on class and gender in political action in Appalachia.

7. See Yarrow (1990). Not all men in the coalfields worked in the mines. The proportion was so large, however, that I feel comfortable with this generalization. Women did not start working in the mines until 1973, and then only in small numbers.

8. Most infamously in the Tony Boyle administration; see Hume (1971).

9. Ibid.

10. Montrie (2003: 142–50).

11. Ibid., 176–77.

12. Roberts, "Responsible Mining: UMWA Wants Communities, Environment Protected."

13. Bragg v. Robertson, 72 F. Supp. 2d 642, 661–62 .

14. Condon (2003).

15. Interview with John Taylor, August 19, 2003.

16. The strike against Pittston Coal Company was an eleven-month standoff in 1989 that drew UMWA participation from around the region, including Coal River. The strike is remembered for, among other things, the dramatic nonviolent takeover of a Pittston preparation plant by camouflaged union miners. See Sessions and Ansley (1993).

17. Interview with Elaine Purkey, October 14, 2003.

18. Interview with Freda Williams, August 4, 2003.

19. In chapter 4.

20. See Couto, Sessions and Ansley, Judkins, Anglin, and Fisher in Fisher (1993) for importance of community in organizing struggles in Appalachia. Purkey's comments also resemble comments in Allen (ibid.).

21. Personal communication with Judy Bonds, August 20, 2003.

22. This theme is taken up in chapter 8.

23. The effort made by a broad spectrum of West Virginians in the late 1960s and early 1970s combined protests over lost jobs and physical destruction caused by increased strip mining. See Montrie (2003: 115–19).

24. The 2004 poll was sponsored by the Appalachian Center for the Economy and the Environment, a member of the broad coalition against mountaintop removal that focuses on law and policy issues.

25. Doreen Massey (1994: 168–72) discusses the shifting notion of "home" historically and along lines of race, class, and gender.

26. Hufford (2003) describes this distinction in greater detail.

27. The new battle of Blair Mountain has gone back and forth between 2005 and 2010. The original battle site has been listed and delisted on the National Register of Historic Places.

28. Voted Song of the Year by the International Bluegrass Music Association in 1994.

29. The Goldman Environmental Prize is the most prestigious prize awarded for environmental activism and is often referred to as the Nobel Prize for the environment. The prize is awarded annually to one activist from each of six regions of the world. MTR activist Maria Gunnoe was among the recipients in 2009.

30. The Clean Water Protection Act has been introduced in the House of Representatives in each session since 2002, most recently as H.R. 1310 in the 111th Congress. During the 110th Congress, a companion bill in the Senate was introduced, and is currently pending reintroduction.

Chapter 8. Commons Environmentalism and Community Activism

1. Interview with Patty Sebok, March 11, 2004.

2. Interview with Patty Sebok, March 11, 2004.

3. Interview with Freda Williams, August 3, 2003.

4. Interview with Judy Bonds, July 3, 2003.

5. See "American Ginseng and the Idea of the Commons."

6. Reid (2006) calls this "Appalachian environmentalism."

7. Interview with Freda Williams, April 30, 2003.

8. Interview with John Taylor, July 2, 2003.

9. Comments in this section are drawn from interview with Robert Washington [pseud.], June 15, 2003, and Dottie Washington [pseud.], May 18, 2004.

10. Interview with Paul Nelson and Nanette Nelson, June 4, 2003.

11. Synfuel is also a scandalous tax loophole. During the 1970s, the federal government offered a tax credit for innovative fuels that use material previously considered waste. By the late 1990s, coal companies were claiming the credit by spraying chemicals on otherwise perfectly good coal. Essentially, they got paid twice for the same ton of coal—once by the customer and once by the government.

12. Now defunct, the West Virginia Organizing Project offered help organizing communities all across southern West Virginia.

13. Interview with Pauline Canterberry and Mary Miller, April 8, 2003.

14. Martinez-Alier (2002: 14). I use the term "field" in the tradition of Bourdieu (1985).

15. Martinez-Alier (2002: 14).

16. My reading of social practice theory of identity is based on Holland et al. (1998) and Holland and Lave (2001). The academic lineage traces back to Bourdieu (1977, 1990).

17. This is a combination of wilderness and conservation perspectives, properly speaking. Recreation could be considered a "wise use," but the examples I employ are more closely related to wilderness rather than corporate development.

18. Interview with Julian Martin, March 21, 2003.

19. Essays by Cronon and White appear in Cronon (1996).

20. Wise use describes economic and efficient management of environmental resources and protection of property rights for "common" good. See Harvey (1996: 383–85).

21. "Seasonal Round of Activities on Coal River."

22. Satterfield (2002: 8).

23. "Kirkendoll." 2001.

24. Martinez-Alier (2002: 13).

25. See Cole and Foster (2001).

26. Race in central Appalachia is a subject too large to be treated adequately here. Because nearly all Coal River residents are white, race would not appear to be a salient issue at first glance. Rather than treat it superficially, I have chosen to simply state that race is by no means irrelevant, but beyond the scope of this project.

27. Harvey (1996: 333).

28. Ibid.

29. Nonini (2007).

30. I follow Hufford's lead in interpreting into the commons concepts from both Arendt and Habermas.

31. Reid (2006).

32. Osterweil (2005), quoted in Gibson-Graham 2006 (xix–xxi).

Conclusion: John Henry, Efficiency, and Community

1. Recent research disputes the origin of the John Henry legend, suggesting that it originated in Alabama. See Garst (2002).

2. Interview with Roderick Pickett, August 8, 1997.

3. Green (1993: 72).

4. Among Berry's extensive body of work, I draw from *The Great Work* (1999) and a personal interview.

5. Wolf (1982).

6. Gudeman (2001).

7. I base my approach to landscape as a social artifact on work by Lefebvre (1976, 1991), Harvey (1996), Mitchell (1996, 2000), and Neil Smith (1996, 1998). Landscapes are not understood as simply the form of the physical environment, but the way that the physical environment is known and appropriated by the humans living on it.

8. This is what Bourdieu calls *habitus* (1977, 1985).

9. Gudeman (2001) describes this as the "base" of community.

10. Bourdieu calls this concept "doxa" (1977: 164).

11. Bourdieu asserts that *habitus* is where the products of social history are "naturalized" (1977: 78). Neil Smith (1998: 277) suggests that *habitus* is also the site where nature is made social and historical.

12. Among the many writers on experience and place, I draw from Tuan (1977), Tilley (1994), and Basso (1996).

13. Neil Smith (1998: 277). Also, see Osterweil (2005) and Gibson-Graham (2006) on transcending the divide between the local and the global, termed "localized globalism."

14. Gudeman (1986: 26).

15. Gramsci (1971); Arendt (1951); Habermas (1991).

16. Most recently, Republicans in the 111th Congress have proposed cutting funds and other maneuvers to block the Environmental Protection Agency from restricting MTR.

17. O'Dell (2004).

18. Fraser (1992) calls this "actually existing democracy."

19. Dudley (2002: 63).

20. Greider (2003).

Epilogue

1. After the initial Mountain Justice Summer in 2005, the organization persisted and subsequently dropped the word Summer from its name to indicate ongoing efforts.

2. Manchin, a Democrat, was elected to the U.S. Senate in 2010, taking the seat of the deceased longtime Senator Robert Byrd. "Manchin Plans No Investigation of Coal, Health," *Sunday Gazette-Mail*, 30 March 2008.

Bibliography

Interviews by Author

Judy Bonds, July 3, 2003.
Pauline Canterberry, April 8, 2003.
Mike Caputo, December 3, 2003.
Elizabeth Casto, August 29, 2003.
Ernie Harless [pseud.], October 15, 2003.
Ken Hechler, June 27, 2003.
Danny Howell and Kay Howell, April 9, 2003.
Jimmy Jackson [pseud.], June 5, 2003.
David Jarrell and Kathy Jarrell [pseud.] April, 2003.
Randy Jarrold [pseud.], July 16, 2000.
Joe Lovett, June 6, 2003.
Julian Martin, March 21, 2003.
Clyde McKnight, June 19, 2003.
Mary Miller, April 8, 2003.
Janice Nease, September 18, 2003.
Paul Nelson and Nanette Nelson, June 4, 2003.
Elaine Purkey, October 14, 2003.
Patty Sebok, March 11, 2004.
George Snodgrass and Mary Snodgrass [pseud.], June 2003.
Jack Spadaro, December 10, 2003.
Bernie Stanley [pseud.], July 5, 2003.
John Taylor, July 2, August 19, 2003.
Dottie Washington [pseud.], May 18, 2004.
Robert Washington [pseud.], June 15, 2003.
Ronnie White [pseud.], July 2000.
Freda Williams, July 11, 2000; April 30, August 3, 4, 2003.

References

Alinsky, Saul. [1949] 1970. *John L. Lewis: An Unauthorized Biography.* New York: Vintage.

Alvarez, Sonia, Evelina Dagnino, and Arturo Escobar, eds. 1998. *Cultures of Politics/Politics of Cultures: Re-Visioning Latin American Social Movements.* Boulder, CO: Westview Press.

"American Ginseng and the Idea of the Commons." Tending the Commons: Folklife and Landscape in Southern West Virginia. Library of Congress. American Memory Home. http://tinyurl.com/4wzcbon.

Amherst Coal Company v. United Mine Workers of America et al. 1975. Civil Action No. 75-0510-CH (S. D. W. Va.).

Anglin, Mary K. 1993. "Engendering the Struggle: Women's Labor and Traditions of Resistance in Rural Southern Appalachia." In Fisher, *Fighting Back,* 263–81.

———. 2002. "Lessons from Appalachia in the 20th Century: Poverty, Power and the 'Grassroots.'" *American Anthropologist* 104, no. 2: 565–82.

Apollo Alliance. "The New Apollo Project." www.apolloalliance.org.

Appadurai, Arjun. 1996. "The Production of Locality." In *Modernity at Large: Cultural Dimensions of Globalization,* 178–99. Minneapolis: University of Minnesota Press.

Appalachian Center for the Economy and the Environment. "Mountaintop Removal Poll Data." http://tinyurl.com/4j5gzka.

Appalachian Land Ownership Task Force. 1983. *Who Owns Appalachia? Landownership and Its Impact.* (Lexington, KY: University Press of Kentucky).

Appleby, Monica Kelly. 1999. "Women and Revolutionary Relations: Community-Building in Appalachia." In Barbara Ellen Smith, *Neither Separate Nor Equal,* 171–81.

Arendt, Hannah. [1951] 1973. *The Origins of Totalitarianism.* New York: Harcourt Brace Jovanovich.

Basso, Keith. 1996. *Wisdom Sits in Places: Landscape and Language Among the Western Apache.* Albuquerque: University of New Mexico Press.

Berry, Thomas. 1999. *The Great Work: Our Way into the Future.* New York: Bell Tower.

Billings, Dwight B., and Kathleen M. Blee. 2000. *The Road to Poverty: The Making of Wealth and Hardship in Appalachia.* Cambridge: Cambridge University Press.

Billings, Dwight B., Gurney Norman, and Katherine Ledford, eds. 1999. *Back Talk from Appalachia: Confronting Stereotypes.* Lexington: University of Kentucky Press.

Boone County Land Use Master Plan. 2002. Charleston, WV: E.L. Robinson Engineering Co. Print.

Bourdieu, Pierre. 1977. *Outline of a Theory of Practice.* Cambridge: Cambridge University Press.

———. 1983. "The Field of Cultural Production, or the Economic World Reversed." Trans. Richard Nice. *Poetics* 12: 29–73.

———. 1984. *Distinction: A Social Critique of the Judgment of Taste.* Cambridge, MA: Harvard University Press.

———. 1985. "The Genesis of the Concepts of 'Habitus' and 'Field.'" *Sociocriticism* 2, no. 2: 11–24.

———. 1990. *The Logic of Practice.* Stanford, CA: Stanford University Press.

———. 1996. *The Rules of Art: Genesis and Structure of the Literary Field.* Stanford, CA: Stanford University Press.

Bragg v. Robertson, 72 F. Supp. 2d 642, 661—62 (S.D. W. Va. 1999), *vacated sub nom.* Bragg v. W. Va. Coal Ass'n, 248 F.3d 275 (4th Cir. 2001).

Braun, Bruce, and Noel Castree, ed. 1998. *Remaking Reality: Nature at the Millennium.* London: Routledge.

Breed, Allen. 2003. "Little Sympathy for Rudolph, N.C. Locals Say." *Charleston Gazette.* June 2. www.wvgazette.com.

Brown, Beverly. 1995. *In Timber Country: Working People's Stories of Environmental Conflict and Urban Flight.* Philadelphia: Temple University Press.

———. 1996. "Fencing the Northwest Forests: Decline of Public and Accustomed Rights." *Cultural Survival Quarterly.* (Spring): 50–52.

Brown, Edwin L., and Colin J. Davis, eds. 1999. *It Is Union and Liberty: Alabama Coal Miners and the UMW.* Tuscaloosa: University of Alabama Press.

Burns, Shirley Stewart. 2007. *Bringing Down the Mountains: The Impact of Mountaintop Removal Surface Coal Mining on Southern West Virginia Communities, 1970-2004.* Morgantown: West Virginia University Press.

Calhoun, Craig. 1993. "New Social Movements of the Early Nineteenth Century." *Social Science History* 3, no. 11: 385–427.

Calhoun, Craig, ed. 1992. *Habermas and the Public Sphere.* Cambridge: MIT Press.

Castells, Manuel. 1996. *The Rise of Network Society.* Malden, MA: Blackwell.

———. 1997. *The Power of Identity.* Malden, MA: Blackwell.

Caudill, Harry. 1963. *Night Comes to the Cumberlands: A Biography of a Depressed Area.* Boston: Little, Brown & Co.

Center for Advancing Health. 2000. "Young Users of Smokeless Tobacco Lack Awareness of its Dangers." December 17. http://tinyurl.com/4kotpg6.

Clark, Paul F. 1981. *The Miners' Fight for Democracy: Arnold Miller and the Reform of the United Mine Workers.* . Ithaca, NY: New York State School of Industrial and Labor Relations, Cornell University.

———. 1996. "Legacy of Democratic Reform: The Trumka Administration and the Challenge of the Eighties." In John H. M. Laslett, *The United Mine Workers of America: A Model of Industrial Solidarity?* University Park, PA: Pennsylvania State University Press. 459–483.

"Coal Operator Makes Case over Buffet." 2000. *Charleston Gazette.* August 1. www.wvgazette .com.

Cole, Luke, and Sheila Foster. 2001. *From the Ground Up: Environmental Racism and the Rise of the Environmental Justice Movement.* New York: New York University Press.

Comaroff, Jean, and John L. Comaroff, eds. 2001. *Millennial Capitalism and the Culture of Neoliberalism.* Durham, NC: Duke University Press.

Condon, Bernard. 2003. "Not King Coal." *Forbes* (May 26): 80–82.

Corbin, David Alan. 1981. *Life, Work, and Rebellion in the Coal Fields: The Southern West Virginia Miners, 1880-1922.* Champaign: University of Illinois Press.

Couto, Richard. 1993. "The Memory of Miners and the Conscience of Capital: Coal Miner's Strikes as Free Spaces." In Fisher, *Fighting Back,.* 165–94.

Couto, Richard, and Catherine S. Guthrie. 1999. *Making Democracy Work Better: Mediating Structures, Social Capital, and the Democratic Prospect.* Chapel Hill: University of North Carolina Press.

Cronon, William, ed. 1996. *Uncommon Ground: Rethinking the Human Place in Nature.* New York: W.W. Norton.

Crumley, Carole, ed. 1994. *Historical Ecology: Cultural Knowledge and Changing Landscapes.* Santa Fe, NM: School of American Research Press.

———. 1996. "Historical Ecology." In *Encyclopedia of Cultural Anthropology.* Ed. David Levinson and Melvin Ember. 2 vols. New York: Henry Holt & Co.

de Certeau, Michel. 1984. *The Practice of Everyday Life.* Berkeley: University of California Press.

Dicken, Peter. 1998. *Global Shift: Transforming the World Economy.* New York: Guilford Press.

Di Leonardo, Micaela. 1998. *Exotics at Home: Anthropologies, Others, American Modernity.* Chicago: University of Chicago Press.

Dudley, Kathryn. 1994. *The End of the Line: Lost Jobs, New Lives in Postindustrial America.* Chicago: University of Chicago Press.

———. 2000. *Debt and Dispossession: Farm Loss in America's Heartland.* Chicago: University of Chicago Press.

Edelman, Marc. 2001. "Social Movements: Changing Paradigms and Forms of Politics." *Annual Review of Anthropology* 30: 285–317.

Eller, Ronald D. 1982. *Miners, Millhands and Mountaineers: Industrialization of the Appalachian South, 1880–1930.* Knoxville: University of Tennessee Press.

Engelhardt, Elizabeth. 2003. *The Tangled Roots of Feminism, Environmentalism, and Appalachian Literature.* Athens: Ohio University Press.

Epstein, Barbara. 1990. "Rethinking Social Movement History." *Socialist Review* 20: 35–65.

Erikson, Kai T. 1976. *Everything in Its Path: Destruction of Community in the Buffalo Creek Flood.* New York: Simon and Schuster.

Escobar, Arturo. 1998. "Whose Knowledge, Whose Nature? Biodiversity, Conservation, and the Political Ecology of Social Movements." *Journal of Political Ecology.* 5: 53–82.

———. 1999a. "After Nature: Steps to an Antiessentialist Political Ecology." *Current Anthropology* 40, no. 1 (February): 1–30.

———. 1999b. "An Ecology of Difference: Equality and Conflict in a Glocalized World." *World Culture Report* 2: 1–20. Lourdes Arizpe, ed. Paris: UNESCO.

———. 2001. "Culture Sits in Places: Reflections on Globalism and Subaltern Strategies of Localization." *Political Geography*: 139–74.

Farmer, Paul. 2003. *Pathologies of Power: Health, Human Rights, and the New War on the Poor.* Berkeley: University of California Press.

Fisher, Stephen. 2004. "Building Social Movements from the Inside Out: From the Grassroots to the Regional and Wider Coalitions, Networks, and Solidarities." Paper delivered to the Social Movements Conference. Boone, NC. October.

Fisher, Stephen, ed. 1993. *Fighting Back in Appalachia: Traditions of Resistance and Change.* Philadelphia: Temple University Press.

Fox, Richard G., ed. *Recapturing Anthropology.* Santa Fe, NM: School of American Research Press. 1991.

Frankel, Todd C. 2000a. "Coal Operators Get Chance to Talk with Candidate." *Charleston Gazette.* August 2. www.wvgazette.com.

———. 2000b. "Workplace Changing at Dizzying Pace." *Charleston Daily Mail*, July 24. www.dailymail.com.

Fraser, Nancy. 1992. "Re-Thinking the Public Sphere: A Contribution to the Critique of Actually Existing Democracy." In Calhoun, *Habermas,* 109–42.

Gallagher, Andrew. 1981. "'Sheer Acts of Terrorism' Cited by President of Elk Run Coal Co." *Sunday Gazette-Mail* (Charleston, WV). May 24, 2A.

Garst, John. 2002. "Chasing John Henry in Alabama and Mississippi: A Personal Memoir of Work in Progress 'Tributaries." *Journal of the Alabama Folklife Association* 5: 92–129.

Gaventa, John. 1980. *Power and Powerlessness: Quiescence and Rebellion in an Appalachian Valley.* Urbana: University of Illinois Press.

———. 2002. "Appalachian Studies in Global Context: Reflections on the Beginnings— Challenges for the Future." *Journal of Appalachian Studies* 8, no. 1: 79–90.

Gaventa, John, Barbara Ellen Smith, and Alex W. Willingham. 1990. *Communities in Economic Crisis: Appalachia and the South.* Philadelphia: Temple University Press.

Gettleman, Jeffrey. 2003. "Sympathy for Bombing Suspect May Cloud Search for Evidence." *New York Times.* June 1. www.nytimes.com.

Gibson-Graham, J. K. 2006. *A Postcapitalist Politics.* Minneapolis: University of Minnesota Press.

Gillespie, Alexander. 2001. *The Illusion of Progress: Unsustainable Development in International Law and Policy.* London: Earthscan Press.

Gorn, Elliott J. 2001. *Mother Jones: The Most Dangerous Woman in America.* New York: Hill & Wang.

Gramsci, Antonio, Quintin Hoare, and Geoffrey Nowell-Smith. 1971. *Selections from the Prison Notebooks of Antonio Gramsci.* New York: International Publishers.

Green, Archie. 1993. *Wobblies, Pile Butts, and other Heroes: Laborlore Explorations.* Urbana: University of Illinois Press.

Gregory, Steven. 1998. *Black Corona: Race and the Politics of Place in an Urban Community.* Princeton, NJ: Princeton University Press.

Greider, William. 2003. *The Soul of Capitalism: Opening Paths to a Moral Economy.* New York: Simon & Schuster.

Gross, James A. 1995. *Broken Promise: The Subversion of U.S. Labor Relations Policy, 1947–1994.* Philadelphia, PA: Temple University Press.

Gudeman, Stephen. 1986. *Economics as Culture: Models and Metaphors of Livelihood.* London: Routledge & K. Paul.

———. 2001. *The Anthropology of Economy: Community, Market, and Culture.* Malden, MA: Blackwell.

Habermas, Jurgen. 1991. *The Structural Transformation of the Public Sphere: An Inquiry into a Category of Bourgeois Society.* Cambridge: MIT Press.

Harcourt, Wendy, and Arturo Escobar, eds. 2005. *Women and the Politics of Place.* Bloomfield CT: Kumarian Press.

Hardt, Michael, and Antonio Negri. 2000. *Empire.* Cambridge, MA: Harvard University Press.

Harrington, Michael. [1962] 1981. *The Other America: Poverty in the United States.* New York: Penguin.

Harvey, David. 1973. *Social Justice and the City.* Baltimore: Johns Hopkins University Press.

———. 1989a. *The Condition of Postmodernity: An Enquiry into the Origins of Cultural Change.* Cambridge, MA: Blackwell.

———. 1989b. *The Urban Experience.* Baltimore: Johns Hopkins University Press.

———. 1996. *Justice, Nature and the Geography of Difference.* Cambridge, MA: Blackwell Publishers.

———. 2000. *Spaces of Hope.* Berkeley: University of California Press.

———. 2003. *The New Imperialism.* Oxford: Oxford University Press.

———. 2005. *A Brief History of Neoliberalism.* Oxford: Oxford University Press.

———. 2006. *Spaces of Global Capitalism.* London: Verso.

Hasler, Richard. 2006. "The Tragedy of Privatization: Moving Mountains in Appalachia, a Southern African Critique." *Journal of Appalachian Studies* 11, no. 1 & 2: 95–103.

Heys, John, and Paul Wison. 2004. "Wal-Mart Tops State CHIP List." *Sunday Gazette-Mail* (Charleston, WV). December 26, 1A.

Hinson, Glenn. 2000. *Fire In My Bones: Transcendence and the Holy Spirit in African American Gospel.* Philadelphia, PA: University of Pennsylvania Press.

Hohmann, George. 2000. "Residents Want Input on Economy." *Charleston Daily Mail.* July 17. www.dailymail.com.

Holland, Dorothy, and Jean Lave, ed. 2001. *History in Person: Enduring Struggles, Contentious Practice, Intimate Identities.* Santa Fe, NM: School of American Research Press.

Holland, Dorothy, William Lachicotte Jr., Debra Skinner, and Carole Caine. 1998. *Identity and Agency in Cultural Worlds.* Cambridge, MA: Harvard University Press.

Howell, Benita, ed. 2002. *Culture, Environment, and Conservation in the Appalachian South.* Champaign: University of Illinois Press.

Hufford, Mary. 1995. "Context." *Journal of American Folklore.* 108: 528–49.

———. 2001. "Stalking the Forest Coeval: Fieldwork at the Site of Clashing Social Imaginaries." *Practicing Anthropology* 23 (2001): 29–32.

———. 2002a. "Interrupting the Monologue: Folklore, Ethnography, and Critical Regionalism." *Journal of Appalachian Studies* 8, no. 1: 62–78.

———. 2002b. "Reclaiming the Commons: Narratives of Progress, Preservation, and Ginseng." In Howell, *Culture, Environment, and Conservation.*

———. 2003. "Out of the Overburden, Onto the Map: Cultural Assessment and the Case of Mountaintop Removal Coal Mining." Paper presented at Sustaining the Mountains: Ecological Citizenship for the 21st Century, Center for Folklore and Ethnography and the Institute for Environmental Studies at the University of Pennsylvania, April 24.

Hume, Brit. 1971. *Death and the Mines: Rebellion and Murder in the United Mine Workers.* New York: Grossman.

Jamison, Frederic. 1984. "Postmodernism, or, the Cultural Logic of Late Capitalism." *New Left Review* 146 (July/August): 53–92.

Johnston, Barbara Rose. 1995. "Human Rights and the Environment." *Human Ecology* 23: 111–23.

Jordan-Bychkov, Terry G., and Matti Kaups. 1989. *The American Backwoods Frontier: An Ethnic Interpretation.* Baltimore: Johns Hopkins University Press.

Judkins, Bennett M. 1993. "The People's Respirator: Coalition Building and the Black Lung Association." In Fisher, *Fighting Back,* 225–41.

Katz, Cindy, and Andrew Kirby. 1991. "In the Nature of Things: The Environment and Everyday Life." *Transactions, Institute of British Geographers* 16: 259–71.

Kilborn, Peter T. 2000. "U.S. Cracks Down on Rise in Appalachia Moonshine." *New York Times.* March 23, A18.

"Kirkendoll." 2001. Editorial. *Charleston Gazette.* January 10. www.wvgazette.com.

Lefebvre, Henri. 1976. "Reflections on the Politics of Space." Trans Michael J. Enders. *Antipode* 8: 30–37.

———. 1991. *The Production of Space.* Oxford: Blackwell.

Lewis, Helen, Linda Johnson, and Don Askins, eds. 1978. *Colonialism in Modern America: The Appalachian Case.* Boone, NC: Appalachian Consortium Press.

Lewis, Ronald L. 1998. *Transforming the Appalachian Countryside: Railroads, Deforestation and Social Change in West Virginia: 1880–1920.* Chapel Hill: University of North Carolina Press.

Loeb, Penny. 1997. "Sheer Madness." *U.S. News and World Report* (Aug. 11): 26–36.

Maggard, Sally Ward. 1999. "Gender, Race, and Place: Confounding Labor Activism in Central Appalachia." In Barbara Ellen Smith, *Neither Separate Nor Equal*, 185–206.

Martinez-Alier, Joan. 2002. *The Environmentalism of the Poor: A Study of Ecological Conflicts and Valuation.* Cheltenham, UK: Edward Elgar.

Massey, Doreen. 1994. *Space, Place and Gender.* Cambridge: Polity Press.

McNeil, Bryan T. 2005a. "Global Forces, Local Worlds: Mountaintop Removal and Appalachian Communities." In Peacock, Watson, and Matthews, *The American South*, 99–110.

———. 2005b. "Social Movements and the Epistemology of Pragmatism." Paper presented at the meeting of the American Anthropological Association, Washington DC, December 4.

Melucci, Alberto. 1988. "Getting Involved: Identity and Mobilization in Social Movements." *International Social Movement Research* 1. 329–40.

———. 1989. "New Perspectives on Social Movements: An Interview with Alberto Melucci." In *Nomads of the Present*. Philadelphia: Temple University Press. 180–232.

Mitchell, Don. 1996. *The Lie of the Land: Migrant Workers and the California Landscape.* Minneapolis: University of Minnesota Press.

———. 2000. *Cultural Geography: A Critical Introduction.* Malden, MA: Blackwell.

———. 2003. *The Right to the City: Social Justice and the Fight for Public Space.* New York: Guilford.

Montrie, Chad. 2003. *To Save the Land and People: A History of Opposition to Surface Coal Mining in Appalachia.* Chapel Hill: University of North Carolina Press.

Morgan, John G. 1981. "Oil Firm Holdings in State Extensive." *Sunday Gazette-Mail* (Charleston, WV). May 10, 1A.

Nesbitt, J. Todd, and Daniel Weiner. 2001. "Conflicting Environmental Imaginaries and the Politics of Nature in Central Appalachia." *Geoforum* 32: 333–49.

Newfont, Kathryn. 2001. "Moving Mountains: Forest Politics and Commons Culture in Western North Carolina." Unpublished Thesis. University of North Carolina.

Newman, Katherine. 1995. "Deindustrialization, Poverty, and Downward Mobility: Toward an Anthropology of Economic Disorder." In Shepard Foreman, ed., *Diagnosing America: Anthropology and Public Engagement*, 121–48. Ann Arbor: University of Michigan Press.

Nonini, Donald. 2007. *The Global Idea of "the Commons."* New York: Berghahn.

Nyden, Paul. 1990. "Super Tax Credits: a Boon or Boondoggle for Economic Development?" *Sunday Gazette-Mail* (Charleston, WV). May 27, 1B.

Oberhauser, Ann M., and Anne-Marie Turnage. 1999. "A Coalfield Tapestry: Weaving the Socioeconomic Fabric of Women's Lives." In Barbara Ellen Smith, *Neither Separate Nor Equal*, 109–22.

O'Connor, James. 1998. *Natural Causes: Essays in Ecological Marxism.* New York: Guilford.

O'Dell, Gary. 2004. Paper presented at the meeting of the Appalachian Studies Association, Cherokee, NC, May.

Ortner, Sherry. 1991. "Reading America: Preliminary Notes on Class and Culture." In Fox, *Recapturing Anthropology*, 163–89.

Osterweil, Michal. 2005. "Place-based Globalism: Locating Women in the Alternative Globalization Movement." In Harcourt and Escobar, *Women and the Politics of Place*, 174–89.

Peacock, James L., Harry L. Watson, and Carrie R. Matthews, eds. 2005. *The American South in a Global World.* Chapel Hill: University of North Carolina Press.

Peet, Richard, and Elaine Hartwick. 1999. *Theories of Development.* New York: Guilford.

Peters, Dillon, et al. v. West Virginia Department of Environmental Protection. 2003. West Virginia Surface Mine Board.

Progressive Policy Institute. "The 2002 State New Economy Index." www.neweconomyindex .org/states/2002/westvirginia.html [URL no longer in service].

Purdy, Jedediah. 1998. *For Common Things: Irony, Trust, and Commitment in America Today.* New York: Vintage.

Ragsdale, Jim. 1981. "Coal Firm Damaged in UMW Rampage." *Charleston Gazette.* May 17, 1.

"Ramp Suppers, Biodiversity, and the Integrity of 'The Mountains.'" Tending the Commons: Folklife and Landscape in Southern West Virginia. Library of Congress. American Memory Home. http://tinyurl.com/45qmdtp.

Reed-Danahay, Deborah. 1997. *Auto/Ethnography: Rewriting the Self and the Social.* Oxford: Berg.

Reid, Herbert G. 2006. "Appalachia and the 'Sacrament of Co-Existence': Beyond Post-Colonial Trauma and Regional Identity Traps." *Journal of Appalachian Studies* 11, no. 1 & 2: 164–81.

Reid, Herbert, and Betsy Taylor. 2002. "Appalachia as a Global Region: Toward Critical Regionalism and Civic Professionalism." *Journal of Appalachian Studies* 8, no. 1: 9–32.

Rist, Gilbert. 1997. *The History of Development: From Western Origins to Global Faith.* London: Zed.

"Roads to Nowhere?" 2000. Editorial. *Charleston Gazette.* July 16. www.wvgazette.com.

Roberts, Cecil. 1998. "Responsible Mining: UMWA Wants Communities, Environment Protected. *Charleston Gazette.* October 12.

Robertson, George, Melinda Mash, Lisa Tickner, Jon Bird, Barry Curtis, and Tim Putnam, eds. 1996. *Future Natural.* London: Routledge.

Satterfield, Terre. 2002. *Anatomy of a Conflict: Identity, Knowledge, and Emotion in Old-Growth Forests.* Vancouver: University of British Columbia Press.

"Seasonal Round of Activities on Coal River." Tending the Commons: Folklife and Landscape in Southern West Virginia. Library of Congress. American Memory Home. http://tinyurl.com/4cervnd.

Sen, Amartya. 1992. *Inequality Reexamined.* Cambridge, MA: Harvard University Press.

———. 1999. *Development as Freedom.* New York: Anchor Books.

Sessions, Jim, and Fran Ansley. 1993. "Singing Across Dark Spaces." In Fisher, *Fighting Back*, 195–224.

Slocum, Karla. 2006. *Free Trade and Freedom: Neoliberalism, Place, and Nation in the Caribbean*. Ann Arbor: University of Michigan Press.

Smith, Barbara Ellen. 1987. *Digging Our Own Graves: Coal Miners and the Struggle over Black Lung Disease*. Philadelphia: Temple University Press.

Smith, Barbara Ellen, ed. 1999. *Neither Separate Nor Equal: Women, Race, and Class in the South*. Philadelphia, PA: Temple University Press.

Smith, Herb E. 1984. *Strangers and Kin: A History of the Hillbilly Image*. Whitesburg, KY: Appalshop.

Smith, Neil. 1984. *Uneven Development: Nature, Capital and the Production of Nature*. Oxford: Blackwell.

———. 1996. "The Production of Nature." In Robertson et al., *Future Natural*, 35–54.

———. 1998. "Nature at the Millennium: Production and Re-Enchantment." In Braun and Castree, *Remaking Reality*, 271–285.

———. 2005. *The Endgame of Globalization*. New York: Routledge.

Stewart, Kathleen. 1996. *A Space on the Side of the Road: Cultural Poetics in an "Other" America*. Princeton, NJ: Princeton University Press.

Stiglitz, Joseph E. 2002. *Globalization and Its Discontents*. New York: W.W. Norton.

Tilley, Christopher. 1994. *A Phenomenology of Landscape: Places, Paths, and Monuments*. London: Berg.

Tuan, Yi-Fu. 1977. *Space and Place: The Perspective of Experience*. Minneapolis: University of Minnesota Press.

United Health Foundation. "America's Health: State Health Rankings: West Virginia 2010." http://tinyurl.com/4b4qoov.

U.S. Census Bureau. 2007. *Statistical Abstract of the United States* (print).

———. "Educational Attainment by State: 1990 to 2005," 145.

———. "Individuals and Families Below Poverty Level—Number and Rate by State 2000 and 2004," 457.

———. Table 687. "Household Income—Distribution by Income Level and State: 2004," 454.

Waller, Altina. 1988. *Feud: Hatfields, McCoys, and Social Change in Appalachia, 1860–1900*. Chapel Hill: University of North Carolina Press.

Ward, Ken. 2000. "Bush Hauling in Coal Contributions." *Charleston Gazette*. June 24.

Warren, Kay B. 1998. *Indigenous Social Movements and Their Critics*. Princeton: Princeton University Press.

Watts, Michael. 1998. "Nature as Artifice and Artifact." In Bruan and Castree, *Remaking Reality*.

Weise, Robert. 2001. *Grasping at Independence: Debt, Male Authority, and Mineral Rights in Appalachian Kentucky, 1850–1915*. Knoxville: University of Tennessee Press.

Weller, Jack. 1965. *Yesterday's People: Life in Contemporary Appalachia*. Lexington, KY: University of Kentucky Press.

West Virginia Coal Association. www.wvcoal.com.

West Virginia Department of Environmental Protection. 2011. Surface Mine Board Members. http://tinyurl.com/49plef4.

Whisnant, David E. 1983. *All That Is Native & Fine: The Politics of Culture in an American Region*. Chapel Hill: University of North Carolina Press.

———. 1994. *Modernizing the Mountaineer*. Knoxville: University of Tennessee Press.

White, Richard. 1996. "Are You an Environmentalist or Do You Work for a Living." In Cronon, *Uncommon Ground*, 171–85.

Williams, Raymond. 1973. *The Country and the City*. New York: Oxford University Press.

Wills, Ken, Orie Loucks, Paul Kalisz, Al Fritsch, Alan Rees, and Wade Davidson. 1997. "Patterns of Forest Health: A Report on Citizen Monitoring In the Eastern Mountains 1994–1997" (September). Tending the Commons: Folklife and Landscape in Southern West Virginia. http://tinyurl.com/6xukljs.

Wolf, Eric. 1982. *Europe and the People Without History*. Berkeley: University of California Press.

Woodrum, Robert H. 1999. "Wildcats, Caravans, and Dynamite: Alabama Miners and the 1977–1978 Coal Strike." In Brown and Davis, *It Is Union*, 111–30.

World Bank. 2005. *World Bank Development Report 2006: Equity and Development*. Washington DC: The International Bank for Reconstruction and Development/The World Bank.

"W.VA Had Record 27 ATV Deaths In 2002." 2003. *Charleston Gazette*. February 14. www.wvgazette.com.

Yarrow, Mike. 1990. "Voices from the Coalfields: How Miners' Families Understand the Crisis of Coal." In Gaventa, Smith, and Willingham, *Communities in Economic Crisis*, 38–52.

Zukin, Sharon. 1991. *Landscapes of Power: From Detroit to Disney World*. Berkeley: University of California Press.

———. 1995. *The Culture of Cities*. Oxford: Blackwell.

Index

Bryan T. McNeil is an assistant professor of anthropology at American University.

The University of Illinois Press
is a founding member of the
Association of American University Presses.

Composed in 10.5/13 Adobe Minion Pro
with Memphis display
by Jim Proefrock
at the University of Illinois Press
Manufactured by Thomson-Shore, Inc.

University of Illinois Press
1325 South Oak Street
Champaign, IL 61820-6903
www.press.uillinois.edu

Never a man without his vices.
If any man doubts it
He has not sunk to the whoredom of his heart,
Nor tongued his own flesh.

Our loves betray us.
We give ourselves to God
And in our faithlessness
Play strumpet to the devil.

Thus it is that my hate is scribbled about my mouth
And my lust rings my eyes.

My guilt is blistered upon my hands.
They have prized blood.
They are dabbed with sin.

O my God, my God, what can I say
Except that Thou hast touched me?

In sleep, in deep slumber,
In the raw desert night,
Thou didst send Thy holy devils
There to accost me.
As Thy terrible henchmen
They did show me me.

What visions of vastness on the moon-sunken wastes?
So dry is the night the dust-devils wander,
They whisper me out.

I will go back once more to the city of man,
Will abase myself before the sinner
For he is cleaner than I.

At least he never has claimed to be good,
Nor supposed himself righteous.

At least he does not swear by Thy truth
And live by his lies.

At least he does not bless with the one hand
While he horribly defiles with the other.

Forgive me, dear Christ, and make me as Thyself,
Who knew Thy true Self.

Hot night. The crude desert stars. The devouring distances.
There is not a coyote's howl to quaver the darkness.
There is not the scuttle of a deermouse nor the slow drag of a
    serpent.
There is not the mutter of a single leaf
So heavy hangs the air.

O my soul, my soul, what deaths, what pits, what savageries, what
    wastes!

If I could touch so much as a piece of human dung
That some hapless wanderer dropped by a yucca
I should consider myself not friendless.

But my thoughts return upon me
And I dare not sleep,
For I am in dread of my dreams.

Therefore in the morning will I go forth
And return to the ways of man.

I will seek God henceforth in the shameful human face.
I will serve God in the wretched human act.
I will savour God in the salt of human tears.

In the body's corruptness will He be revealed to me,
In the postures of defloration,
In the deeds of wrath.

Where the murderer strangles his hope,
Where the thief plunders his heart,
Where the ogler gloats and gloats on his own self
And gloating profanes.

Out of these, out of these, will Thy peace shine forth
If I show pity.

No day? No dawn? No water? No wet?
A drop of grace for my parched tongue,
One drop would suffice me.

Forgive me, that my heart was vicious.
In my viciousness of heart
I coupled the bitch.

But in the spate of such hardness
Thou didst come to redeem me.
Hadst Thou not discovered my sin to myself
Thou couldst never have touched me to forgive me.
Therefore blessed is my sin.

I will seek out a human face that I may know pity.
That I might betray and be forgiven.
That I might be betrayed and forgive.

I will seek love in the face of a man
And pity in the eyes of a woman.

I will seek faith in the brow of a child.

I will return to my mother,
To the breasts of her that nursed me,
To the lap of her that bore me.

And I will find my father.
He will bless my head.
He will forgive me.

Therefore will I be whole again,
And be made new again,
And again be made as a child.

For the night is dark.
But off in the east I see low light.
I smell the dawn.

And will find my God in the thwarted love that breaks between
    us!